T H E
COMPLETE
FILMS OF
ALFRED
HITCHCOCK

THE COMPLETE FILMS OF ALFRED HITCHCOCK

ROBERT A. HARRIS & MICHAEL S. LASKY

CITADEL PRESS
Kensington Publishing Corp.
www.kensingtonbooks.com

ACKNOWLEDGMENTS

The authors would like to express their sincerest gratitude to the many splendid people who assisted us in one way or another in the ultimate creation of this volume. Without their aid, encouragement, suggestions, and yes, photographs, this book would be yet a long time coming. Thank you, then, to Robert W. Evans and Elizabeth Thomson of the Library of State University of New York, College at Purchase; Gene Andrewski; Mark Ricci of the Memory Shop; Ernest Burns, Cinemabilia; the staff of the Film Stills Archive, British Film Institute; Robert C. Holzer; Mary Corliss, Museum of Modern Art; John Poole and Peter Meyer, Janus Films; the staff of the Lincoln Center Library for the Performing Arts; Hal Samis; Lou Marino and John Sutherland of Warner Bros.; Steve Sally; Dr. Stanley Solomon of Iona College; Roy Frumkes; Sara Taffet; Martin Bresnick of Audio-Brandon Films; a special thanks to Janis Okon and Ray Harris, who typed the final manuscript; and- to Barbara Goldman, Mary Schmidt and Roslyn Kramer, fond affection for their continued psychic comfort and support during the many months of "frenzy."

And finally, we wish to thank Chris Simon, our designer, for his support and genuine interest.

CITADEL PRESS BOOKS are published by

Kensington Publishing Corp.
850 Third Avenue
New York, NY 10022

All Kensington titles, imprints, and distributed lines are available at special quantity discounts for bulk purchases for sales promotions, premiums, fund-raising, educational, or institutional use. Special book excerpts or customized printings can also be created to fit specific needs. For details, write or phone the office of the Kensington special sales manager: Kensington Publishing Corp., 850 Third Avenue, New York, NY 10022, attn: Special Sales Department, phone 1-800-221-2647.

CITADEL PRESS and the Citadel logo are Reg. U.S. Pat & TM Off.

First Kensington printing: December 2002

10 9 8 7 6 5 4 3 2 1

Printed in the United States of America

Cataloging data may be obtained from the Library of Congress.

ISBN: 0-8065-2427-8

In memory of my father,
David M. Harris

     —RAH

• • •

To my parents,
Jesse and Vivien Lasky,
who took me to see
my first Hitchcock movie

     —MSL

Contents

6590-P4

Preface

Hitchcock (hich' kok), N. Alfred Joseph. **Born** England August 13, 1899. English-American film and television director-producer.

An entertainer at heart, Alfred Hitchcock delighted millions of TV viewers with his choice words and unabashed hamming before the camera in the late 1950s and early 1960s. By accident he had begun a custom of appearing in a cameo in each of his films. It finally became necessary for him to appear as early as possible so audiences wouldn't be distracted from the plot while watching for him. And the originality of his appearances was just one small manifestation of his devotion to understatement and his abhorrence of cliché. As he has said repeatedly, his films are not slices of life but pieces of cake—they are made strictly for us to enjoy. He likes to tell a good story, both on the screen and off, no matter how absurd it may be, but for Hitchcock it must be dramatic, moving, and human to be worthwhile. So for him *content* has never been as important as the accent on *technique* to make the content more interesting. Hitchcock thoroughly understands his craft and its varied uses. He knows that rhythm and beauty are important but that they are worthless if not coordinated to specific purposes. He is a consummate director and an engaging personality as well, both reflected in his work and his style of living.

The Films of Alfred Hitchcock attempts to cover the more than fifty years he has spent as a film director. In a showcase of stills from his many films and in a text which examines the background of each production, how it was critically received and what it was about, we have tried to illustrate the genius of the artist and the humaneness of the man. For further detailed discussion, the authors recommend *Hitchcock,* by François Truffaut (New York: Simon & Schuster, 1967) and *Focus on Hitchcock,* edited by Albert J. LaValley (Englewood Cliffs, N. J.: Spectrum Books, Prentice-Hall, 1972).

Foreword
by Pat Hitchcock O'Connell

The audience.

It was the audience that came first and foremost to my father's mind. Whether he was creating a scene of terror or suspense or leading filmgoers toward a more romantic mood, it was always concern for the audience that affected each element of his films.

That's why he created his films. Or more correctly, why he and my mother did. When they met, it was she who had the stronger foothold in the fledgling British film industry. But he moved quickly up the ladder. His earliest work is lost. Ten years after he began, he was one of the most important filmmakers in the industry, and my mother was there beside him. People probably don't realize how much of her is in his films. He seldom made an important decision without her.

The interesting thing is during those early days—and of course, I wasn't there even near the beginning—neither he nor any of his fellow filmmakers ever really considered the life of a film. Photographed on fragile nitrate film stock and often copied to death, the films of the '30s and '40s were never expected to have a long life. A few hundred prints went to theaters worldwide and after playing second and third run houses it was over.

The concept of people watching his work—some of it now over seventy-five years old—let alone studying it and considering its merits—would have seemed very much a joke back then. His films were made as entertainment—to give pleasure to an audience. Were he still with us today, I'm certain that he would find the humor in, and have a huge dose of appreciation for, the fact that members of those audiences still study and discuss his work. Even down to individual elements like the camera moves in *Notorious* or *Young and Innocent.* Or the fact that students will pull apart the classic shower scene from *Psycho,* breaking it down into its individual pieces, each shot or strip of film—to learn how it was created. An illusion that still has a magical and frightening hold over an audience forty years after it was created.

When his 1958 film *Vertigo* was re-released in 1996, it was exposed to a very different audience. Or more correctly, to a number of different audiences. There were those who had seen it thirty-eight years before, who remembered the terror and the passion and wanted to see it again—this time restored in 70mm and with Bernard Herrmann's brilliant score in stereo. There were those who had seen it on television, with pieces missing and the intricate storyline intercut with commercials for deodorants and nylons. And there was a new audience—a young audi-ence—there because of the Hitchcock legend—who come to a theater to see a film that, strangely enough, was considered a failure in 1958—and was now his masterpiece. It was the members of this very special audience—the young people being exposed to his work for the first time—who would animatedly show the fear, the shock—as the tale unfolded before them for the very first time. And it would have pleased him to see that his work had not only not lost its power over the years, but had gained and grown in its ability to take an audience to a different and unknown world for one hundred twenty-eight minutes.

While the actual film materials may age, with a scratch showing here or there; while the wonderful actors and craftspeople who made up his working family may be disappearing one by one, his films not only survive, but continue to bring pleasure to new audiences. When he received his AFI Lifetime Achievement Award it was noted that, like those of recipients before him, his films had "stood the test of time." What more could a filmmaker ask?

"People Think I'm a Monster"
The Life and Career of Alfred Hitchcock

He's a man who always looks like he's just come from a funeral. His rotund Santa Claus body is never without a dark navy blue suit, white shirt, and banker's tie. His face, in public, is usually void of any distinct expression. A man of mystery—an enigma. But for Alfred Hitchcock, the Master of Suspense, this seems right, doesn't it?

As French director François Truffaut once said in the *auteur* magazine he helped found, *Cahiers du Cinema*, "Hitchcock revels in being misunderstood, more so because it is on misunderstandings that he has constructed his life. . . . Hitchcock is a Hitchcockian character; he loathes having to explain himself. He must realize, however, that one day he will have to behave like his characters who assure their salvation by admitting this. But to admit that he is a genius is difficult, particularly when it is true. We can never dispute the formal genius of Hitchcock even though we are still squabbling over his responsibility for the scenarios he shoots."

Hitchcock sparkles with menacing glee, especially when he has pulled off one of the practical jokes he delights in. Hitchcock's humor is with him constantly. He feels his pièce de résistance was achieved by what he did to the hundreds of millions of people who viewed *Psycho*, many of whom were afraid to take showers for weeks after.

But it's probably the Hitchcock of television fame that most people have come to know: a man unperturbed by anything short of a world holocaust. His public persona then, whether shaped intentionally or naturally, is one of an obese Englishman who is cool, calm, and collected. Another practical joke? Perhaps.

In 1973 Hitchcock was to receive an honorary degree from Columbia University. He agreed to speak to a group of film students for the occasion. His latest film, *Frenzy*, had just been released, and some clever students got the idea of creating a table decoration consisting of a bag of potatoes and a striped tie—the two important motifs of the picture. The table was placed directly in front of the director's chair so there would be no way of its being overlooked. The students anxiously waited to assay his reaction, but not once during the entire proceedings did he give the slightest indication of recognition. Perhaps it's because Hitchcock thinks he has been irreversibly typed. "It has been said of me," he notes, "that if I made *Cinderella*, the audience would start looking for a body in the pumpkin coach. That's true. If an audience sees one of my productions with no spine-tingling, they're disappointed."

Even when Alfred Hitchcock stood up in his box at New York's Avery Fisher Hall on April 29, 1974, and accepted the loving applause of the 2,700-odd people that had come to the gala evening in his honor, he didn't seem to be visibly affected. The Film Society of Lincoln Center in New York created an entire evening devoted to his career of expert film-making, and at the end of what seemed to be a too-short selection of highlights from his fifty-three films, the entire audience rose en masse to show their gratitude. After many minutes he raised his hand to still the crowd, and in his inimitable monotone said, "As you have seen on the screen, scissors are the best way." This was a reference to the murder scene from *Dial M for Murder* that had particularly shocked the black-tie and evening-gown gathering. That's all he said except for a brief filmed section at the end of the clips in which he declared how deeply touched he was at the honor. Like a drowning man, he had just seen his whole life flash before his eyes, he stated, but this time without so much as getting his feet wet.

ALFRED JOSEPH HITCHCOCK was born in London on August 13, 1899, to William Hitchcock, a poultry dealer and fruit-importer, and Emma Whelan Hitchcock. As a young boy he was possessed by wanderlust, and by the time he was eight he had ridden every bus line in London and explored all its docks and shipping terminals.

One of his pet hobbies was keeping tabs on the British merchant fleet by purchasing *Lloyd's Bulletin*, a shipping newspaper, and then scurrying home to plot the ship positions on a huge wall chart.

His parents were devout Catholics and made sure their son had a proper Jesuit upbringing. Once, as a child, when he had done something of which his father disapproved, he was given a note to take to the police chief. The officer read it and put Alfred in a jail cell for ten minutes. "That's what we do to boys who are naughty," he reprimanded. Ever since then Hitchcock has had a phobia for police and police stations, and this fear has manifested itself in many of his films.

He attended St. Ignatius College, a Jesuit preparatory school in London, where he started on a course that would prepare him to become an electrical engineer. He eventually was forced to give up his courses at the University of London to help support his family by working as a technical clerk in a cable-manufacturing concern. Not to be deterred, he rose from the lowly job to the advertising department, where he showed talent for producing advertising layouts. He soon took a job as an assistant layout man in the advertising office of a London department store at a meager salary of fifteen shillings per week.

Upon learning one day that the Famous Players–Lasky Company was planning to open London studios, Hitchcock "went to work on a pet idea," according to Walter Wanger, the producer of Hitchcock's 1940 film, *Foreign Correspondent*. He felt that film title cards were atrocious and decided to design some to present to the new producers. He worked for five days and nights, carefully lettering art title cards using the names of the first announced production, *The Sorrows of Satan*, to fill out the list of credits.

After battling past the army of secretaries and assistants to the assistants, he somehow managed to wrangle his way to the top man, who looked at Hitchcock's work and informed him that he was in England to make not *The Sorrows of Satan* but another film altogether. Persistent as ever, Hitchcock created a whole new batch of title cards for the right film, *The Great Day*, which the producer saw and liked.

In his new job as a title writer for Famous Players–Lasky, Hitchcock added symbolic drawings to the otherwise unadorned titles. This was something novel and attracted attention. By 1923, he was a scenario writer for Gainsborough Pictures in Islington, England, and that same year he saw his first credit as art director for *Woman to Woman*. This came after he had tried his hand at directing a comedy about London low-life called *Number Thirteen*. The star of the picture, Clare Greet, put up some of the money for the project, but apparently it was not enough to sustain it and the film was never completed. He returned to Famous Players–Lasky, where he became co-director on the film *Always Tell Your Wife* after the first director became ill and could not complete shooting. He then acted as designer, script collaborator, and assistant director on *The White Shadow* for Gainsborough and continued there with *The Passionate Adventure* (1924) in the same three jobs. *The Blackguard* and *The Prude's Fall* both followed in 1925. Then Hitchcock got his first break.

He was asked to direct *The Pleasure Garden*, which would be his first complete film as director. It was to be made in Munich, and Hitchcock brought the cast and crew to Germany on a $50,000 budget. During the shooting the producers wired him, "Come home—use sets," but he was able to finish the film before returning.

The picture was a slight melodrama, but it obtained good reviews and brought attention to Hitchcock as a capable director. His background in advertising layout was to help Hitchcock in his directorial duties. In planning each film he would make hundreds of sketches illustrating the camera angles and the facial expressions he wanted from the main characters. In fact, the now-famous caricature of his profile was his own creation. In an interview in the *Saturday Evening Post* many years later, he explained, "I began to draw it years ago when I was a movie art director. With one exception there's been little change to it since then. At one time I had more hair. All three of them were wavy."

Following *The Pleasure Garden*, Hitchcock returned to the German studio Emelka for his second film, *The Mountain Eagle*, which was also shot on location in the Austrian Tyrol. In 1926 he made his first suspense yarn, *The Lodger*, a story about a man mistaken for Jack the Ripper. The film was praised by critics and audiences alike.

Hitchcock married Alma Reville on December 2, 1926, at Brompton Oratory. He knew Alma from Famous Players–Lasky, where she had been a writer. He had first proposed to her on the ship from Germany to England during the production of *The Blackguard*, almost two years earlier. Alma Revelle's name would appear on the credits of many of Hitchcock's later British and American productions, for her adaptations and original scenarios.

After completing *The Lodger*, Hitchcock was offered American directorial stints, but he chose to stay at Islington. Somehow his next film didn't measure up to his previous success. It was appropriately, and ironically, called *Downhill*. A modest soap opera, it was out of Hitchcock's league and did not do well. He went to work on another film, *Easy Virtue*, based on a play by Noel Coward. The playwright, who is known for his verbal wit, was obviously better on the stage, and the silent film proved boring without sound.

It was 1927, and upon completion of *Easy Virtue* he quit Gainsborough and went to the Elstree studio of British International Pictures. The box-office success of *The Lodger* assured him the then-phenomenal salary of £10,000, raised to £15,000 three years later.

The story of his first film for British International Pictures, his own, was about the boxing world. *The Ring*, released in 1927, was a creative effort which brought both him and his studio praise. But his next two films were insignificant and only his direction saved them from being total

Hitchcock and *Lady Vanishes* star Margaret Lockwood watch Patricia Hitchcock play with her dog.

Hitchcock in early publicity still "directing." To his right Alma Reville, the future Mrs. Hitchcock (c. 1926).

Circa 1939

Alfred Hitchcock talks with Warner Bros. President Jack L. Warner as the latter was invested as a Commander of the Order of the British Empire.

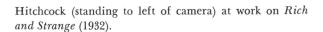

Hitchcock (standing to left of camera) at work on *Rich and Strange* (1932).

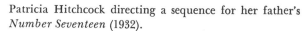

Patricia Hitchcock directing a sequence for her father's *Number Seventeen* (1932).

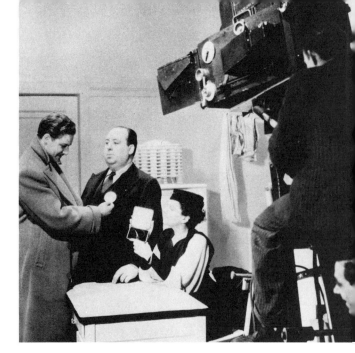

Hitchcock with Robert Donat and Lucie Mannheim on the set of *The 39 Steps*.

Mr. and Mrs. Hitchcock with daughter Pat upon arrival in New York for location work on *The Wrong Man*.

Hitchcock and wife Alma tour Egypt just before he commenced shooting of *The Man Who Knew Too Much* in Morocco.

Lunch time at work on *The 39 Steps* in an obviously chilly studio.

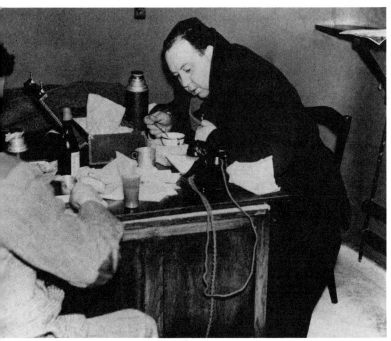

bores. The first was *The Farmer's Wife,* which concerned a man's selection of a wife from the community. Following that was a film that was not as bubbly as it sounded. *Champagne* originally had a Hitchcock story but was rejected by studio executives. The result was a filmed hodgepodge.

British International Pictures then assigned Hitchcock a Hall Caine novel, *The Manxman,* which was definitely not material that interested him. Accordingly, it was less than successful, but the studio had savvy enough to hold it from release until after his next film had received a gratifying box-office. *Blackmail* was to be his last silent film; it was 1929 and the talkies had arrived. For Alma and Alfred Hitchcock, 1929 also meant the arrival of their first and only child, Patricia. Hitchcock had almost completed shooting *Blackmail* when the studio told him that they wanted to remake it as a sound picture. He has always enjoyed, even invited, challenge to his work, and sound gave him the opportunity to invent new methods to overcome its problems. Even though *Blackmail* was his first dealing with sound, his innovations proved successful. He had exploited a new invention of a mechanical art which had proven deadly to others.

Not yet known as the master of suspense, Hitchcock next directed a sequence in a musical revue called *Elstree Calling.* In 1930 it was the British equivalent of the *Broadway Melodies* of Hollywood. Hitchcock directed only a small sequence in which Gordon Harker, a British actor, did a couple of sketches.

Hitchcock then returned to the format of the more serious stage-play adaptation. *Juno and the Paycock* was a film based on the Sean O'Casey play. This was nothing more than a photographed stage play. It was followed by *Murder* which, because of its technical innovations in sound, was a melodrama that went above its class.

In 1931 he directed only one film, *The Skin Game,* based on the John Galsworthy play about the English class system. Meanwhile, Hitchcock and his wife enjoyed the amenities his prominence as a director brought. They lived in comfort in a luxury flat in London and in a second home, an old and modest manor house at Shamley Green near Guildford, Surrey. His fondness for Shamley Green was one reason why he did not accept the American offers that he constantly received.

Rich and Strange, his first 1932 production, was part comedy, part drama, which Hitchcock enjoyed doing but which apparently audiences didn't appreciate. *Number Seventeen,* his final film for British International Pictures, was based on a stage play and was a comedy-thriller, a genre in which he felt at home.

It seems Hitchcock had performed every function on a movie production except to act as producer. He got that chance with *Lord Camber's Ladies,* which he produced but did not direct. It was quickly made and starred the marvelous Gertrude Lawrence.

The idea of getting caught up in independent productions made him decide to return to Michael Balcon, head of Gaumont-British, where his first film was a Viennese pastry called *Waltzes from Vienna,* a film he considers to be his worst. His six finest British thrillers were the result of this union. The first, released in 1934, was the highly praised *The Man Who Knew Too Much,* followed in 1935 by *The Thirty-Nine Steps,* which outdid it. *The Secret Agent* (1936) was based remotely on a novel by Somerset Maugham. *Sabotage* (released in America as *A Woman Alone*), also produced in 1936, was based, ironically, on *The Secret Agent* by Joseph Conrad but had absolutely no connection to the previous film. *Young and Innocent,* a delightful 1937 production, starred the now-grown

Publicity shot for *Notorious.*

9

Madeleine Carroll is visited on the set of *The 39 Steps* by scenarist Alma Reville Hitchcock and friend.

Nova Pilbeam, child actress of *The Man Who Knew Too Much*. It was followed by the remarkable *The Lady Vanishes* in 1938.

This completed his contract with Gaumont-British—conveniently so. After many entreaties from the United States, he finally accepted David O. Selznick's offer to make five films for $800,000. It meant selling his beloved Shamley Green, but the pastures did indeed look greener in America. When he began his television series in the 1950s, he named the production company after Shamley.

Selznick did not need Hitchcock until late in 1939, so the director decided to make one more picture in England to keep busy. He returned to Elstree, where he was coaxed into working on *Jamaica Inn* with Charles Laughton and Erich Pommer, the German tyrant of a producer he had not worked with since *The Pleasure Garden* in

1925. *Jamaica Inn* was one of his many productions based on material by Daphne du Maurier. It was an unenjoyable experience which, halfway through production, he realized he should never have gotten into. He completed the film, which did surprisingly well at the box-office, and then set sail for his new country. Besides his wife and daughter, Hitchcock took along his secretary, Joan Harrison, who had progressed to help him with the script of his last film and who would eventually become the producer of his famous TV series in the fifties.

"HOORAY FOR HOLLYWOOD!" seemed appropriate once Hitchcock arrived in 1939. His first film for Selznick was supposed to be *Titanic*. This was scrapped, and instead he directed a British Gothic based on Daphne du Maurier's novel of the same name, *Rebecca,* starring Joan Fontaine. Although he didn't win an award for his expert direction, he did help the film win the Best Picture of the Year Award for 1940.

The war had begun in Europe, and Hitchcock yearned to return to Britain. But he was urged to remain in America and use his talents for the Allied cause in his films. The result was a flag-waving but sensational film called *Foreign Correspondent.* Made for Walter Wanger and United Artists, it was his first film on loan from Selznick. It was also the first of an unrelated trilogy of war propaganda films he would direct.

Hitchcock relished the Hollywood high-life and became good friends with many of the leading stars and craftsmen. One enduring relationship was with the beguiling Carole Lombard, who insisted that Hitch direct her in a film. The result was the fast-paced 1941 screwball comedy called *Mr. and Mrs. Smith.* In addition to the talented Lombard, he was ably assisted by Robert Montgomery. Lombard matched wits with Hitch and, poking fun at his misunderstood remark, "all actors are cattle," she had a corral stocked with three calves bearing star nameplates built on the set. This practical joke has since become one of the great Hollywood legends.

The comedy was another loan-out picture, this one for RKO. It was followed with another RKO production, a British locale thriller called *Suspicion.* Once again he used Joan Fontaine, who picked up an Oscar for her performance. Starring with her was another young actor who would become one of Hitchcock's favorites, Cary Grant.

In 1942, Hitchcock made his second war-effort film, a cross-country chase thriller, *Saboteur.* This time he was assigned Robert Cummings and

Hitchcock and daughter in his library during pre-production work on one of his films.

Priscilla Lane, actors he felt were not of Hitchcock caliber. Since his arrival in Hollywood he had learned that front-office tampering was to be expected. He would not escape it until he went into independent production in 1948.

Saboteur was for Universal, as was his 1943 film, *Shadow of a Doubt,* which remains one of his favorites. He says it's one of the only films where the characters are allowed to develop and because of this is more successful and plausible than his other thrillers.

That same year he went to work with Tallulah Bankhead on his last war-oriented drama, *Lifeboat.* Always the craftsman and technician, Hitchcock was excited by the challenge of shooting a film within the confines of a single set. Throughout his career he would continually strive to create situations in which he would manipulate his medium in a new way to maintain interest and plausibility.

Secret agents Madeleine Carroll, Peter Lorre and Robert Young get information from their contact, Alfred Hitchcock.

A patriot, Alfred Hitchcock was released from his Selznick contract so that he could return to England to direct two documentary shorts for the Ministry of Information. The cast for these films consisted of French actors who worked as the Molière Players. Made in French, the films were shown throughout France after the Liberation, but no prints were released in English-speaking countries.

It was 1945, and he decided the next three pictures would be for Selznick so that he could complete his contract. *Spellbound,* with Ingrid Bergman and Gregory Peck, was the first; *Notorious,* in 1946, with Bergman and Grant, was second; and 1947's *The Paradine Case,* with Peck, was the third. Originally he was supposed to do five films in his seven-year contract, but this was reduced to four. *The Paradine Case* was the poorest of the package and Selznick lost money on it. *Spellbound* and *Notorious* well made up for the loss, however, bringing millions of dollars into the Selznick coffers.

But now Hitchcock was free—free to do what he pleased. His choice was a partnership with producer Sidney Bernstein in a company they called Transatlantic Pictures. The idea was to produce films in Hollywood and London. As it worked out, the company made only two films, one in Hollywood and the other in England. The first was made at Warner Bros. in Burbank. It was Hitchcock's first color film, but the experiments did not end there. *Rope* was also shot with ten-minute takes, another restriction on the director, who was working in a single setting. The story was about two youths who kill another, just for the thrill of it. Since the ten-minute takes were not completely successful, Hitchcock tried slightly shorter ones of seven minutes in his next effort, a costume drama filmed in Technicolor called *Under Capricorn.* It, too, was a slow, plodding film, due not so much to the long takes as to a verbose scenario. It was filmed in England, where Hitchcock remained to make *Stage Fright* in 1950, with Marlene Dietrich and Jane Wyman, which was a dull affair with little suspense. It seemed that England no longer held the magic it once did for Hitchcock, for *Stage Fright* was his fourth straight loser. He was to regain his mastery of suspense with his next superb 1951 production, *Strangers on a Train.*

Strangers on a Train, like *Stage Fright,* was made under contract to Warners, but unlike the latter, it was critically and financially his most successful film in five years. Like *Shadow of a Doubt, Strangers on a Train* employed real loca-

James Stewart and Kim Novak, stars of *Vertigo,* cajole Hitch into eating an egg appetizer, which he is repelled by.

Hitchcock with smiling saboteur (Oscar Homolka) in *Sabotage.*

On the set of *Waltzes From Vienna.*

Circa 1960.

The Hitchcock clan watch some off-scene action on the set of *Strangers on a Train.*

tion shooting which helped sustain the enormous amount of suspense that the film created. Hitchcock was obviously interested in what he was doing, and the result was one of his finest films.

His strict Jesuit upbringing is reflected somewhat in his next Warners film, *I Confess*. Montgomery Clift appears in this film as a priest who cannot exonerate himself of a murder charge because the actual murderer has revealed himself to Clift in the sanctity of the confessional. The problems of Church and State play a major part in this detailed film, and on the whole, proved more frustrating than suspenseful to the audience.

Frederick Knott's well-oiled stage play, *Dial M for Murder*, was next on the Hitchcock agenda at Warners and was filmed in the technical marvel of the day, 3-D. Hitchcock had lots of experience with filming stage plays, and his philosophy was, "why open up any drama originally intended for a confined space?" The result is a talky film, but suspenseful nonetheless.

After *Dial M for Murder*, Hitchcock returned to Paramount, which had developed from the original Famous Players–Lasky. This time he was producer and could be the obligatory "tampering executive." For the first Paramount film he created what some critics consider to be his best work, *Rear Window*. Once again he met the challenge of a confined set, a one-room flat overlooking the rear court of an apartment complex. Besides James Stewart, Grace Kelly, and Thelma Ritter, the real star in this thriller is the camera, which becomes the eyes of the audience. Hitchcock was always the voyeur in his films, and for *Rear Window* he created a voyeur's paradise, complete with binoculars and telephoto lens. But if any film shows us how Hitchcock manipulates his characters and his audiences for the particular effect he wants, this one does.

Grace Kelly returned to Hitchcock the following year, 1955, in the enchanting *To Catch a Thief*, a light-hearted chase across the azure coast of the Riviera, as good a place as any for location photography. Cary Grant was on hand as well, in his third appearance under Hitchcock's direction. It was an auspicious change of pace for the director, who had felt the pangs of wanderlust from an early age. That same year he ventured into another disciplining experiment in the form of a TV series, *Alfred Hitchcock Presents*, weekly half-hour programs with twist endings (to be called "Hitchcock endings") with only a handful directed by himself. He remained executive producer and assigned Joan Harrison, his ex-secretary, to do the actual produc-

tion. The program lasted eight years and was eventually lengthened, for its last season, to an hour.

His droll introductions on the show were fashioned by a writer who was instructed to watch Hitch's 1955 film, *The Trouble with Harry*, a black comedy about a dead man whom everybody seemed to feel responsible for slaying. Filmed in Vermont, *The Trouble with Harry* was one of Hitchcock's pet projects but unfortunately didn't prove successful with audiences. Perhaps its humor was a bit too personal or contrived for moviegoers.

The Man Who Knew Too Much, produced in 1956, was a remake of his 1934 classic but was far from a déjà vu experience. The plot remained substantially the same but was lengthened from a little over one hour to two hours. In addition, the widescreen VistaVision and Technicolor added a new brilliant gloss and spectacle to the production filmed in England and on location in the Mideast. Doris Day, whom Hitchcock had seen and liked, was cast in the role of a retired singer turned worried mother. The plot was hinged in part on her singing of the song "Que Sera Sera," an Academy Award winner, which was dramatically used at the climax of the film.

Back at Warner Bros. in 1957, now as an independent producer, Hitchcock dabbled with a new idea, a suspense story based on fact. *The Wrong Man*, a black-and-white semidocumentary, starred Henry Fonda and Vera Miles, an actress who appeared often on Hitch's TV show. The title of the film echoed one of the director's favorite themes, the wrong man accused of a crime he didn't commit. But as much as the theme of compassion was built up, the real-life quality of the story actually hurt the box office. After *The Wrong Man*, Hitchcock returned to Paramount to make one of his more complex and absorbing mysteries, *Vertigo*. James Stewart was cast in his third Hitchcock film opposite Kim Novak, who was given the opportunity to prove her acting ability. The 1958 production received mixed reactions but did well at the box office and exemplified Hitchcock's meticulous planning before actual shooting.

In 1959 Hitchcock made one film for M-G-M which he considers to be the epitome of all his productions. *North by Northwest* was an original screenplay by Ernest Lehman. He and Hitchcock worked on it for a year. It starred Cary Grant and Eva Marie Saint, a replacement for the retired Grace Kelly. It is an outrageous fantasy with the now-familiar theme of the innocent man who pursues, and is pursued, across country in order to prove his innocence. The Technicolor Vista-Vision production hit a peak for suspense thrillers and was a brilliant way to end the decade. *North by Northwest* was filled with Hitchcock's subtle, but always black, humor; still, it could not compare with the sadistic trickery he employed on the audience in what most people agree is his tour de force in horror, *Psycho*. Hitchcock used all his knowledge and experience to manipulate audience emotion. *Psycho* was a return to black-and-white and was filmed quickly by the same crew that shot his TV series. While many films are gimmicky, *Psycho* is simple and unassuming. Its advertising, however, employed a brilliant ruse. Because the heroine was killed a third of the way into the film, people who arrived late wondered where Janet Leigh was. Thus Hitchcock appeared in the advertising and demanded that audiences show up on time before the film began as no one would be admitted thereafter.

Psycho proved to be his most successful film with both critics and the box office and in its first run grossed $16 million on an $800,000 budget. Pat Hitchcock made a brief appearance in *Psycho*, as she had in *Strangers on a Train, Stage Fright,* and a number of the television plays. She has since married and is busy with her family.

The 1960 film *Psycho* was the last he would make for Paramount. He then signed a long-term contract for five films with Universal, one of the only studios left in Hollywood with a busy back lot. It wasn't until 1963 that *The Birds* was released. Two years of diligent planning were spent on the horror film. Probably the most unintentional horror of the film, though, is the acting of the lead actress, a Hitchcock discovery, Tippi Hedren, a former model who couldn't understand that she was no longer a mannequin. *The Birds*, based on a Daphne du Maurier story, surpassed the technical artistry that seemed to peak with *North by Northwest* and *Psycho*. The film is full of ambiguities, but that was as Hitchcock designed it.

The following year, 1964, saw the release of *Marnie,* again with Miss Hedren. This was a pure and simple soapy melodrama, so there wasn't all that much to ruin. In the tradition of *Spellbound,* it was a Freudian, analytical study of a kleptomaniac and a man in love with her because of her illness. The production was disappointing, if only because it appeared to be slapped together hastily without the loving care Hitchcock had devoted to his last few efforts.

Another two-year wait for the next Universal fiasco, in the shape of *Torn Curtain,* did not add

Hitchcock in Australia during movie promotion, 1960.

15

much to the master's reputation. With the exception of a detailed murder sequence, the fiftieth Hitchcock film lacked the spark and urbane wit that added so much class and suspense to earlier spy and chase films.

When three years had gone by with no Hitchcock release, people began to think that Hitchcock had retired. He, too, was getting restive without a project that could be filmed. For convenience only, he purchased the rights to Leon Uris's best-seller, *Topaz*. Apparently Hitch hadn't learned his lesson very well with *Torn Curtain*. *Topaz* was just another, ever-more-complicated Cold War spy story. Once again, with the exception of a few sequences and details, the film was a failure.

Returning to England, where he hadn't produced a film in almost twenty years, Hitchcock concocted what critics called "a gem of a picture." The project was one that had been in mind for many years but was an on-again-off-again affair. *Frenzy* was the title, and it was clear that the master of suspense was once again in full control. He was now seventy-three but his age did not manifest itself in this briskly paced suspense story about a man accused of a crime his best friend committed. *Frenzy* was released by a very pleased Universal and made $6.5 million in net rentals on its first run in the United States and Canada alone.

EARLY IN HIS CAREER in the United States, Hitchcock became a millionaire, but his tastes were never overly elaborate, as his conservative apparel proves. A good bottle of wine, a home-cooked meal, a modest collection of paintings—especially ones by his favorite artist, Klee—and a fat cigar were the amenities of life that suited Alfred Hitchcock. His wealth had not come from films and television alone. In 1956 a magazine based on his name and concept of suspense and the macabre was started. *Alfred Hitchcock's Mystery Magazine* was, and is, edited by professionals who were given license to use Hitchcock's name. During the run of his television show he was given first rights to the stories for TV adaptation. Pat Hitchcock acted as liaison between the magazine and her father and was given the title of associate editor on the masthead.

A long and profitable series of anthology volumes produced by Random House and then reissued in paperback by Dell was endorsed with his name as editor, although mystery writers chose the stories. Some of the titles reflect his brand of humor: *Alfred Hitchcock Presents Stories My Mother Never Told Me; Stories to Be Read with the Lights On;*

and *Stories That Scared Even Me.*

Although shy, he had appeared on talk shows, especially when a new film was about to be released. Dick Cavett devoted an entire ninety-minute program to his career, and several film festivals have held retrospectives of his films. It is at these showings that one discovers that multiple viewings of Hitchcock films are never tiring.

HITCHCOCK. The single name is enough to tell people what type of film they can expect. Hitchcock: the only director whose name alone can sell a film and very often save it from an otherwise bad box-office. Few directors ever achieve the status of a superstar with their name above the title. Americans have always considered the thriller, the mystery, the suspense film, and the black comedy to be plebeian. Hitchcock took these genres, gave them dignity, and made them acceptable as art forms.

An Englishman with an admittedly English humor, Alfred Hitchcock said his film-making had always been influenced more by Americans than by his British compatriots. Of his fifty-three feature films, twenty-eight were British (counting four that were American-produced, but made in England). While each is unique, they share a common bond of vitality. Hitchcock was a director who did not like to actually *make* or *shoot* films. He liked to create them on paper, figuring out every shot, every technical problem, and every movement of camera and actor. Once it was down on paper he felt his work was done and the actual shooting was only going through the motions, a mere formality. His productions were pre-cut.

"Many films are pieces of life, mine are slices of cake," he had said. Hitchcock had always seen himself as a master of ceremonies, directing the entertainment that will amuse, thrill, titillate, and otherwise occupy the audience. Because his mastery of his craft always resulted in something new and exciting on the screen, whether it works or not, his films have been the constant subject of controversy. To the French, he was an auteur director, the single master creator of a film, its author, so to speak. To the Americans, he had always been represented as the cherubic master of suspense, the man who could take thrills to new heights, the portly master of the involuntary scream. Today's generation knows Hitchcock from his obligatory cameos in his films and from his controlled, acerbic wit and deadpan introductions for eight years on his TV series.

But he is still elusive to us, no matter how well we think we know him. "I'm in competition with

Not that Hitchcock cared. He said he never read the critics. He made films to satisfy himself and his audiences. Even off the job, he was always trying to keep the people around him amused or in a dither. One of his favorite practical jokes, and he was known to have pulled many in his day, was describing a particularly bloody killing while he was riding a crowded elevator. Perhaps he was more amused than anyone. Nevertheless, his films have grossed well over $200 million, and he had been the impresario of some 350 popular TV shows.

Part of his mystique, his public sobriety, had to do with his shyness and unerring modesty. In fact, he rarely sat in a theater with an audience watching one of his films. The first time he had done this in a long while was at Lincoln Center at his Gala Tribute in 1974. He had the opportunity to hear them scream and squeal and watch them squirm in their seats.

You would think that he would have missed this after so many glorious thrillers, but no, Hitchcock said slyly, "I can hear them screaming when I'm making the picture." His theory of mystery *v.* suspense has been applied to almost every one of his pictures. In an interview in *Life* magazine he was able to explain it simply:

"Let us suppose that three men are sitting in a room in which a ticking bomb has been planted. It is going to go off in ten minutes. The audience does not know it is there either, so they go on talking inanely about the weather or yesterday's baseball game. After ten minutes of desultory conversation the bomb goes off. What's the result? The unsuspecting audience gets a surprise.... That's all. But suppose the story were told differently. This time, while the men still do not know the bomb is there, the audience does know. The men still talk inanities, but now the most banal thing they say is charged with excitement. When one finally says, 'Let's leave,' the entire audience is praying for them to do so. But another man says, 'No. Wait a minute. I want to finish my coffee.' The audience groans inwardly and yearns for them to leave. That is suspense."

Hitchcock frightened millions of people around the world. Did he himself scare easily? "Very easily," he admitted. "Here's a list in order of adrenalin production: 1. Little children; 2. Policemen; 3. High places; 4. That my next picture won't be as good as the last one."

He liked to keep everyone in the audience interested. He did all right. Well, more than all right.

Sir Alfred Hitchcock died April 28, 1980.

myself," he ruefully surmised. People expect him to out-Hitchcock Hitchcock and to stay above the many directors who tried to imitate him. When he made a personal film that satisfied himself but let his audiences down, it is clear that he had seriously tried to create more than just another expected "entertainment." Even his entertainments have always had something to say about mankind, society, politics, or human nature. Many of his films seem obvious and superficial, and occasionally that's all they were intended to be. Because of the mystique he created for and of himself, because of the protective cover he maintained, the people he excited with his provocative work have attempted to find meanings never intended in his films.

19

The Early Years

1922-1933

The Lodger.

22

In eleven short years Alfred Hitchcock directed nineteen features * in a variety of genres ranging from whodunit mysteries to stagey musicals. Taken as a whole, they reveal to us the primal Alfred Hitchcock. Or, as animator Al Kilgore, creator of Bullwinkle and other characters, has noted, "the early English works of Hitchcock are to his later, glossier productions as a cartoonist's roughs are to his completed artwork."

There is a steady progression of improvement and sophistication in techniques with each new film—although some of the material with which Hitchcock had to work was not inspired. He was able to transcend limited budgets and severely restricted scenery and equipment by exploiting the illusions of the medium. And in the rare instances in which he had some say in what property he would direct, the differences are apparent.

Eleven of the nineteen early films were silents. *Blackmail* would have been the twelfth, but British International Pictures informed Hitchcock that he was to remake the entire film, which had been shot as a silent. Sound had arrived and *Blackmail* was chosen as the first talkie to be made in England. For this alone it is a curiosity piece in the history of British cinema. But it did offer some clues to the style of director Hitchcock.

In 1922, at twenty-three, Hitchcock became a director and producer—albeit for an ill-fated production. His first directorial stint was an uncompleted independent production called *Number Thirteen*. As unlucky as this number was for him then, three years later he was given his first full assignment, to direct *The Pleasure Garden*. When it was released, critics agreed that the film had the look and feel of an American-made picture, although it had been produced in Munich. But this was to be expected, since Hitchcock had used American lighting techniques and know-how from his apprentice experiences at Famous Players–Lasky.

The story of *The Pleasure Garden* tells of a naïve chorus girl, Patsy, who works at the Pleasure Garden Theatre. She arranges a job for her friend Jill. Patsy marries Levett, who is a friend of Jill's fiancé, Hugh. After they honeymoon at Lake

---

* Of the nineteen films, one was not completed due to lack of funds and the other was a contribution to a multi-director production. During this period he had also acted as a producer, scriptwriter, scenic director, etc.

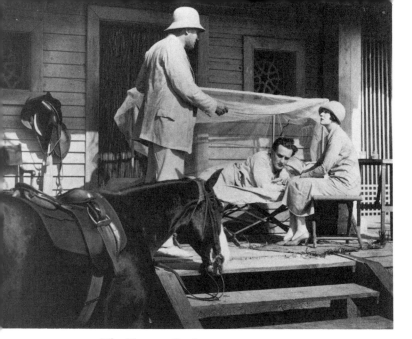

The Pleasure Garden

Como, Levett leaves for the colonies. Patsy returns home to find Jill fooling around with other men while she stalls her trip to the islands, where fiancé Hugh awaits. Patsy finally leaves but arrives only to find him making love to a native woman. Patsy, shocked and outraged, declares she is leaving him. He kills the native but makes it look like suicide. As he is about to kill Patsy, he is himself shot down by a local doctor. Hugh, abandoned by Jill, and Patsy decide they need each other.

This was typical of the messy melodramas which Hitchcock was repeatedly assigned in his first years as a director. His next film was *The Mountain Eagle,* released in 1926 in England and also presented in the United States as *Fear o' God.* All that remains from this film are a half-dozen photographs. The nitrate print has long been the victim of decomposition. *The Mountain Eagle* concerns the manager of a store who fancies a young schoolteacher. She runs to the mountains, where she is rescued by a hermit, who finally marries her. Shot in the studio and on location in the Tyrol, the picture starred Nita Naldi, supposedly the new Theda Bara.

The first true Hitchcock film was made later that same year. *The Lodger* was ostensibly about Jack the Ripper, but this is left open. The concept of suspicion, though, was the crux of the picture and the basis for suspense. Adapted from the novel of the same name, the plot was basically: Was the

new boarder in the lodging house Jack the Ripper? The suspense mounts until even the audience—who up to that time considered the boarder innocent—thinks he is the killer. This is the first appearance of the theme of many later Hitchcock films: that of the wrong man accused of a crime and his escape from the people in pursuit. The distribution company, Wardour, on first viewing thought *The Lodger* was terrible and canceled its bookings. Even with the drawing power of its matinée-idol star, Ivor Novello, *The Lodger* just could not interest the distributor. A few months later a new screening was arranged. After Wardour asked Hitchcock to make some small changes, it released *The Lodger* to reviews calling it about the best British picture ever made. No doubt this was due to the many technical tricks Hitchcock created for the film. For example, when the landlady hears the lodger's footsteps above, she "sees" them in what looks like a double-exposure but is actually a plate-glass floor. The use of lighting to create the suggestive shadows which haunt the film, and the gripping mob scene at the end of the film—with the lodger in handcuffs hanging on an iron fence, alluding to the crucifixion—are also significant. All of these trendsetting innovations were controversial in their day, but they worked then as they do now. Luckily the boarder has been discovered to be innocent and is saved from the mob which surrounds him. He too is after the killer, as his sister was a victim.

Downhill, made at Gainsborough Studios in 1927, was written by its star, Ivor Novello, in collaboration with Constance Collier. Released in the United States as *When Boys Leave Home,* it was the story of a young boy accused of stealing at his school. Although completely innocent, he is expelled from school. His father, outraged at what the boy has supposedly done, rejects him, and the boy leaves home. He goes to Paris, has an affair with an actress, and eventually comes home to his parents. They are remorseful after learning their son was innocent. Hitchcock experimented with some dream sequences by shooting them in superimpositions and blurred images; this was unlike the work of most other directors of that time except possibly the early work of René Clair *(Entr' Acte)* and Abel Gance *(La Folie de Docteur Tube, Napoléon).*

A Noël Coward play was the basis for Hitchcock's next film, *Easy Virtue* (1927). It is the tale of Laurita (Isabel Jean), a married woman who falls in love with a young artist. The young man kills himself and she divorces her alcoholic hus-

The Lodger: Ivor Novello—Is he or isn't he?

The Lodger: Ivor Novello and Daisy Jackson.

Downhill.

Ivor Novello and Daisy Jackson in *Downhill.*

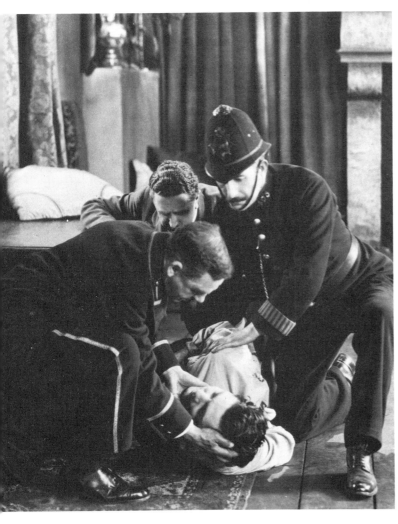

band. To forget her woes, she travels abroad and meets another young man, John Whittaker (Robin Irvine), whom she marries. But his stuffy upper-class family investigates her background and compels him to divorce her. At the end we see she has nothing left but misery.

Easy Virtue is possibly the finest example of the purely literary film-making so prevalent in England during the twenties. It is a well-produced, basically straightforward filming of the Noël Coward stage play. Yet Hitchcock raises it above the norm. One scene of note involves a proposal of marriage expected during a midnight phone call. The sequence opens with a closeup of a wristwatch. It belongs to a switchboard operator. We know that this is the call in question and can judge the outcome by the expression on the operator's face as she listens in. The camera does not linger over long silent shots of the couple broken by titles, but stays with the simple, workable premise of the switchboard operator.

The next picture was *The Ring* (1927), directed for British International Pictures. It was about Jack Sander, a fighter called "One Round Jack" (Carl Brisson), and Bob Corby, the champion from Australia (Ian Hunter), both of whom are in love with Nelly (Lillian Hall-Davies). Included in the film were many original flourishes of detail and style that charmed the critics but went unnoticed by the regular audiences. The title refers to the arena in which the boxing matches took place, to the wedding ring, and also to a snakelike bracelet that Bob gives to Nelly.

Easy Virtue: the arrival of help.

Isabel Jeans and Robin Irvine in *Easy Virtue.*

Gordon Harker, Carl Brisson and Harry Terry in *The Ring*.

In 1928, Hitchcock directed and wrote *The Farmer's Wife* based on a play by Eden Philpotts. It was about a farmer whose previous wife died and who looks for a new one. He considers various women as possibilities but in the end realizes that it is his housekeeper, who is secretly in love with him, who is the right wife for him. The film relies too heavily on dialogue, and the title cards interrupt the action more than they should. Supposedly a comedy, it lost much of its intimacy that it had as a live performance play. The New York *World* reviewed it by recommending it "on the strength of its scenic and photographic virtues. It is a travelogue of the English countryside depicting with rare effect, the salient features of landscape among which may be cited a foxhunt with the hounds in full cry."

Champagne, which followed, was made in English and German versions. The story line is as thin as mountain air and is basically boy meets girl, boy loses girl, boy finally gets girl. Hitchcock thinks that this is one of his worst films ever, but it does

have some funny bits, such as a drunk who walks with a stagger from side to side on a ship that is very steady. When the ship starts to roll, though, the drunk walks straight and everybody else staggers. The film was trivial but not unlike some of the other losers with which Hitchcock was connected in his early years.

The Manxman was his next project, although *Harmony Heaven* is credited to him as a 1929 musical in color. It was his last silent film, but alas, another one that Hitchcock considered worthless and banal. It concerns two men in love with the same woman—Peter, an indigent fisherman, and Philip, a rich lawyer. Peter proposes to Kate but her father says no, because the man can't support her. In search of fortune, he leaves the Isle of Man where the trio lives. Philip begins to court Kate after they hear of Peter's reported death, but Peter returns and she keeps her promise to marry him. She gives birth to a child, but Philip is the father. The film moves downhill through attempts of suicide, confessions, and pleas for happiness and rightful family ties for the child.

The sound era entered with *Blackmail* in 1929. Two versions of the film are known to exist: the first is silent except for the last reel, and the second is completely sound. The story concerns a girl who is in love with a young police officer. During dinner at a large restaurant, Alice flirts with an artist (Cyril Ritchard) who sits at a nearby table. Frank, her detective boyfriend, is not totally pleased by her games, but she enjoys the interest

Carl Brisson and Lillian Hall-Davies with the second meaning of *The Ring*.

Jameson Thomas (right), Gordon Harker (left), and Lillian Hall-Davies, *The Farmer's Wife*.

Gordon Harker, Jameson Thomas and Lillian Hall-Davies, *The Farmer's Wife*.

Betty Balfour is interviewed in *Champagne*.

of the artist. When an argument ensues, Frank leaves her to be picked up by the artist and escorted to his flat to see his etchings. After an initial art lesson, in which the artist teaches Alice to draw a nude, she becomes his model for the evening.

Reconsidering the premise of the film to this point, Alice has flirted with the artist, gone to his flat, and removed most of her clothing in order to put on a flimsy outfit in which to model. It would seem that any negative reactions to the artist's advances at this point would be only as a bit of morning-after excuse of "I tried to be good but . . ." In any case, the artist assumes that any woman who has put herself in Alice's position is interested in more than his etchings and that any negative response on her part is simply a front for her actual desires.

For Alice, however, the game has gone too far and her protestations are not only real but on the verge of panic. When the artist does make his move, her reaction is acute, violent, and reflex. The artist is killed with a bread knife as a painting of a jester leers down mockingly as a silent witness.

As may be expected by the audience, Frank is assigned to assist in the case. While searching for

Anny Ondra in the arms of
Malcolm Keen in *The Manxman*.

Malcolm Keen framed by the natural sets of *The Manxman*.

The chase after the blackmailer. (Donald Calthrop) through and above the British Museum in *Blackmail.*

clues, he finds one of Alice's gloves and contrary to his Scotland Yard training pockets the clue. When he arrives at Alice's shop, we find that he does not have the only clue. The other glove is in the possession of a blackmailer. Frank recognizes the blackmailer and, remembering him to be a member of the local crime element, phones the station house. Frank explains to the blackmailer that he may be arrested for the crime, and he flees as the police arrive to question him, later to fall to his death during a chase through and above the British Museum.

Alice arrives at the police station ready to confess her part in the crime, but is interrupted several times and finally never gets a chance to tell her story. She is escorted out of the station by Frank without involving herself. The case is closed. In this second film of the true Hitchcock style, we see that there are no truly black or white characters. Alice has put herself in a position in which she would either have to defend herself or give in to the artist's desires. The artist may or may not have lured Alice into the flat for nonartistic mo-

Hitchcock makes his appearance in *Blackmail* seated next to John Londgen and Anny Ondra.

Blackmail

tives. The detective has withheld evidence in order to protect Alice whom he assumes is strictly innocent. The blackmailer wants a free meal and a bit of quick cash to forget everything, and the detective has put him in a position for which he dies for his ambitions. Our characters are gray, and the truths and deceptions of crime and justice exist somewhere in a zone of love, desire, survival, and the fates of everyday existence.

To take advantage of the new-fangled device which made pictures talk, Hitchcock showed how the repetition of the word *knife* made the girl feel guilty about her killing. The word *knife* is repeated over and over again but in innocuous dialogue such as "Pass the bread knife, please," until it gnaws at the audience's nerves. For the chase sequence in the British Museum, he used the forerunner of rear projection, a method involving mirrors and other deceptions to camouflage the lack of real scenery.

In 1930 he directed a few scenes with Gordon Harker for a musical revue called *Elstree Calling.* He then went on to direct the film version of Sean O'Casey's distinguished *Juno and the Paycock.* The

Sara Allgood as Juno and other players in *Juno and the Paycock.*

scenario was written by Mr. and Mrs. Hitchcock. More of a play than a film, *Juno and the Paycock* interested Hitchcock for its mood, characters, humor, and pace. The story is about a poor family about to inherit some money during the Dublin uprising. The money doesn't come after all; the daughter is about to give birth to an illegitimate child; and the son is shot as an informer. The critics raved about the picture and Hitchcock, but the director was unhappy with the work because it was based on another person's success, in this case Sean O'Casey's.

Hitchcock prepared two versions—English and German—of his next effort, *Murder* (1930). In a capsule review in *The New Yorker,* the picture is summed up as a "handsomely designed early Hitchcock whodunit set among theatre people; not in the class of his mid-thirties work, but with inventive tricks. Herbert Marshall in his first talking picture is a fancy big time actor serving on a jury; convinced of the innocence of a young actress (Norah Baring) who is on trial for murder, he tries to solve the case to save her life. There are some snobbish bits that appear to ridicule the 'lower

Norah Baring (left) and the prison attendants in *Murder*.

Herbert Marshall as Sir John begins to realize that he is questioning the real killer in *Murder*.

The Skin Game: The suicide

Helen Haye, Edmund Gwenn and Jill Esmond in *The Skin Game*.

Hitchcock and Jill Esmond.

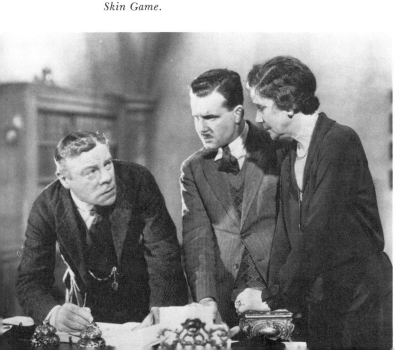

orders'—apparently the unfortunate results of attempts at improvisation. Hitchcock experimented with a stream of consciousness monologue and there's a tricky sequence in which Marshall listens to *Tristan* on the radio while he shaves. (The entire orchestra was behind the set playing simultaneously with the scene, since music could not be dubbed in later.) The actual murderer turns out to be a transvestite—daring at the time. Hitchcock called the film "the first important who-done-it picture I ever made." The German version was called *Mary* and was also made at Elstree.

The Skin Game, which followed *Murder* in 1931, was taken from the play by John Galsworthy and adapted by Hitchcock and his wife, Alma Reville. Edmund Gwenn starred as Mr. Hornblower, who is at odds with an aristocratic landowner, Hillcrest, played by C. V. France. The film is more Galsworthy than Hitchcock and seems very stagy. *The New York Times* said of it, "Mr. Hitchcock's imagination is never particularly keen during this production and frequently there are lengthy discourses between two characters without the slightest sem-

blance of movement to the picture—now and then this director has a fairly good idea but it is never brilliant and several of his scenes are not helped by much footage."

Rich and Strange was Hitchcock's first production in 1932 and had many more interesting aspects. "The film is more an episode than a story. A small town couple come into money and take a world cruise. They drift apart on the ship, flirt, get seasick, love, plan and quarrel and so on. Finally, they are reunited when the ship is wrecked. They are saved by a Chinese junk and eventually reach England and the fireside." Safe at home they return to their everyday lives as if nothing had happened, neither sadder nor wiser from their experiences. Apparently *Rich and Strange* was the director's reaction against some of his past talky dramas. Only about one fifth of the film contains dialogue. In the United States the picture was released as *East of Shanghai,* but that didn't help it from flopping at the box office as it did in England.

Affairs weren't going too well for British International Pictures, and in 1932 the studio gave

Rich and Strange: Harry Kendall and Joan Barry.

Hitchcock a meager budget to make *Number Seventeen.* Essentially a detective story, the picture runs about an hour and is rather confusing. It takes place in a spooky old house and ends with an exciting cross-country car chase, for which miniatures were used. It looked like a picture that had to be made to fill a quota. But it was the last he directed for BIP, although he produced one more, called *Lord Camber's Ladies.* Then he went over to Gaumont-British to direct *Waltzes from Vienna.* Hitchcock describes this period as "his lowest ebb," which in fact it was. His last two films were poorly received and he wasn't getting any constructive criticism. He took on *Waltzes* just to have something to do. It was a cheap musical without music; of course Strauss waltzes are included, as the budget couldn't afford anything else. The story concerns young Strauss, who leaves his music to join his sweetheart's father's confectionery business. A fortuitous encounter with a countess revives his dreams of fame; with her encouragement he composes the "Blue Danube" waltz. There's not much more after that, which might explain why it was released in the United States as *Strauss' Great Waltz.*

The year was 1933 and Hitchcock was approached by Michael Balcon, who asked if he had anything he would really like to do. Since Balcon trusted Hitchcock enough to give him his first film, *The Pleasure Garden,* he knew that whatever Hitchcock wanted would be acceptable. Hitchcock's answer was the following year's release, *The Man Who Knew Too Much.* The rest, as they say, is history.

NUMBER THIRTEEN (unfinished) 1922

Production: Wardour & F.; *Producer:* Alfred Hitchcock; *Director of Photography:* Rosenthal; *Studio:* Islington; *Principal Actors:* Clare Greet, Ernest Thesiger; *16mm Rental Source:* Unavailable.

THE PLEASURE GARDEN 1925

Production: Michael Balcon (Gainsborough), Eric Pommer (Emelka–G.B.A.); *Screenplay:* Eliot Stannard, from the novel by Oliver Sandys; *Director of Photography:* Baron Ventigmilia; *Assistant Director and Script Girl:* Alma Reville; *Studio:* Emelka, at Munich; *Distributors:* Wardour & F.; U.S.A., Amyon Independent; *Principal Actors:* Virginia Valli (*Patsy Brand, the dancer*), Carmelita Geraghty (*Jill Cheyne*), Miles Mander (*Levet*), John Stuart (*Hugh Fielding*), Frederic K. Martini, Florence Helminger, George Snell, C. Falkenburg; *Length:* 7,058 feet: *16mm Rental Source:* Raymond Rohauer.

THE MOUNTAIN EAGLE (U.S.A.: Fear o' God) 1926

Production: Gainsborough, Emelka; *Producer:* Michael Balcon; *Screenplay:* Eliot Stannard; *Director of Photography:* Baron Ventigmilia; *Studio:* Emelka, at Munich; *Location Work:* Austrian Tyrol; *Distributors:* Wardour & F.; U.S.A.; Artlee; Independent Distributors; *Principal Actors:* Bernard Goetzke (*Pettigrew*), Nita Naldi (*Beatrice, the governess*), Malcolm Keen (*Fear o' God*), John Hamilton (*Edward Pettigrew*); *Length:* 7,503 feet; *16mm Rental Source:* Unavailable.

THE LODGER (A Story of the London Fog) 1926

Production: Gainsborough, Michael Balcon; *Screenplay:* Alfred Hitchcock and Eliot Stannard, from the novel by Mrs. Belloc-Lowndes; *Director of Photography:* Baron Ventigmilia; *Sets:* C. Wilfred Arnold and Bertram Evans; *Editing and Subtitles:* Ivor Montagu; *Assistant Director:* Alma Reville; *Studio:* Islington; *Distributor:* Wardour & F.; *Principal Actors:* Ivor Novello (*The*

Number Seventeen: At the top of the staircase (still intact) are Donald Calthrop and friends.

A tense moment.

Jessie Matthews.

Jessie Matthews in the musical *Waltzes From Vienna.*

Lodger), June (*Daisy Jackson*), Marie Ault (*Mrs. Jackson, her mother*), Arthur Chesney (*Mr. Jackson*), Malcolm Keen (*Joe Betts, the policeman, Daisy's fiancé*); *Length:* 7,500 feet; *16mm Rental Source:* Janus.

DOWNHILL   (U.S.A.: *When Boys Leave Home*)
1927

Production: Michael Balcon, Gainsborough, G.B.; *Screenplay:* Eliot Stannard, from the play by Ivor Novello and Constance Collier, written under the pseudonym David Lestrange; *Director of Photography:* Claude McDonnell; *Editing:* Ivor Montagu; *Studio:* Islington; *Distributors:* Wardour & F.; U.S.A., World Wide Distributors; *Principal Actors:* Ivor Novello (*Roddy Berwick*), Ben Webster (*Doctor Dowson*), Robin Irvine (*Tim Wakely*), Sybil Rhoda (*Sybil Wakely*), Lillian Braithwaite (*Lady Berwick*), and Hannah Jones, Violet Farebrother, Isabel Jeans, Norman McKinnel, Jerrold Robertshaw, Annette Benson, Ian Hunter, Barbara Gott, Alfred Goddard; *Length:* 7,600 feet; *16mm Rental Source:* Unavailable.

EASY VIRTUE   1927

Production: Michael Balcon, Gainsborough Production; *Screenplay:* Eliot Stannard, from the play by Noel Coward; *Director of Photography:* Claude McDonnell; *Editing:* Ivor Montagu; *Studio:* Islington; *Distributors:* Wardour & F.; U.S.A., World Wide Distributors; *Principal Actors:* Isabel Jean (*Larita Filton*), Franklin Dyall (*M. Filton*), Eric Bransby Williams (*The Correspondent*), Ian Hunter (*Plaintiff's Counsel*), Robin Irvine (*John Whittaker*), Violet Farebrother (*his mother, Mrs. Whittaker*), and Frank Elliot, Darcia Deane, Dorothy Boyd, Enid Stamp-Taylor; *Length:* 7,392 feet; *16mm Rental Source:* Images.

THE RING   1927

Production: British International Pictures, G.B.; *Producer:* John Maxwell; *Screenplay:* Alfred Hitchcock; *Adaptation:* Alma Reville; *Director of Photography:* Jack Cox; *Assistant Director:* Frank Mills; *Studio:* Elstree; *Distributors:* Wardour & F.; *Principal Actors:* Carl Brisson (*Jack Sander, called "Round One"*), Lillian Hall-Davies (*Nelly*), Ian Hunter (*Bob Corby, the champion*), Forrester Harvey (*Harry, the traveling showman of the ring*) and Harry Terry, Gordon Harker, Billy Wells; *Length:* 8,454 feet; *16mm Rental Source:* Janus.

THE FARMER'S WIFE   1928

Production: British International Pictures, G.B.; *Producer:* John Maxwell; *Screenplay:* Alfred Hitchcock,

from the play by Eden Philpotts; *Director of Photography:* Jack Cox; *Assistant Director:* Frank Mills; *Editing:* Alfred Booth; *Studio:* Elstree; *Location Work:* Wales; *Distributors:* Wardour & F.; *Principal Actors:* Lillian Hall-Davies (*Araminta Dench, the young maid*), James Thomas (*Samuel Sweetland*), Maud Gill (*Thirza Tapper*), Gordon Harker (*Cheirdles Ash*), and Louise Pounds, Olga Slade, Antonia Brough; *Running Time:* 67 minutes; *16mm Rental Source:* Janus.

CHAMPAGNE   1928

Production: British International Pictures, G.B.; *Screenplay:* Eliot Stannard; *Director of Photography:* Jack Cox; *Studio:* Elstree; *Distributor:* Wardour & F.; *Principal Actors:* Betty Balfour (*Betty*), Gordon Harker (*Her Father*), Ferdinand Von Alten (*The Passenger*), Jean Bradin (*The Young Man*), and Jack Trevor, Marcel Vibert; *Length:* 8,038 feet; *16mm Rental Source:* Janus.

THE MANXMAN   1929

Production: British International Pictures, G.B.; *Producer:* John Maxwell; *Screenplay:* Eliot Stannard, from the novel by Sir Hall Caine; *Director of Photography:* Jack Cox; *Assistant Director:* Frank Mills; *Studio:* Elstree; *Distributors:* Wardour & F.; U.S.A.: Ufa Eastman Division; *Principal Actors:* Carl Brisson (*Pete*), Malcolm Keen (*Philip*), Anny Ondra (*Kate*), Randle Ayrton (*Her Father*), and Clare Greet; *Length:* 8,163 feet; *16mm Rental Source:* Janus.

BLACKMAIL   1929

Production: British International Pictures, G.B.; *Producer:* John Maxwell; *Screenplay:* Alfred Hitchcock, Benn W. Levy, and Charles Bennett, from the play by Charles Bennett; *Adaptation:* Alfred Hitchcock; *Dialogue:* Benn W. Levy; *Director of Photography:* Jack Cox; *Sets:* Wilfred C. Arnold and Norman Arnold; *Music:* Campbell and Connely, finished and arranged by Hubert Bath and Henry Stafford, performed by the British Symphony Orchestra under the direction of John Reynders; *Editing:* Emile de Ruelle; *Studio:* Elstree; *Distributors:* Wardour & F.; U.S.A.: Sono Art World Wide Pict.; *Principal Actors:* Anny Ondra (*Alice White*), Sara Allgood (*Mrs. White*), John Londgen (*Frank Webber, the detective*), Charles Paton (*Mr. White*), Donald Calthrop (*Tracy*), Cyril Ritchard (*the artist*), and Harvey Braban, Hannah Jones, Phyllis Monkman, ex-detective Sergeant Bishop; *Length:* 7,136 feet; *16mm Rental Source:* Janus.

JUNO AND THE PAYCOCK   1929

Production: British International Pictures; *Producer:* John Maxwell; *Screenplay:* Alfred Hitchcock and Alma Reville, from the play by Sean O'Casey; *Director of Photography:* Jack Cox; *Sets:* Norman Arnold; *Editing:* Emile de Ruelle; *Studio:* Elstree; *Distributors:* Wardour & F.; U.S.A.: British International by Capt. Harold Auten; *Principal Actors:* Sara Allgood (*Juno*), Edward Chapman (*Captain Boyle*), Sidney Morgan (*Joxer*), Marie O'Neill (*Mrs. Madigan*), and John Laurie, Dennis Wyndham, John Longden, Kathleen O'Regan, Dave Morris, Fred Schwartz; *Running Time:* 85 minutes; *16mm Rental Source:* Museum of Modern Art, New York.

MURDER   1929

Production: British International Pictures, G.B.; *Producer:* John Maxwell; *Screenplay:* Alma Reville, from the work by Clemence Dane (pseudonym of Winifred Ashton) and Helen Simpson, ENTER SIR JOHN; *Adaptation:* Alfred Hitchcock and Walter Mycroft; *Director of Photography:* Jack Cox; *Sets:* John Mead; *Editing:* René Harrison; *Supervision:* Emile de Ruelle; *Studio:* Elstree; *Distributor:* Wardour & F.; *Principal Actors:* Herbert Marshall (*Sir John Menier*), Nora Baring (*Diana Baring*), Phyllis Konstam (*Dulcie Markham*), Edward Chapman (*Ted Markham*), Miles Mander (*Gordon Druce*), Esme Percy (*Handel Fane*), Donald Calthrop (*Ion Stewart*), and Amy Brandon Thomas, Joynson Powell, Esme V. Chaplin, Marie Wright, S. J. Warmington, Hannah Jones, R. E. Jeffrey, Alan Stainer, Kenneth Kove, Guy Pelham, Matthew Boulton, Violet Farebrother, Ross Jefferson, Clare Greet, Drusilla Vills, Robert Easton, William Fazan, George Smythson; *Running Time:* 92–108 minutes; *16mm Rental Source:* Janus.

THE SKIN GAME   1931

Production: British International Pictures; *Producer:* John Maxwell; *Screenplay:* Alfred Hitchcock and Alma Reville, from the play by John Galsworthy; *Additional Dialogues:* Alma Reville; *Director of Photography:* Jack Cox, assisted by Charles Martin; *Editing:* René Harrison and A. Gobett; *Studio:* Elstree; *Distributors:* Wardour & F.; U.S.A.: British International; *Principal Actors:* Edmund Gwenn (*Mr. Hornblower*), Jill Esmond (*Jill*), John Longden (*Charles*), C. V. France (*Mr. Hillcrest*), Helen Haye (*Mrs. Hillcrest*), Phyllis Konstam (*Chloe*), Frank Lawton (*Rolfe*), and Herbert Ross, Dora Gregory,

Edward Chapman, R. E. Jeffrey, George Bancroft, Ronald Frankau; *Running Time:* 85 minutes; *16mm Rental Source:* Janus.

RICH AND STRANGE   (U.S.A.: *East of Shanghai*) 1932

Production: British International Pictures, G.B.; *Producer:* John Maxwell; *Screenplay:* Alma Reville and Val Valentine, from a theme by Dale Collins; *Adaptation:* Alfred Hitchcock; *Directors of Photography:* Jack Cox and Charles Martin; *Sets:* C. Wilfred Arnold; *Music:* Hal Dolphe, directed by John Reynders; *Editing:* Winifred Cooper and René Harrison; *Sound Engineer:* Alec Murray; *Studio:* Elstree; *Location Work:* Marseilles, Port Said, Colombo, Suez; *Distributors:* Wardour & F.; U.S.A.: Powers Pictures; *Principal Actors:* Henry Kendall (*Freddy Hill*), Joan Barry (*Emily Hill*), Betty Amann (*The Princess*), Percy Marmont (*Gordon*), Elsie Randolph (*The Old Lady*); *Running Time:* 83 minutes; *16mm Rental Source:* Janus.

NUMBER SEVENTEEN   1932

Production: British International Pictures; *Producer:* John Maxwell; *Screenplay:* Alfred Hitchcock, from the play and the novel by Jefferson Farjeon; *Director of Photography:* Jack Cox; *Studio:* Elstree; *Distributor:* Wardour & F.; *Principal Actors:* Léon M. Lion (*Ben*), Anne Grey (*The Young Girl*), John Stuart (*The Detective*), and Donald Calthrop, Barry Jones, Garry Marsh; *Running Time:* 63 minutes; *16mm Rental Source:* Janus.

WALTZES FROM VIENNA   (*Strauss' Great Waltz*) 1933

Production: Gaumont-British, G.F.D., G.B.; *Screenplay:* Alma Reville and Guy Bolton, from the play by Guy Bolton; *Sets:* Alfred Junge and Peter Proud; *Music:* Johann Strauss the Elder and Johann Strauss the Younger; *Studio:* Lime Grove; *Distributors:* G.F.D.; U.S.A.: Tom Arnold; *Principal Actors:* Jessie Matthews (*Rasi*), Esmond Knight (*Shani Strauss*), Frank Vosper (*The Prince*), Fay Compton (*The Countess*), Edmund Gwenn (*Johann Strauss the Elder*), Robert Hale (*Ebezeder*), Hindle Edgar (*Leopold*), Marcus Barron (*Drexter*), Charles Heslop, Sybil Grove, Billy Shine, Junior, Bertram Dench, B. M. Lewis, Cyril Smith, Betty Huntley Wright, Berinoff and Charlot; *Running Time:* 80 minutes; *16mm Rental Source:* Unavailable.

Becoming the Master of Suspense

1934-1939

Derek deMarney, Edward Rigby, and Nova Pillbeam in
Young and Innocent.

42

If Alfred Hitchcock ever chose to direct a musical comedy—which he wouldn't—his choice of material certainly would not be as flimsy as his 1933 Gaumont-British assignment, *Waltzes from Vienna*. The film registers in celluloid the boredom Hitchcock felt with a vehicle that was totally alien to his interests. He had been thinking about *The Man Who Knew Too Much* at the time the studio told him to direct the musical. The result was that *Waltzes from Vienna* was a mediocre picture. The following film, *The Man Who Knew Too Much,* was the film that triggered Hitchcock's reputation as the master of suspense.

Producers Michael Balcon and Ivor Montagu gave Hitchcock carte blanche to do what he wanted with his project. The product was acclaimed around the world, and established a new high in the thriller genre. It was only a preview, however, of the films Hitchcock would make from then on. The following year in 1935 he reached new heights with a film he still regards as one of his best, *The Thirty-Nine Steps.* Loosely based on the best-selling Canadian novel, Hitchcock's film succeeds because of the plethora of intrigue and atmosphere he inserts into the plotline.

Following this satisfying venture, Hitchcock put together a film based on a spy novel by Somerset Maugham called *Ashenden*. The film, retitled *The Secret Agent,* was about spies, like the previous two, and had its share of romance, but in the end it failed to please audiences as much as the two previous efforts. The reason lay in the inadequacies of plot.

Sabotage followed, based on *Secret Agent* by Joseph Conrad. Hitchcock dared to show the ruthlessness of political criminals and has regretted it ever since. He feels it was a mistake to build the audience's tension and then not relieve it.

His next feature was almost featherweight by comparison. Based on a Josephine Tey novel, Hitchcock dealt with plot more than character here, with the wrong man theme woven into a chase across England. *Young and Innocent* was entertaining and included many unused technical tricks which perhaps made the film more exciting than it actually was. His following venture was also a very light affair but possessed much more vitality. *The Lady Vanishes* is considered a classic of suspense today and in fact much of its overt humor seems timely today. *The Lady Vanishes* was a spy film and a chase story, but in the end we see that all the running, chaos, and bother is centered around one

With Sylvia Sidney and John Loder, stars of *Sabotage*.

thing: a government secret disguised in a silly children's rhyme. It was this thing (usually intangible) that the spies or bad guys are after which Hitchcock refers to as the "MacGuffin." What exactly is a MacGuffin? Nothing really. But it is the reason that gives Hitchcock an opportunity to build an incredible plot. Or, as he explained it once: Two men were sitting on a train. One man asked the other, "What is that over your head?" pointing to a bag. "Oh, that's my MacGuffin." What's a MacGuffin? "It's used to capture lions in the Scottish highlands," the man replied. "But there are no lions in the Scottish Highlands!" "Well, then that's no MacGuffin," the man retorted.

And so you see a MacGuffin isn't much of anything. But it is what Hitchcock has employed in virtually every one of his cloak-and-dagger films. Most of the late British pictures, the very ones that

earned for Hitchcock the reputation he still carries, were relatively short, running less than one hundred minutes and frequently less than ninety. In America his features tended to be much longer running from an hour and forty minutes to more than two hours. As he began to master his style and know his subject, he was able to fill in more of the details.

His last film in England was unnecessary. David O. Selznick had called him to America. But he had time and preferred to remain occupied, so he took on *Jamaica Inn*, a pirate adventure. Even though he began to detest the assignment, he completed it. Totally unlike his previous pictures, it was a costume drama with all the trimmings that was nevertheless entertaining. Only one other Hitchcock film can be equated to it: *Under Capricorn* which he would direct at the end of the next decade.

44

The Man Who Knew Too Much

1934

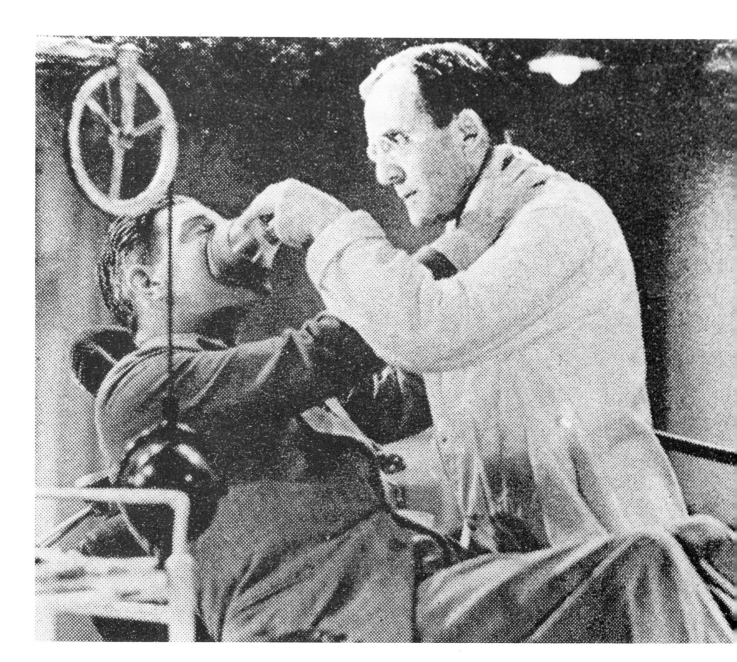

Production: Gaumont-British Pictures, G.B.; *Producers:* Michael Balcon; Associate, Ivor Montagu; *Screenplay:* A. R. Rawlinson, Charles Bennett, D. B. Wyndham Lewis, Edwin Greenwood, from an original theme by Charles Bennett and D. B. Wyndham Lewis; *Additional Dialogue:* Emlyn Williams; *Director of Photography:* Curt Courant; *Sets:* Alfred Junge and Peter Proud; *Music:* Arthur Benjamin, directed by Louis Levy; *Editing:* H. St.C. Stewart; *Studio:* Lime Grove; *Distributors:* G.F.D.; *Principal Actors:* Leslie Banks (*Bob Lawrence*), Edna Best (*Jill Lawrence*), Peter Lorre (*Abbot*), Frank Vosper (*Ramon Levine*), Hugh Wakefield (*Clive*), Nova Pilbeam (*Betty Lawrence*), Pierre Fresnay (*Louis Bernard*), and Cicely Oates, D. A. Clarke Smith, George Curzon; *Running Time:* 84 minutes; *16mm Rental Source:* Images.

Released directly after *Waltzes from Vienna, The Man Who Knew Too Much* was Hitchcock's comeback to the genre he knew best. Actually, the screenplay had already been prepared when he was asked to take on the directing chore of *Waltzes from Vienna* in 1933.

The Man Who Knew Too Much was in many ways indicative of what we could expect from Hitchcock from then on. It is a small, tightly woven film—only 84 minutes—which includes a generous portion of Hitchcockian humor and a more than adequate amount of suspense. Although he was given only a limited budget, he knew the technical tricks which could camouflage the fact. The gripping Albert Hall sequence in which a diplomat is about to be assassinated was actually shot in the Lime Grove studio. A painting by the academician Fortunino Matania reflected with a mirror into the camera lens served as most of the Albert Hall audience.

While the script is not as polished as the screenplays for his later pictures, it did capture one's attention. Playwright Emlyn Williams, who later appeared in *Jamaica Inn,* assisted by writing some additional dialogue. The story is about Bob and Jill Lawrence (Leslie Banks and Edna Best), who are on vacation in Switzerland with their daughter Betty (Nova Pilbeam). They are befriended by a Frenchman, Louis Bernard (Pierre Fresnay). When he is killed, he whispers to Bob an international secret about the intended assassination of a diplomat, which will embarrass the British government. To prevent Bob from revealing what he knows, the conspirators kidnap Betty as a hostage. The hired assassin is Abbott (Peter Lorre), who will shoot the diplomat during a concert at Albert Hall.

The film is primarily concerned with the dilemma of kidnaping—how to get Betty back safely. The subplot about the assassination is just the setup, or MacGuffin, as Hitchcock refers to it. Jill goes to Albert Hall and at the last minute foils the assassination by screaming in the auditorium. A chase follows to the hideout where Betty is held captive,

Frank Vosper with Nova Pilbeam and Edna Best (with gun).

Peter Lorre.

Planning the assassination: Frank Vosper, Leslie Banks, Nova Pilbeam and Peter Lorre.

and a gunfight ensues. The climax is reached when Jill, already established in the first scene as an excellent markswoman, shoots a spy who is about to kill her daughter. This final scene, based on the Sidney street siege, forced Hitchcock into a position in which he had to show the police as being unfamiliar with the weapons delivered to them, supposedly taken from gunshops or possibly sportsmen living in the area. It was thought to be politically improper for the police to be, or seem to be, knowledgeable in the use of firearms.

The Man Who Knew Too Much is a breathless escapade which, considering the infancy of sound film, was far ahead of its time. The death of Louis Bernard comes suddenly and points out that death comes when we least expect it. Hitchcock devised a comic episode leading up to it. We are invited to laugh as we watch Nova Pilbeam and Leslie Banks attach the end of an unraveling sweater onto a dancer in the nightclub. The humor is direct, slapstick, and obvious, but it is cut short by a bullet plunging into the chest of Pierre Fresnay. His death, unexplained and surprising, becomes all the more bothersome in the middle of our laughter.

The Man Who Knew Too Much lacks grace and rhythm between the suspense and the jokes, and Hitchcock concedes that the film was the creation of a "talented amateur." The critics differed, however, and the film has garnered unanimous praise

as one of the best British films and best thrillers ever. "So sure is Hitchcock's touch in creating an electric atmosphere that the audience is enthralled," raved *The New York Times*. Richard Watts, in the New York *Herald Tribune,* noted, "Hitchcock has given his work a machine gun pace, interjected a proper number of homely human incidents that add the required credibility to a wild and furious story . . . it is the best crime melodrama of the season and beats Hollywood in its chosen field, that of shrewd, ominous and dynamic melodrama."

The cast was similarly praised, with special mention of Peter Lorre in his first English-speaking film. Lorre was introduced to the director by Sidney Bernstein, with whom Hitchcock would later be partnered. Lorre had appeared earlier in Fritz Lang's German classic, *M,* and was perfect for the role of the anarchist.

Nova Pilbeam, who appeared as a child, went on to be cast in 1937 as the lead in Hitchcock's *Young and Innocent.*

The Man Who Knew Too Much is an archetype of the Alfred Hitchcock thriller. It was his favorite type of story, which may explain why he remade the film in 1956, adding forty-five minutes onto the story. The debate continues as to which is a better version, but both hold up equally well. No comparisons are really necessary.

Frank Vosper, Peter Lorre and
Cicely Oates.

Frank Vosper, Peter Lorre and Leslie Banks.

The 39 Steps
1935

The chase begins for Robert Donat when he discovers his guest has been murdered.

Production: Gaumont-British; Producer: Michael Balcon; Associate Producer: Ivor Montagu; Screenplay and Adaptation: Charles Bennett and Alma Reville, from the novel by John Buchan; Additional Dialogue: Ian Hay; Director of Photography: Bernard Knowles; Sets: Otto Werndorff and Albert Jullion; Costumes: J. Strassner; Music: Louis Levy; Editing: Derek N. Twist; Sound Engineer: A. Birch, Full Range Recording System at Shepherd's Bush, London; Studio: Lime Grove; Distributors: G.F.D.; Principal Actors: Madeleine Carroll (Pamela), Robert Donat (Richard Hannay), Lucie Mannheim (Miss Smith-Annabella), Godfrey Tearle (Professor Jordan), Peggy Ashcroft (Mrs. Crofter), John Laurie (Crofter, the farmer), Helen Haye (Mrs. Jordan), Frank Cellier (the Sheriff), Wylie Watson (Memory); Running Time: 81 minutes; 16mm Rental Source: Janus.

With the smashing financial and critical success of *The Man Who Knew Too Much* to his credit, Alfred Hitchcock was in a position to negotiate for control over his next production. *The 39 Steps,* based on the famous John Buchan novel of 1915, was freely adapted and changed by Hitchcock until very little of the original plot remained. Writer Buchan, who doubled as the British Governor General of Canada, was, at first, naturally upset that his book was used only as a foundation but later, after viewing the film, admitted that it was actually much better than his version.

Hitchcock rates *The 39 Steps* as one of his favorite films. He feels that its tempo is perfect. There is no dead footage, and the audience's absorption in the web of intrigue creates the impression of extremely fast pace. In an interview with Peter Bogdanovitch, Hitchcock once commented, "What I liked about *The 39 Steps* were the sudden switches and the jumping from one situation to another with such rapidity. Donat leaping out of the window of the police station with half of a handcuff on, and immediately walking into a Salvation Army band, darting down an alleyway into a room. 'Thank God you've come, Mr. so-and-so' they say and put him on to a platform. A girl comes along with two men, takes him into a car to the police station, but it's not really to the police station. . . . You know the rapidity of the switches, that's the great thing about it. If I did *The 39 Steps* again, I would stick to the formula, but it really takes a lot of work. You have to use one idea after another, and with such rapidity." The film is rich in details and that indescribable sense of the macabre.

Perhaps one of the reasons why *The 39 Steps* is one of the director's favorites is that it was his first to tackle his now-classic theme—the innocent man, framed by circumstantial evidence, who must run cross-country from police and spies alike in his frantic attempt to clear himself and find the real enemies of the people.

Fortunate casting provided Hitchcock with the dashing Robert Donat who was promoted as a matinee idol (that "Monte Cristo Man"). Paired with him was the beguiling Madeleine Carroll.

The Charles Bennett script is literate and balanced with a fair share of romantic banter. Hitchcock said in interviews at the time of release that he makes his talkies as if they were silent with a minimum of dialogue and a maximum of action. (He would change this point of view when he directed the witty *North by Northwest,* which while covering the same basic plot was close to an hour longer than *The 39 Steps.*)

The story revolves about Richard Hannay, who finds he must escape from his London flat after he discovers that the mysterious woman to whom he had given refuge the night before has been murdered. The killers are now after him, although he really isn't sure why, and he flees, following a single clue, to Scotland. Eluding his pursuers by jumping from the train on Forth Bridge, Hannay makes his way to the home of Professor Jordan (Godfrey Tearle) who, unknown to him, is the mastermind behind the spy ring. Again he is almost trapped, but he manages to escape to the heather moors with the girl he met on the train, Pamela (Madeleine Carroll), to whom he is handcuffed by the spies masquerading as police. The couple make it to a theater, where they find Mr. Memory (Wylie Watson), whom the spies use to transmit government secrets. Mr. Memory is shot and the spy's plans are foiled. Hannay is cleared of the murder and gets Pamela. The plot really doesn't matter much, although it is interesting, because it is what Hitchcock does with the situations he gets his hero into that create the excitement and suspense.

By combining the now-famous sound edit of the landlady's scream as she finds the body in Hannay's apartment linked with the shot of the train carrying Hannay toward his adventures, Hitchcock breached the "one-should-see-what-one-hears" barrier. The landlady's scream replaced the train whistle and connected the two scenes, adding shock value.

The entire production was shot at the Lime Grove Studio of Gaumont-British, and again it was the director's technical expertise that gave *The 39 Steps* a polished tone. The scene on the

Scottish moors created some problems, though; sixty-two sheep brought to the set for authenticity also brought havoc. The scene had to be shot before the sheep ate the sets.

Another fine point in the film is Donat's meeting with the insidious Professor Jordan, played with relish by Godfrey Tearle. Donat has learned that the leader of the spy ring is missing a finger on his right hand. He tells this to Tearle, who replies, "You mean this hand, don't you?" Other places where Hitchcock let his hero squirm include

Robert Donat with Peggy Ashcroft.

Donat and Carroll discover the secret of the 39 steps.

52

that of Donat's taking cover in a political rally to escape the police. Forced to give a double-talk speech with his handcuffs hidden, he is wildly applauded by the crowd. Unfortunately, Hannay knows nothing about the candidate about whom he speaks.

The film was enthusiastically greeted in America and England. It was the biggest hit for Hitchcock in the United States at that time. When it opened at the Roxy Theater in New York, *The New York Times* said, "A master of shock and suspense, of cold horror and slyly incongruous wit, he uses his camera the way a painter use his brush, stylizing his story and giving it values which the scenarist could hardly have suspected. Perhaps the identifying hallmark of his method is its apparent absence of accent in the climaxes, which are upon the spectator like a slap in the face before he has set himself for the blow. There is a subtle feeling of menace in Mr. Hitchcock's low-slung, angled use of the camera."

Hitchcock dispenses with credibility. He amends

Robert Donat and Madeleine Carroll under the spotlights of the studio.

Robert Donat meets a pair of lingerie salesmen (Wilfred Bramball, right)

Lucy Mannheim explains to Robert Donat about the leader of the spy ring who has a missing finger.

Robert Donat and Madeleine Carroll.

the plot to serve his purposes, and of course, he puts humor where you would least expect it, in a suspenseful situation. The total effect of all this chicanery is pure unadulterated entertainment. Added to this were high production values and players who "preserve that sureness of mood and that understand the director's intention . . ." as the *Times* reviewer described it.

The 39 Steps was remade in color in 1960 with Kenneth More replacing Robert Donat and Taina Elg substituting for Madeleine Carroll. Director Ralph Thomas took on a difficult assignment in trying to out-Hitchcock Hitchcock and could not match the superlative earlier version. The color helped, with lush cross-country photography, but it only sparkled like a rhinestone when compared to Hitchcock's black-and-white gem.

The Secret Agent
1936

John Gielgud, Peter Lorre, and friend.

Production: Gaumont-British; *Producers:* Michael Balcon and Ivor Montagu; *Screenplay:* Charles Bennett, from the play by Campbell Dixon, adapted from the novel ASHENDEN by Somerset Maugham; *Adaptation:* Alma Reville; *Dialogues:* Ian Hay and Jesse Lasky, Jr.; *Director of Photography:* Bernard Knowles; *Sets:* Otto Werndorff and Albert Jullion; *Costumes:* J. Strasser; *Music:* Louis Levy; *Editing:* Charles Frend; *Studio:* Lime Grove; *Distributors:* G.F.D., U.S.A.: G.B. Prod.; *Principal Actors:* Madeleine Carroll (Elsa Carrington), John Gielgud (Richard Ashenden), Peter Lorre (The General), Robert Young (Robert Marvin), and Percy Marmont, Florence Kahn, Lilli Palmer, Charles Carson, Michael Redgrave; *Running Time:* 86 minutes; *16mm Rental Source:* Janus.

Alfred Hitchcock's reputation as a master of suspense had been long confirmed and his last two pictures had done nothing to alter this image. For the first of his two 1936 productions, he combined two Somerset Maugham *Ashenden* adventure stories with a play by Campbell Dixon based on yet other stories from the series. The result was a pastiche of too many plots and subplots presented in helter-skelter fashion.

Unlike the American studios, the British did not tamper very much with Hitchcock's product, no matter how good or bad it may have been. Casting was also left open to his needs. His cast was truly all-star, although many of the actors did not achieve full prominence until after *Secret Agent* was released. Madeleine Carroll, fresh from her satisfying role in *The 39 Steps,* was opposite John Gielgud. Peter Lorre, Robert Young, Lilli Palmer, and Michael Redgrave also joined the action, of which there was more than enough.

The New York Times, reviewing the picture after its Roxy Theater opening, remarked: "*Secret Agent* for all its Somerset Maugham base is one of those affairs in which practically every member of the cast turns out to be a spy, not even excepting Robert Young, whom you are asked to picture as an American spy in the pay of the Central Powers. After this it will not be too hard to think of Miss Carroll as a dilettante who has joined the intelligence service for a thrill, and who, sent to Geneva to play the wife of John Gielgud for espionage reasons, falls in love with him while being pursued by Mr. Young."

Madeleine Carroll and John Gielgud.

Peter Lorre, John Gielgud, Madeleine Carroll, and Robert Young.

Peter Lorre, John Gielgud, Robert Young, and Madeleine Carroll.

Lilli Palmer, Peter Lorre, and John Gielgud.

Secret Agent concerns Richard Ashenden (John Gielgud), a novelist army hero turned agent, whose assignment is to hunt down and kill a spy. By mistake, he kills an innocent tourist instead. He and his pretended wife, Elsa Carrington (Madeleine Carroll), feel guilty for this dirty work. Their comrade-in-arms, the General (Peter Lorre), takes it all as part of the job but in the end is accidentally shot himself. The chase takes us to Geneva where the spies are headquartered in a chocolate factory. As always, Hitchcock made sure that the ingredients of the action are related to the location where they occur. Typically Swiss associations are welded throughout the picture. At the end, in a tremendous train wreck, the real spy Robert Marvin (Robert Young) is killed.

If the scenario itself did not contribute to the credibility of the action, the acting did. The New York *Herald Tribune* noted that "Madeleine Carrol is appealing and utterly human in her loathing of the job she has chosen to perform. Robert Young plays the German agent with guile and remarkable power when he is finally cornered in a smashing climax that involves bombardment and derailing

Madeleine Carroll, John Gielgud, Robert Young and Peter Lorre.

of a train. Overshadowing their characterizations is that of Peter Lorre. As a Mexican 'general,' with a heart of a butcher, he contributes most of the terrifying qualities to the production. One regrets that Mr. Hitchcock did not throw away the disconnected and annoying romantic passages and give Lorre more to do.''

When the film first opened, critics were reportedly disgruntled about the bad soundtrack, but in the end, it was not the soundtrack that proved to be the failing of *Secret Agent,* but a lack of heroics on the part of Gielgud. As Hitchcock later reflected, ''You can't root for a hero who doesn't want to be one.'' The actor did a competent job, but it was his characterization that gave the audience little to identify with.

Although the film as a whole does not succeed because of inconsistencies and loose ends, Hitchcock does provide us with some delicious touches that audiences were coming to expect from him. There is the single continued organ note which rings out across a Swiss valley—until it is discovered within the church that a body is slumped across the keyboard. Then too, there is a chase through a Swiss chocolate factory which is being used as cover for spies, and the wailing of a dog that knows its master has been killed. As always, Hitchcock has used his locale to advance the storyline and heighten the impact. For Hitchcock a city is not simply an area for the story to take place: it is an additional character in the drama.

Sabotage

(U.S.A.: A Woman Alone)   1936

Matthew Bolton and John Loder.

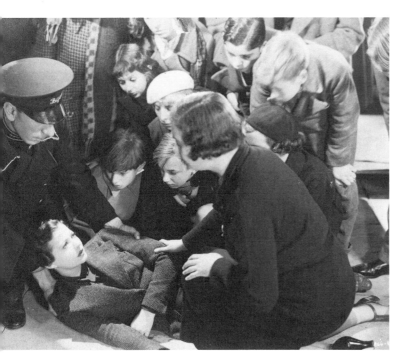

Sylvia Sidney.

Desmond Tester, bomb in hand, is delayed.

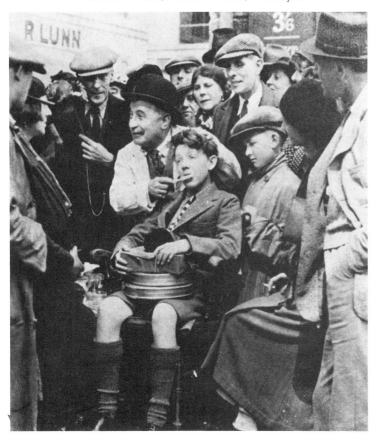

Production: Shepherd, Gaumont-British Pictures; *Producers:* Michael Balcon and Ivor Montagu; *Screenplay:* Charles Bennett, from the novel THE SECRET AGENT by Joseph Conrad; *Adaptation:* Alma Reville; *Dialogues:* Ian Hay, Helen Simpson, and E. V. H. Emmett; *Director of Photography:* Bernard Knowles; *Sets:* Otto Werndorff and Albert Jullion; *Music:* Louis Levy; *Costumes:* J. Strassner; *Editing:* Charles Frend; *Studio:* Lime Grove; *Cartoon:* Sequence of "Who Killed Cock Robin?" a Silly Symphony of Walt Disney, used with his permission; *Distributors:* G.F.D., U.S.A.: G.B. Prod.; *Principal Actors:* Sylvia Sidney (*Sylvia Verloc*), Oscar Homolka (*Verloc, her husband*), Desmond Tester (*Sylvia's brother*), John Loder (*Ted, the detective*), Joyce Barbour (*Renee*), Matthew Boulton (*The Superintendent*), and S. J. Barmington, William Dewhurst, Peter Bull, Torin Thatcher, Austin Trevor, Clare Greet, Sam Wilkinson, Sara Allgood, Martita Hunt, Pamela Bevan; *Running Time:* 76 minutes; *16mm Rental Source:* Janus.

Based on the Joseph Conrad novel *The Secret Agent, Sabotage* received its title because of the confusion that would have ensued with the previous film called *Secret Agent.* Confusion with titles resulted anyway when Hitchcock directed the American *Saboteur* with Robert Cummings.

Conrad's story was updated when Verloc, the anarchist who wants to destroy London, became the owner of a small cinema. Played by Oscar Homolka, Verloc is a man we pity and hate at the same time. His wife was portrayed by Sylvia Sidney, an actress whose screen career had been ebbing. Hitchcock gave her a role in which she was able to do some of her best work. The detective, posing as a vegetable salesman, was played by John Loder for whom Hitchcock had to settle when he couldn't get his first choice, Robert Donat.

The plot of the film is uncomplicated. Verloc (Homolka) is a saboteur who uses his cinema as a front. His wife (Sidney) and her small brother (Desmond Tester) live with him. Ted, a detective in disguise as a grocery clerk, becomes friendly with Mrs. Verloc and her brother. When it is revealed that he is a detective and that Verloc is suspected of sabotage, Verloc gives the young boy a package containing a bomb. The boy gets delayed in delivering it and the bomb explodes on the bus. Mrs. Verloc, repelled by the truth, kills Verloc with a carving knife. The murder to which she is about to confess remains undisclosed when other saboteurs get into the Bijou and blow it up.

If there is any single scene about which Hitchcock had regrets, it is the time bomb sequence. He

Sylvia Sidney.

now concedes that he was wrong to build up the audience's suspense and then not relieve it. The explosion, killing the child and all the people on the bus, is anticlimactic. Public opinion turned against Hitchcock, not so much for letting the bomb go off, but for allowing a child to be killed in such a grisly manner.

Actually the film gains in realism as it continues. It demonstrated the total lack of compassion of saboteurs and the senselessness of loss of human life and property as a means to fulfill political ideologies.

Another sequence that stands out is that in which Mrs. Verloc, while cutting meat on a plate, decides to kill her husband. There is no dialogue, no music, just quick successive shots of faces and hands clutching the knife. Sylvia Sidney thought that this, her big scene, should have dialogue, but Hitchcock proved to her that without it the scene plays more powerfully. The result is one of her best moments on the screen.

Sabotage was banned from exhibition in Brazil because it upset public order, according to the South American government. The censor declared that it taught conspiracy and terroristic technique. In the United States it was released under the title *A Woman Alone*, which certainly didn't help box-office receipts.

The reasons for the sabotage are never actually explained. Throughout the film the tension is maintained, but when it is over, the audience never really understands what it was all about.

The performances helped to maintain interest. John Loder, as the detective, did not meet Hitchcock's standards. Miss Sidney returned to the U.S. to make *Dead End* and Homolka continued his career in brilliant character roles.

Hitchcock got permission from Walt Disney to include a sequence from *Who Killed Cock Robin?* a Silly Symphony cartoon. It is shown just as Mrs. Verloc learns of her brother's death. She sits in the darkened theater listening to the laughter and almost laughs against her will with them.

Variety said, "The competent and experienced hand of the director is apparent throughout this production, which is a smart one and executed in a businesslike manner."

61

Young and Innocent
(U.S.A.: The Girl Was Young) 1937

Derek deMarney, Edward Rigby extricate Nova Pilbeam from her car as it plummets
during a cave-in.

Production: Gainsborough, Gaumont-British; *Producer:* Edward Black; *Screenplay:* Charles Bennett and Alma Reville, from the novel A SHILLING FOR CANDLES by Josephine Tey; *Director of Photography:* Bernard Knowles; *Sets:* Alfred Junge; *Music:* Louis Levy; *Editing:* Charles Frend; *Studios:* Lime Grove and Pinewood; *Distributors:* G.F.D., U.S.A.: G.B. Prod.; *Principal Actors:* Derrick de Marney (*Robert Tisdall*), Nova Pilbeam (*Erica*), Percy Marmont (*Colonel Burgoyne*), Edward Rigby (*Old Will*), Mary Clare (*Erica's aunt*), John Longden (*Kent*), George Curzon (*Guy*), Basil Radford (*Uncle Basil*), and Pamela Carme, George Merritt, J. H. Roberts, Jerry Verno, H. F. Maltby, John Miller, Torin Thatcher, Peggy Simpson, Anna Konstam, Beatrice Varley, William Fazan, Frank Atkinson, Fred O'Donovan, Albert Chevalier, Richard George, Jack Vyvian, Clive Baxter, Pamela Bevan, Humberston Wright, Gerry Fitzgerald, Syd Crossley; *Running Time:* 80 minutes; *16mm Rental Source:* Janus.

Edward Rigby and Nova Pilbeam.

The English and American titles for Hitchcock's fifth film for Gainsborough are equally innocuous and bland. But then, *Young and Innocent* was an especially smooth thriller for Hitchcock. It is a film chock full of touches Hitchcock wanted to include in other productions but could never find a way to fit in. In a very real sense, the title describes the kind of film *Young and Innocent* is.

By the time of its release in the United States in 1938, some of the critics had finally come to understand that a Hitchcock film was a team project. Howard Barnes put it aptly in the New York *Herald Tribune:* "Another stunning film from Mr. and Mrs. Hitchcock."

Alma Reville and Charles Bennett created a screenplay based on Josephine Tey's novel *A Shilling for Candles,* and the result was a breathlessly paced movie which offers gripping suspense and melodrama.

Nova Pilbeam and Percy Marmount.

It begins the way Hitchcock's 1973 hit, *Frenzy,* was to begin. A woman's body is washed ashore with the belt of a man's raincoat, obviously the murder weapon. The body is found, and we're off on a double chase, the kind Hitchcock knows best. Robert Tisdall (Derrick de Marney) is accused of the murder. He escapes to the Cornish countryside to search for the true killer, the man who stole his raincoat. With the police in pursuit, he is helped by a "young and innocent" girl, Erica (Nova Pilbeam). In the course of their chase the young fugitives call on the girl's aunt (Mary Clare) and uncle (Basil Radford), ostensibly to establish some sort of alibi. They find themselves trapped in a game of blindman's buff at a children's party. The scene slows the chase down but adds frustrating suspense and, at the same time, humor. You can't

Mary Clare leading the birthday party.

This scene was cut from the original ending.

help laughing at the pair's predicament, yet you still worry about the time they are losing from their escape. It is a well-timed scene, lasting about five minutes but seeming much longer to the viewer. De Marney noted in an interview that Hitchcock used a stopwatch to time scenes. "Too slow," he would murmur. "I had the scene marked for thirty seconds and it took you fifty seconds flat. We'll have to retake." In later films, timing would become second nature to Hitchcock and stopwatches wouldn't be needed.

Erica and Robert finally find a hobo who can identify the man who gave him the beltless raincoat, the real murderer. Now the police are almost on top of them. A car chase ensues, ending with a climactic cliff-hanging coal mine cave-in. But it's probably the finale of the movie that most audiences will remember: a single scene created with such remarkable technique that it is worth the entire film. The hobo says that the man they are looking for has twitching eyes. Hitchcock takes us, in one sweeping and flowing single shot, across what was at the time Pinewood's largest sound stage—from 145 feet away to just 4 inches from the twitching eyes of the murderer. He is a drummer in a large hotel ballroom, where looking for a pair of eyes is like looking for the proverbial needle in a haystack. Hitchcock needed two days to complete the sequence, which required a special crane-mounted camera on tracks. It is a dramatic shot and probably does more to excite the audience than any other sequence.

Young and Innocent has "a quiet charm," as the New York *Times* said, and there is never a clash between its realism and romanticism. Hitchcock was never one to quibble over plausibility, but *Young and Innocent* remains one of his more credible storylines.

The performances are all convincing, if slight. Nova Pilbeam was England's major child star, and Derrick de Marney, a current matinee idol, fit into his role the way Cary Grant later filled similar American parts.

Basil Radford, who makes a cameo appearance as the flustered Uncle Basil here, went on the following year to give one of his greatest performances in Hitchcock's *The Lady Vanishes*.

The film runs eighty minutes, but the American version had a full ten minutes chopped from it, much to Hitchcock's dismay. It was a cut that was to prepare the master of suspense for all the tampering with his films by studio executives in America. Not until he was his own man, his own producer, was he able (and then not always) to get exactly what he wanted, and what was usually best for his films.

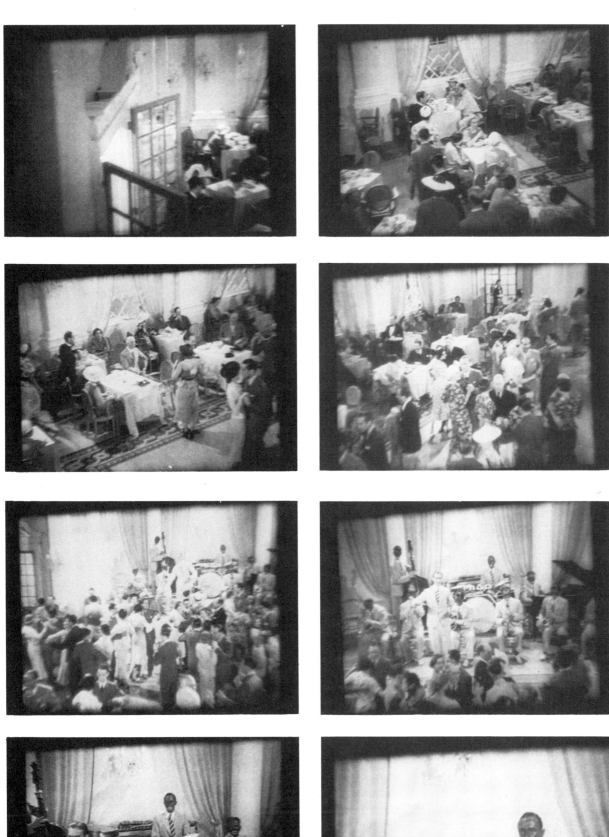
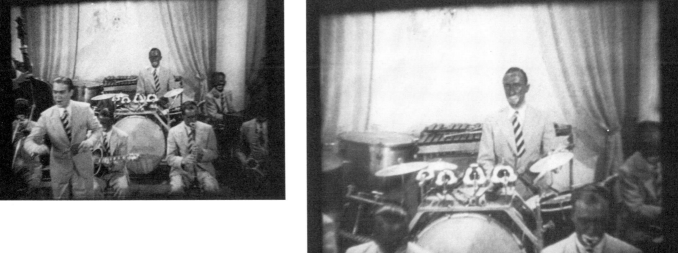

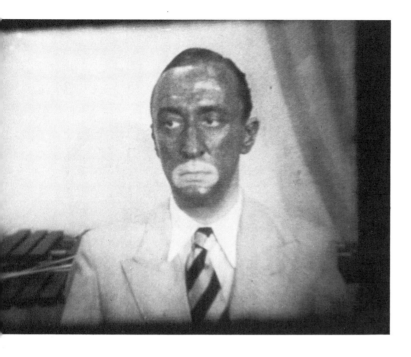
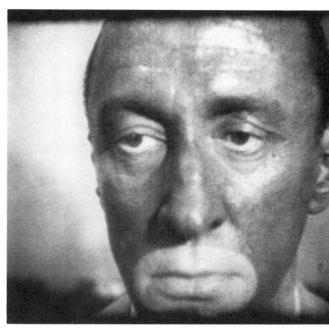
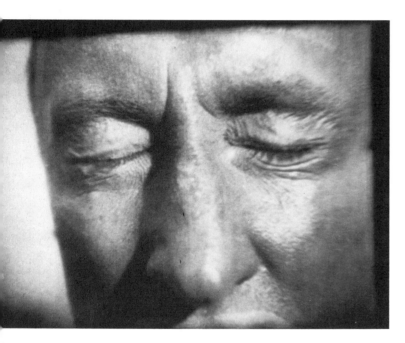
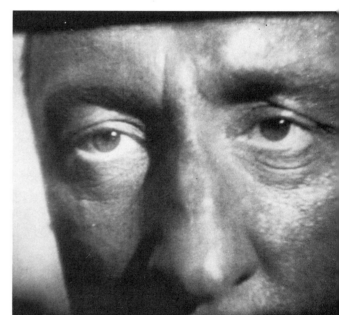

66

The Lady Vanishes

1938

Michael Redgrave and Naughton Wayne help a wounded spy, dressed as a nun, who has changed sides.

Michael Redgrave and Margaret Lockwood.

Production: Gainsborough Pictures, G.B.; *Producer:* Edward Black; *Screenplay:* Sidney Gilliat and Frank Launder, from the novel THE WHEEL SPINS by Ethel Lina White; *Adaptation:* Alma Reville; *Director of Photography:* Jack Cox; *Sets:* Alec Vetchinsky, Maurice Cater, and Albert Jullion; *Music:* Louis Levy; *Editing:* Alfred Roome and R. E. Dearing; *Studio:* Lime Grove; *Sound Engineer:* Sidney Wiles; *Distributors:* G.B., U.S.A.: G.B. Productions; *Principal Actors:* Margaret Lockwood (*Iris Henderson*), Michael Redgrave (*Gilbert*), Paul Lukas (*Dr. Hartz*), Dame May Whitty (*Miss Froy*), Googie Withers (*Blanche*), Cecil Parker (*Mr. Todhunter*), Linden Travers (*Mrs. Todhunter*), Lary Clare (*The Baroness*), Naunton Wayne (*Caldicott*), Basil Radford (*Charters*), and Emil Borco, Zelma Vas Dias, Phillipe Leaver, Sally Stewart, Catherine Lacey, Josephine Wilson, Charles Oliver, Kathleen Tremaine; *Running Time:* 97 minutes; *16mm Rental Source:* Janus.

A film's plausibility is Hitchcock's least concern, and he is the first to admit it. Like so many of his films, *The Lady Vanishes* works on an improbable premise. If the lady of the title, played by the great Dame May Whitty, had merely sent a tele-gram or made a phone call, we would be without a classic Hitchcockian chase across Eastern Europe.

The Lady Vanishes has more overt humor than any other Hitchcock suspense film, with the possible exception of *The Trouble With Harry*. In fact, the first 20 minutes of the film are completely comic, subdued British humor that is at once witty and full of subtle nuance. As the film progresses, there is less and less comedy and more gripping suspense. The initial innocence is merely a disguise which magnifies the later thrills. As *Newsweek* pointed out when the film first opened: "Characteristically Hitchcock lets his audience in on his secrets early and piles one thrilling sequence on another as his characters grope slowly and dangerously toward the truth."

The critics were ecstatic, calling Hitchcock "England's greatest director." The New York Critic's Award for 1938 went to *The Lady Vanishes* and to Hitchcock as the best director for that year. Howard Barnes of the *New York Herald Tribune* summed up how the critics and audiences felt about Hitchcock upon the release of *The Lady Vanishes:* "Even in so synthetic a medium as the screen, it is possible to recognize the work of a master craftsman. *The Lady Vanishes* is a product of individual imagination and artistry quite as much as a Cezanne canvas or a Stravinsky score." Orson Welles reportedly saw the film eleven times and James Thurber twice more than that.

The story of this much acclaimed film concerns a young English girl on a train going home from a vacation in the Balkans. The girl, Iris Henderson (Margaret Lockwood), meets a kindly old lady named Miss Froy (Dame May Whitty) who befriends her when Iris is hit on the head by a falling flowerpot which, we later learn, was meant for Miss Froy. Iris naps on the train and upon awakening from her doze finds that Miss Froy has mysteriously vanished from the train and has been replaced by an impostor in Miss Froy's clothing. Almost all of the passengers deny ever having seen the old lady and contend that she was an illusion brought on by Iris's accident with the falling flowerpot. A sincere young musican, Gilbert (Michael Redgrave), comes to her assistance.

Our young couple meet up with a parade of sinister and bizarre characters as they search the train for a clue to Miss Froy's whereabouts. There is a circus magician and his family, an "eastern European" baroness, an over-friendly brain surgeon (Paul Lukas) and his nurse dressed as a nun. Slowly, Iris and her musical cohort discover that most of the people on the train are in the employ

Margaret Lockwood and Michael Redgrave attack th magician with more than tricks up his sleeve.

Linden Travers, Naughton Wayne and Basil Radford fend off the attacking spies.

of or have a decided interest in the success of the apparently evil brain surgeon. But there is a handful of passengers who are on the couple's side and finally their interactions come into play.

There is the wealthy British official, away for the weekend with his mistress and obviously not desiring to be seen or involved in a case that might give his whereabouts publicity. He has seen Miss Froy and only speaks up when his life seems in danger. Two other men, supplying a bit of comedy relief, are played with perfect understatement by Naunton Wayne and Basil Radford. They only want to get back to England in time for "the game" —the cricket match must go on and they are not about to miss it, no matter what crisis is developing on the train.

The major break for the young couple and the mystery comes when they realize the nurse-nun is wearing high heel shoes—not exactly a Sister's proper attire. They discover that she is an actress hired by the doctor to guard a fully bandaged "patient" who is supposedly being taken to a distant hospital for surgery. The patient under wraps is

The ambushed train defends itself against attackers.

Michael Redgrave, Margaret Lockwood, and Paul Lukas.

Dame May Whitty, Margaret Lockwood, Naughton Wayne, Michael Redgrave and the spy who came in from the cold.

Cecil Parker attempts to wave a white flag at Paul Lukas' attacking forces—in vain.

Miss Froy. The heightening tension of the film climaxes as the train is ambushed and we learn that Miss Froy was carrying the secrets of a covert treaty between two foreign powers. Miss Froy makes her escape to deliver the message encoded in the tune of a children's lullaby. The couple and other passengers on the train fight off the enemy in a noisy gun battle. Of course, the passengers win and the happy couple gets back to Scotland Yard to deliver the message that will supposedly save freedom around the world.

Hitchcock made clever use of transparencies, rear projection systems and miniatures, disguising the almost nonexistent budget and the small studio. The set on which the entire film was produced was only ninety feet long. Assisting Hitchcock were a cast of highly professional actors who gave the whimsical plot more meaning and deadly seriousness than it really had.

The pacing of the suspense in counterpoint with the pervading comedy made *The Lady Vanishes* more thrilling than its content warranted. While the comedy was handled mostly by the two foils, Wayne and Radford, Michael Redgrave added a significant share as a music "scholar" who is studying eastern European folk dances.

It was while preparing *The Lady Vanishes* that Hitchcock received the bid from Hollywood that was to make him the world's most famous director. David O. Selznick wired him to come into his employ. After making one more film in Britain, Hitchcock was to leave—reluctantly—and not return until 1948 for *Under Capricorn*, except for a brief hiatus for his wartime documentaries.

Lukas attempts to stop the train he feels is carrying Miss Froy.

Jamaica Inn
1939

Leslie Banks and Maureen O'Hara.

Production: Mayflowers Productions, G.B.; *Producers:* Erich Pommer and Charles Laughton; *Production Manager:* Hugh Perceval; *Screenplay:* Sydney Gilliat and John Harrison, from the novel by Daphne du Maurier; *Dialogues:* Sydney Gilliat and J. B. Priestley; *Adaptation:* Alma Reville; *Directors of Photography:* Harry Stradling and Bernard Knowles; *Special Effects:* Harry Watt; *Sets:* Tom N. Moraham; *Costumes:* Molly McArthur; *Music:* Eric Fenby, directed by Frederic Lewis; *Editing:* Robert Hamer; *Sound Engineer:* Jack Rogerson; *Distributors:* Associated British; Paramount; *Principal Actors:* Charles Laughton (*Sir Humphrey Pengaltan*), Horace Hodges (*Chadwick, his butler*), Hay Petrie (*his groom*), Frederick Piper (*His Broker*), Leslie Banks (*Joss Merlyn*), Marie Ney (*Patience, his wife*), Maureen O'Hara (*Mary, his niece*), and Robert Newton, Herbert Lomas, Clare Greet, William Delvin, Mabel Terry Lewis, George Curzon, Basil Radford, Emlyn Williams, Roy Frumkes, Wylie Watson, Morland Graham, Edwin Greenwood, Stephan Haggard, Mervyn Johns; *Running Time:* 98 minutes; *16mm Rental Source:* Raymond Rohauer.

For his last prewar picture in England, Hitchcock directed a pirate adventure based on a soapy gothic tale by Daphne du Maurier. *Jamaica Inn* will be remembered not so much as a Hitchcock picture as it will a Charles Laughton vehicle.

Erich Pommer, a German producer who was a refugee in London, learned of Laughton's wish to be associated with Irving Thalberg. He offered to take the actor into a partnership with John Maxwell of Associated British Producers in a new company, Mayflower Pictures Corporation, which Pommer set up early in 1937. It released three films. The first, *Vessel of Wrath* (*The Beachcomber* in the United States), had Laughton portraying a derelict in the tropics, pursued by a woman missionary. Following that was *St. Martins Lane* (released in America as *Sidewalks of London*), with Laughton opposite Vivien Leigh. The third release was *Jamaica Inn*.

Hitchcock's first association with Pommer was in 1924 on a picture Pommer co-produced called *The Blackguard,* on which Hitchcock served as writer and art director.

In *Jamaica Inn,* Laughton played Sir Humphrey Pengaltan, an obsequious, unctuous squire of a seacoast village. He is the leader of a band of pirates luring ships on the rocks with false signals and then murdering the passengers and crew and plundering the cargos. (Laughton was originally cast as a licentious parson but, because of a possible run-in with the Hays office, the 1930s Federal Censorship Organization, was switched to the squire role.)

Charles Laughton and Maureen O'Hara.

Maureen O'Hara, Leslie Banks, and Marie Ney.

Leslie Banks and his band of pirates.

Leslie Banks, Marie Ney, and Maureen O'Hara.

Maureen O'Hara is directed toward the mysterious Jamaica Inn by the fearful coachman.

Robert Newton, Charles
Laughton, and Leslie Banks.

Maureen O'Hara, then an unknown eighteen-year-old actress, was cast as the leading lady, Mary, who has come to Jamaica Inn to stay with her Aunt Patience (Marie Ney) and her suspicious husband, Joss Merlyn (Leslie Banks). Mary discovers the Inn to be the headquarters of the pirates and saves the life of one of the men when the band unsuccessfully tries to lynch him. It turns out that he is an undercover man. The role was played by Robert Newton, who was to portray the most famous of all pirates, Long John Silver, in Robert Louis Stevenson's *Treasure Island* in 1950. It all ends melodramatically for Sir Humphrey, Merlyn, and Patience after Merlyn is shot by the pirates and Patience is shot by Sir Humphrey, who in turn jumps from a ship's mast.

The film made a sizable profit at the box-office because Hitchcock had developed a loyal following and reputation for entertaining pictures, and because the film had a winning cast and was based on a popular book. Nevertheless, the critics were unkind to *Jamaica Inn;* one called it "a singularly dull and uninspired picture—highly lackadaisical melodrama." For people expecting a Hitchcock picture, it was a letdown, and it was obvious that the director had lost his interest in the property before he completed work on it. If Hitchcock's ennui isn't so apparent on the screen, the phlegmatic acting of Charles Laughton is. One critic called it "Laughtonism," consisting of bombastic gesticulations and assorted *schticks,* all of which made the story drag. For example, Laughton refused to be photographed standing up or walking, until he could perfect the walk he would use. Always the perfectionist, Laughton wore a putty nose because he thought that would make him look more like an indulgent squire—fat, bloated, wicked, mad, and shrewd. Laughton does give a powerful performance but, like the squire he portrays, it is self-indulgent and interferes with the story.

Maureen O'Hara made her screen debut in *Jamaica Inn* and continued with a successful career in Hollywood immediately after. In an interview before the picture opened, Charles Laughton commented, "I told them [other cast members] we must all get behind Maureen and help. If we all tried, we could get her through it some way. Two days later, we were fighting for our scenes. That child was stealing the whole picture from us. She's not just an actress. She's a fine actress."

Another performer was playwright Emlyn Williams, author of *The Corn Is Green* and *Night Must Fall.* Basil Radford, who had charmed audiences the year before in his fetching role in *The Lady Vanishes,* also showed up in Hitchcock's last British picture.

With *Jamaica Inn,* Hitchcock's English period was concluded. He left England for his new country and the beginning of a lucrative and distinguished career in Hollywood.

77

The
Selznick Years
1940-1947

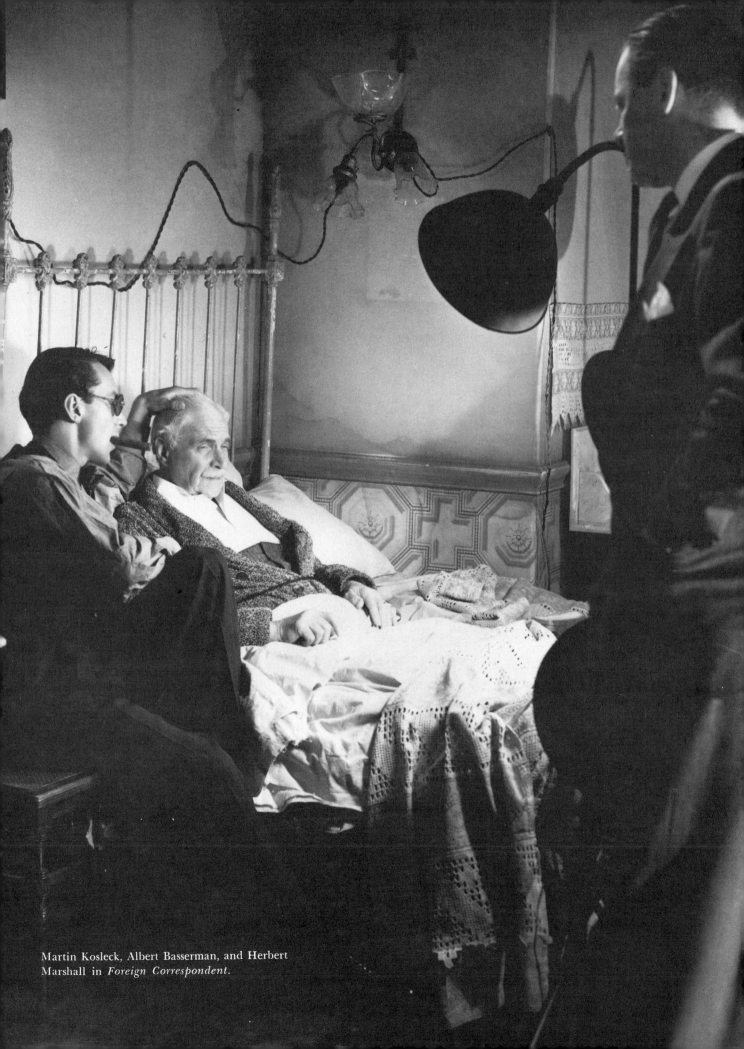

Martin Kosleck, Albert Basserman, and Herbert Marshall in *Foreign Correspondent*.

80

vertures had been made to Alfred Hitchcock to come to Hollywood many times during his fast rise to prominence in England. Each time he refused. Maybe it was out of loyalty to his homeland. Maybe it was because he knew he was on top in England and would be just another director in the United States. Perhaps, in the end, it was because he was comfortable and settled in England and there was no great need to pull up established roots.

Finally, Alfred Hitchcock succumbed to the temptations of Hollywood and accepted David O. Selznick's generous offer to come to America and direct prestigious motion pictures. The deal that brought the director to the United States was in the extravagant tradition of the movie industry—he would receive $800,000 for four pictures. There were disadvantages, too. In England he was more or less his own boss and exercised artistic control over his productions. In America, the producer was the star in the 1940s and the producer's wishes superseded the director's. David O. Selznick prided himself on being the archetype of the American motion picture producer. His contract with Hitchcock, like contracts with stars, treated him as a commodity—as personal property. Excerpts from a letter to Samuel Goldwyn from Selznick in January, 1943, illustrate exactly how Selznick interpreted his control over Hitchcock and his role as producer—a role which would on occasion conflict with Hitchcock's artistic pursuits:

"You recently have sent direct for one of my people, Alfred Hitchcock, and talked with him without so much as either asking us, or even letting us know after the fact. I wonder just how you would behave if I reciprocated in kind—or if any of the big companies did it with your people. I have always maintained that no one is in permanent bondage in this business, and that once a contract has expired, or is soon to expire, every individual in the business should be free to negotiate with anyone he sees fit, without giving offense to the studio to which he or she has been under contract, and regardless of the desire of the original contracting studio to make the bondage permanent. I am not talking about such a case; rather, I am referring to a man who you know full well is still under long-term contract to me. . . .

"Hitchcock has a minimum of two years to go with me, and longer if it takes him more time to finish four pictures, two of which I have sold to Twentieth Century-Fox [*Lifeboat* was the only

On the set of *Suspicion*.

On the set of *Suspicion*.

On the set of *Saboteur*

On location in Santa Rosa, California, for *Shadow of a Doubt*.

Valli, Ann Todd, and Hitchcock during filming of *The Paradine Case*.

picture realized]. And not alone did you try to seduce him, but you tried something which I have never experienced before with any company or individual—you sought to make him unhappy with my management of him. When you told Hitch that he shouldn't be wasting his talents on stories like *Shadow of a Doubt* [Universal, 1943], and that this wouldn't be the case if he were working for you, what you didn't know was that Hitchcock personally chose the story and created the script—and moreover that he is very happy about the picture, which I think he has every right to be. Further, that in the years since I brought Hitchcock over here from England (at a time when nobody in the industry, including yourself, was willing to give him the same opportunity . . .) and established him as one of the most important directors in the world with the production and exploitation of *Rebecca*, he has never once had to do a story that he was not enthusiastic about. This has always been my attitude about directors, and I happen to know that it has not always been your attitude toward directors under contract to you. . . ."

The first picture "England's greatest director" would handle for Selznick was to be *Titanic*, about the "unsinkable" luxury liner that sank on its maiden voyage. The project was scrapped temporarily and Selznick purchased the rights to Daphne du Maurier's *Rebecca* especially for Hitchcock. While in England, Hitchcock had attempted to buy the rights himself, but the asking price was out of his league. Curiously, his first American film has the look and feel of an English production. That was the nature of the project and not the intended style of the director.

Although Hitchcock had to direct four productions for Selznick, he was able to make additional pictures on loanout to other studios. His second picture, *Foreign Correspondent,* was made for Walter Wanger and United Artists. It was while on loan that Hitchcock found he was interfered with less by that particular producer. Accordingly, he always tried to get loaned out by Selznick, and it took eight years to complete his four-picture deal.

In 1942, after directing *Mr. and Mrs. Smith* and *Suspicion* for RKO, Hitchcock was to direct a third film, *Forever and a Day,* but was released from the project which was taken over by another master director, René Clair.

Hitchcock's ingenuity in England had been limited by budgets, but in Hollywood he was able to experiment more with the technical tricks of the trade he enjoyed so much. Money was no object

Publicity shot for *Notorious* by Gaston Longet.

With daughter and wife at the Stork Club.

With Ingrid Bergman and friend.

Cameo appearance in *Rebecca*.

Cameo appearance in *Foreign Correspondent*.

Cameo appearance in *Saboteur*.

Cameo appearance in *Lifeboat*.

and single settings costing as much as $70,000 were not unusual. Perhaps it was because he was forced to work under budgetary handicaps and therefore invent inexpensive devices that he enjoyed the challenge of restrictions and sought projects that crimped his freedom. The single-set production of *Lifeboat* proved that even in America, where cost was no longer a major consideration, the opportunity to *not* take advantage of all that Hollywood offered was more exciting and rewarding to Hitchcock.

In 1944, with World War II in full blast, Hitchcock, eager to help, traveled to England. His contribution was in the form of what he knew best: film. The British Ministry of Information gave him two assignments, *Bon Voyage* and *Adventure Malgache*. Both shorts were performed in French by the Molière Players. They were shot in England

at Associated British Studios, but were never released in any English-speaking countries.

His films were always full of surprises, some of which disturbed the United States Government (notably his fortuitous use of uranium as the MacGuffin in *Notorious* and his shot of the sunken ship *Normandie* in New York harbor in *Saboteur*). It took Selznick to get Alfred Hitchcock to America, for which the Englishman was grateful. In the end, it was Hitchcock himself who established his reputation as "the master of suspense."

The Selznick experience was an apprenticeship for Hitchcock into the ways of American moviemaking. The first thing he learned was that to make a movie the right way, you had to be your *own* boss, which is what Hitchcock became after directing his last picture for Selznick—*The Paradine Case*.

Bon Voyage, Aventure Malgache: Two wartime French-language shorts made for the British Ministery of Information.

Bon Voyage

Aventure Malgache

Rebecca
1940

Joan Fontaine meets the staff of Manderley.

Production: David O. Selznick, U.S.A.; *Producer:* David O. Selznick; *Screenplay:* Robert E. Sherwood and Joan Harrison, from the novel by Daphne du Maurier; *Adaptation:* Philip MacDonald and Michael Hogan; *Director of Photography:* George Barnes; *Sets:* Lyle Wheeler; *Music:* Franz Waxman; *Editing:* Hal C. Kern; *Studio:* Selznick International; *Distributor:* United Artists; *Principal Actors:* Laurence Olivier (*Maxim de Winter*), Joan Fontaine (*Mrs. de Winter*), George Sanders (*Jack Favell*), Judith Anderson (*Mrs. Danvers*), Nigel Bruce (*Major Giles Lacey*), C. Aubrey-Smith (*Colonel Julyan*), and Reginald Denny, Gladys Cooper, Philip Winter, Edward Fielding, Florence Bates, Leo G. Carroll, Forrester Harvey, Lumsden Hare, Leonard Carey, Edith Sharpe, Melville Cooper; *Running Time:* 130 minutes; *16mm Rental Source:* Images.

Daphne du Maurier has supplied Alfred Hitchcock with more stories and novels for screen and TV adaptation than any other writer. *Jamaica Inn,* his last picture in England, was based on a novel by her, and now *Rebecca.* The critical acclaim and popular appeal of the classic novel effectively launched the success of the David O. Selznick production. Just as *Gone with the Wind* changed the lives of many of the artists and craftsmen who worked on the spectacular film version of Margaret Mitchell's blockbuster, so too, the preparation for *Rebecca* had its reverberations. As producer Selznick noted in his memos, the public furor of *Gone with the Wind* far overshadowed the equally grand *Rebecca.*

Selznick relished casting his leading players, and after the publicity for his search for the perfect Scarlett O'Hara, he saw a chance for history to repeat itself with *Rebecca.* Finding the elusive lady for the leading role took some doing. Loretta Young was his first suggestion. Then he decided that even though Vivian Leigh was not right for the role, she could have it anyway. But she refused. Other choices followed: Olivia de Havilland, Margaret Sullavan, Joan Fontaine, and Anne Baxter. By default Joan Fontaine earned the coveted role, even though her reputation as the "wooden woman" preceded her. Selznick decided after consultation with Hitchcock to hire Fontaine for the part. It was on a hunch, similar to the one he had with Vivien Leigh. The male lead was open to many suggestions but choice was narrowed down to Ronald Colman and Laurence Olivier. Olivier won the role. There seemed to be less excitement in choosing a male star in 1940. The women garnered the larger share of glamour.

Selznick lost much of his faith in *Rebecca* as the production proceeded. He was unhappy with the script, displeased with what he thought were unnecessary production expenses, and unsure that the film could sustain the appeal of the best-selling book. After the first preview, which he was against holding, his spirits were bolstered by the deluge of popular support the audience showed. His faith was restored in Hitchcock, with whom he was to rarely consult on future productions, communicating with him only through memos. On *Rebecca,* Hitchcock would have to call Selznick before a final print could be made.

Brought in for just under one million dollars, excluding advertising and print costs, *Rebecca* went on to win not only public and critical approval but the Oscar for "Best Picture of the Year," an award which goes to the producer. The advertising played on the popularity of the book: "You loved the novel, you'll *live* the picture." Besides supplying the brooding undercurrent of evil and tortured romance, Hitchcock—at Selznick's insistance—remained faithful to the du Maurier plot.

A modest and shy young woman (Joan Fontaine), curiously unnamed in the movie or the book (told in the first person), meets and falls in love with Maxim de Winter (Laurence Olivier) while both are on a holiday on the Riviera. They marry. When the new Mrs. de Winter arrives at Maxim's mansion, Manderley, she finds a house of hostile servants, most notably the housekeeper, Mrs. Danvers (Judith Anderson), who always seems to creep from out of the darkness, appearing suddenly and unexpectedly. The memory of the former Mrs. de Winter, Rebecca, while well-guarded, pervades the house and causes the new wife to question Maxim's love for her. The menacing Mrs. Danvers, whose devotion to Rebecca is compulsive, jealously tries to make her new mistress commit suicide. When the investigation into Rebecca's death reveals some ugly facts, Mrs. Danvers sets fire to the house. Manderley's end is signaled by the flames, destroying Mrs. Danvers as well; the love of Maxim and his new wife is realized—the memory of Rebecca now behind him.

Rebecca was made in America, but it is a distinctly English film. The actors are British; the director was imported from England, as was the story. It is only David O. Selznick's Americanization of the picture that makes it a U.S. product. The romantic and universal appeal of the story and the high production values keep *Rebecca* from ever being dated. In fact, it was re-released by Twentieth Century–Fox in 1956, when it had a solid run.

89

Laurence Olivier greets Florence Bates, Joan Fontaine's employer.

Joan Fontaine and Laurence Olivier.

Dame Judith Anderson and Joan
Fontaine.

Dame Judith Anderson,
George Sanders, Joan Fon-
taine, Laurence Olivier, and
C. Aubrey-Smith.

Dame Judith Anderson and Joan Fontaine.

The pervading British style of the film, though, was recognized by the critics. Frank Nugent in *The New York Times* reported, "Hitch in Hollywood on the basis of Selznick's *Rebecca* at Radio City Music Hall is pretty much the Hitch of London's *Lady Vanishes* and *Thirty-Nine Steps,* except that his now famous and widely publicized touch seems to have developed into a firm, enveloping grasp of Daphne du Maurier's popular novel." At 130 minutes, *Rebecca* is second only to *North by Northwest* as the longest film Hitchcock ever made. To get it down even to 130 minutes took a great deal of editing, but Hitchcock creates such a haunting atmosphere that time is suspended for the audience, whose attention remains riveted to the screen.

Hitchcock was to return to another Daphne du Maurier story when he filmed *The Birds* in 1963. As in *Rebecca,* the house of the protagonist in *The Birds* is isolated, which Hitchcock says helps to heighten the suspense. Houses away from the outside world prevent help from arriving. They are places which one leaves never wanting to return.

Rebecca, unlike *The Birds,* is a woman's picture, a Gothic intrigue with little humor. It is not a Hitchcock story, but it has elements that excited Hitchcock's interest and imagination.

Joan Fontaine, Laurence Olivier and Reginald Denny watch Manderley in flames.

Foreign Correspondent
1940

Joel McCrea with Albert Basserman.

Production: Walter Wanger, United Artists; *Screenplay:* Charles Bennett and Joan Harrison; *Dialogues:* James Hilton and Robert Benchley; *Director of Photography:* Rudolph Mate; *Special Effects:* Lee Zavitz; *Sets:* William Cameron Menzies and Alexander Golitzen; *Music:* Alfred Newman; *Editing:* Otto Lovering and Dorothy Spencer; *Assistant Director:* Edmond Bernoudy; *Studio:* United Artists, at Hollywood; *Distributor:* United Artists; *Principal Actors:* Joel McCrea (*Johnny Jones, reporter*), Laraine Day (*Carol Fisher*), Herbert Marshall (*Stephen Fisher, her father*), George Sanders (*Herbert ffolliott, reporter*), Albert Bassermann (*Van Meer*), Robert Benchley (*Stebbins*), Eduardo Cianelli (*Krug*), Edmund Gwenn (*Rowley*), Harry Davenport (*Mr. Powers*), and Martin Kosleck, Eddie Conrad, Gertrude W. Hoffman, Jane Novak, Ken Christy, Crawford Kent, Joan Brodel-Leslie, Louis Borell; *Running Time:* 120 minutes; *16mm Rental Source:* Images.

Leaving the flames of Manderley behind, Hitchcock plunged into the turbulent political controversies of the world as it readied for the upcoming war.

Although *Rebecca* was Hitchcock's first film in Hollywood, *Foreign Correspondent* was his first Hollywood-type production. The film was originally to be based on Vincent Sheean's *Personal History,* for which producer Walter Wanger anted up ten thousand dollars. After three tries to get it into suitable shape as a screen story, Wanger assigned the project to Hitchcock, whom he had "borrowed" from Selznick.

With three months of photography, the film came in on a budget of $1.5 million, the most Hitchock had ever worked with until that time. The spectacle on screen was matched by the production credits for the film. Studio publicity boasts that 558 carpenters, electricians, plumbers, prop men, and technicians in fifty different classifications helped Hitchcock plan the minutest details in advance. Some 240,000 feet of film were shot for the eventual 120 minutes released. The final screenplay, worked over repeatedly by 14 writers for Walter Wanger, was attributed to Charles Bennett and Joan Harrison with dialogue by James Hilton and Robert Benchley. The latter was specially hired by Hitchcock, who enjoyed Benchley's brand of satiric humor. All scenes in which the humorist-actor appeared were written by Benchley himself—the way Hitchcock wanted it.

The physical production of the film is spectacular. "Build me a piece of Amsterdam, a good slice of London, an airplane as big as an Atlantic Clipper, and a few hotels, a Dutch windmill, and a bit of the Dutch countryside," Hitchcock requested. He

got it. The Amsterdam public square, used for an original and daring murder sequence, covered ten acres and took one month to build with three crews working twenty-four hours a day. An elaborate drainage system for the rain was needed for the murder sequence and the subsequent chase under the umbrellas. The next scene at the windmill required more than three hundred linnets, and the birds created messy problems in the studio.

The film contains some of the finest photography and visual design of any of Hitchcock's films. This is due in no small part to the work of William Cameron Menzies, who did production design on *For Whom the Bell Tolls, Things to Come, The Thief of Bagdad,* and *Gone with the Wind.* The windmill sequence with its perfect lighting and interior design would feature some of his greatest work.

Casting was a difficult problem for many Hitchcock films. Thrillers were looked down upon in Hollywood (although Hitchcock was soon to change that), so when the lead was offered to Gary Cooper, the actor rejected it. Joel McCrea was a suitable second choice and did a superb job, but he didn't have the superstar name Hitchcock wanted.

The film was nominated by the Academy for Best Picture and Best Screenplay, but won neither. Hitchcock was able to make the thriller first-class entertainment and, as Howard Barnes in the New York *Herald Tribune* said, *"Foreign Correspondent* blends escapist entertainment with challenging propaganda in the film terms."

Foreign Correspondent is filled with suspense and intrigue but is nevertheless overlong. The story is diverted for theatrical business so often that the picture drags in spots. Johnny Jones (Joel McCrea), a hard-headed, tough-fisted crime reporter, is assigned by his editor to investigate the chances of on outbreak of war in Europe immediately prior to World War II. Jones meets Van Meer (Albert Bassermann), who carries by memory a secret clause in an Allied treaty for his country. Along with Van Meer, the Dutch diplomat are Stephen Fisher (Herbert Marshall) and his daughter (Laraine Day). When the Nazis kidnap Van Meer but make it appear an assassination by killing a double, Jones along with Fisher's daughter Carol search through Holland and England for him. They find that Stephen Fisher has been masquerading as the head of a pacifist group, but is actually a double agent for the Nazis, intent on discovering Van Meer's secret and instrumental in the kidnaping/assassination plot.

War is declared, but Fisher and his daughter,

Robert Benchley and Joel McCrea.

Joel McCrea and Albert Basserman do not realize the photographer is an assassin.

Herbert Marshall sits while Laraine Day, Joel McCrea, George Sanders stand, waiting for their transoceanic plane to crash.

now disillusioned in her romance with Jones, manage to get on the last plane from England to America. Jones is also on the plane, with his English counterpart, played by George Sanders. Sanders had been suspicious of Fisher for some time before Jones arrived. Now they were working together. The transatlantic clipper is attacked by a German ship as it is mistaken for a bomber; it crashes in a scene overflowing with Hitchcockian technical brilliance. Fisher, knowing that he will be arrested upon reaching America, sacrifices his life in order to keep a wing afloat until rescue arrives. Once upon their American rescue ship (the Nazi ship had sped away at its appearance), the two reporters find that they cannot wire the story in which they played the prime roles because the captain insists that his ship remain neutral and that no broadcast of any type come from the vessel. They do succeed, however, in making a personal call and placing the telephone receiver behind them as they explain their exploits to the captain and thereby to the editor in New York. Jones marries Carol and becomes the top European foreign correspondent, with banner headlines and

Joel McCrea hard at work at his office.

Aboard the ship that has rescued them from their plane crash, Laraine Day, Joel McCrea, and George Sanders are interrogated.

97

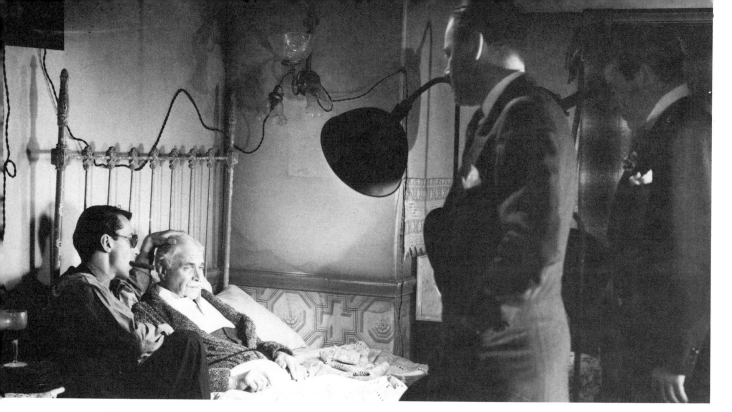

Albert Basserman is interrogated while Herbert Marshall and Eduardo Ciannelli watch.

broadcasts to the states. As the film closes, he is making one such live broadcast as bombs begin to fall around the studio.

The film has proceeded on two levels: The obvious one is the entertaining chase—the cloak-and-dagger work of the New York crime reporter. The second is the flag-waving propaganda calling for an end of American isolationism in World War II. Jones's speech at the end of the film is equal to Chaplin's brilliant oratory at the end of *The Great Dictator* and would seem to be Hitchcock's plea to Americans that England is in desperate trouble and American involvement is essential. It was heard as follows:

JONES: Hello America. I've been watching a part of the world being blown to pieces. A part of the world as nice as Vermont, Ohio, Virginia, California and Illinois lies ripped up bleeding like a steer in a slaughterhouse. And I've seen things that make the history of the savages read like Pollyanna legend.

ANNOUNCER: We're going to have to postpone the broadcast.

(At this point sirens begin to wail and lights flash as bombs begin to burst outside the studio).

JONES: Don't postpone nothing, let's go on as long as we can.

ANNOUNCER: (to Carol) Ma'am, we've got a shelter downstairs.

JONES: How about it, Carol?

CAROL: They're listening in America, Johnny.

JONES: O.K. We'll tell them. I can't read the rest of this speech I have because the lights have gone out. So I'll just have to talk off the cuff. All that noise you hear isn't static, it's death coming to London. Yes, they're coming here now. You can hear the bombs falling on the streets and homes. Don't tune me out—hang on—this is a big story—and you're part of it. It's too late now to do anything except stand in the dark and let them come as if the lights are all out everywhere except in America.

(Music—"America" begins to play softly in background of speech and continues through end credits).

JONES: Keep those lights burning, cover them with steel, build them in with guns, build a canopy of battleships and bombing planes around them and, hello America, hang onto your lights. They're the only lights in the world.

The United States was not to enter World War II for another year and four months but, like Chaplin's film, this was a prophetic statement of what was to come all too soon.

Mr. And Mrs. Smith
1941

Carole Lombard shows Robert Montgomery something in his size.

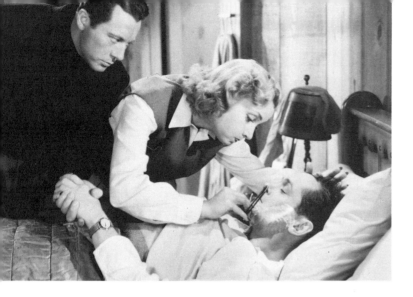

Gene Raymond, Robert Montgomery, and Carole Lombard, shaving hubby during a lull in the feud.

Jack Carson and Robert Montgomery. Mr. Smith conveniently faints.

Robert Montgomery and Carole Lombard meet the new "Mama Lucy."

Production: R.K.O.; *Executive Producer:* Harry E. Edington; *Story and Screenplay:* Norman Krasna; *Director of Photography:* Harry Stradling, A.S.C.; *Sets:* Van Nest Polglase and L. P. Williams; *Music:* Roy Webb; *Special Effects:* Vernon L. Walker; *Editing:* William Hamilton; *Studio:* R.K.O.; *Distributor:* R.K.O.; *Principal Actors:* Carole Lombard (*Ann Smith and Ann Kransheimer*), Robert Montgomery (*David Smith*), Gene Raymond (*Jeff Custer*), Jack Carson (*Chuck Benson*), Philip Merivale (*Mr. Custer*), Lucille Watson (*Mrs. Custer*), William Tracy (*Sammy*), and Charles Halton, Esther Dale, Emma Dunn, Betty Compson, Patricia Farr, William Edmunds, Adela Pearce, Murray Alper, D. Johnson, James Flavin, Sam Harris; *Running Time:* 95 minutes; *16mm Rental Source:* Films, Incorporated.

Comedy in a Hitchcock film is almost always black. Some viewers may interpret it as "sick humor" and others may call it macabre, but Hitchcock makes sure that it is also relevant—if not to the particular story, at least to the characters. Certainly each film Hitchcock has made has its fair share of humor, but it is secondary and never disturbs the main context of the film.

Mr. and Mrs. Smith is a comedy Hitchcock could not really associate himself with, because it was admittedly unfamiliar terrain for the Master of Suspense. He submitted himself to directing it as a favor to close friend Carole Lombard who insisted that he direct her. It was to be the actress-comedienne's second-to-last film before she died in an airplane crash.

The film is a typical forties screwball comedy, but not as fast-paced as such earlier classics as *Bringing Up Baby* or *The Awful Truth*. Parts of it simply don't work. When they don't, though, it is more the fault of the Norman Krasna script than Hitchcock's direction. Hitchcock, who spends months and even years on a film, was given the script of *Mr. and Mrs. Smith* and more or less walked through his role as director, following the scenario and hardly tampering with it. "Despite the performances, despite the endless camera magic with which Mr. Hitchcock tries to conceal the thinness of his material, *Mr. and Mrs. Smith* has its moments of dullness. The result is a chucklesome comedy that fails to mount into a coruscating wave of laughter," said *The New York Times*.

The story is riddled with clichés. David and Ann Smith have a happy, if stormy, marriage. A lawyer visits David to tell him that his marriage to Ann was legally imperfect, so it is not recognized as valid. David tries to conceal this from Ann, who he does not know was visited by the same lawyer. But the

Carole Lombard, Robert Montgomery, and Gene. Raymond. A "drunken" Mr. Smith visits the ski lodge.

Robert Montgomery and Carole Lombard cause a disturbance.

truth comes out and the question is faced: If-you-had-to-do-it-all-over-again-do-you-love-me-enough-to-do-it-again? The rest of the film contains the escapades of the two trying to show they do love each other. In the end, of course, they at least lead us to believe that they will be legally married.

One bit that stands out as particularly Hitchcockian takes place in an old, rather sleazy Italian restaurant where David and Ann first met. David orders soup which even a mangy cat will not eat. It relies heavily, as does most of the film, on pic-torial pantomime, facial expressions, and camera understatement.

Mr. and Mrs. Smith is the director's only American comedy, not counting the macabre *The Trouble with Harry*, which ranks in a different league despite its continuous humor. His direction of the comedy was definitely a fond gift to Carole Lombard. Hitchcock even let her direct him in his obligatory walk-on. While Carole got her wish to appear in a Hitchcock film, for the director it was more of a duty than a pleasure.

102

Suspicion
1941

Cary Grant and Joan Fontaine.

Cary Grant delivers the suspicious glass of milk.

Production: R.K.O.; *Screenplay:* Samson Raphaelson, Joan Harrison, and Alma Reville, from the novel BEFORE THE FACT by Francis Iles (*Anthony Berkeley*); *Director of Photography:* Harry Stradling, A.S.C.; *Special Effects:* Vernon L. Walker; *Sets:* Van Nest Polglase; *Assistant:* Carroll Clark; *Music:* Franz Waxman; *Editing:* William Hamilton; *Sound Engineer:* John E. Tribly; *Assistant Director:* Dewey Starkey; *Studio:* R.K.O.; *Distributor:* R.K.O.; *Principal Actors:* Cary Grant (*John Aysgarth: "Johnnie"*), Joan Fontaine (*Lina MacKinlaw*), Sir Cedric Hardwicke (*General MacKinlaw*), Nigel Bruce (*Beaky*), Dame May Whitty (*Mrs. MacKinlaw*), Isabel Jeans (*Mrs. Newsham*), and Heather Angel, Auriol Lee, Reginald Sheffield, Leo G. Carroll; *Running Time:* 99 minutes; *16mm Rental Source:* Films, Incorporated.

The history of Alfred Hitchcock in Hollywood more often than not is a history of studio tampering with what would have otherwise been an ever better product. In the case of *Suspicion,* an RKO executive, who thought it was wrong to even imply that Cary Grant was a killer, edited Hitchcock's final cut by removing every indication that Grant

Cary Grant and Joan Fontaine.

was the bad guy. This left the studio version with a running time of less than one hour. The head of the studio realized how ridiculous the entire situation was and allowed the rather dismayed Hitchcock to reinstate most of what was butchered from the original version.

Still, Hollywood demanded happy endings in the 1940s, and the ending of the film is not faithful to that of the original novel—*Before the Fact* by Frances Iles—much to the audience's chagrin.

Suspicion in many ways is as British as his first Hollywood film, *Rebecca.* Again he employed Joan Fontaine and a cast of other British actors; again the locale is English, as is the novel upon which the film is based. More than *Rebecca, Suspicion* is definitely a Hitchcockian film, with all the ingenious touches that became his hallmark. Despite these flourishes which only temporarily added to the suspense of the film, *Suspicion* remains a slower-paced, more psychologically oriented film, reflective of *Shadow of a Doubt* and *Spellbound.* It is the case study of how suspicion grows from doubt based on circumstantial evidence.

Lina MacKinlaw is a spinsterish wallflower who

On a lonely country road. Will he kill her?

Gary Grant and Joan Fontaine.

Joan Fontaine, Cary Grant, Nigel Bruce, and Heather Angel.

Cary Grant arrives late at a formal affair to which he has not been invited. Sir Cedric Hardwick, as Joan Fontaine's father, looks on.

Cary Grant and Joan Fontaine.

Cary Grant and Joan Fontaine.

wants to escape the home of her stuffy parents. She meets and falls in love with a reckless playboy, Johnny Aysgarth, whose reputation as a lady's man is well-known. Disregarding the rumors about his past, she marries him. Through accumulated evidence she begins to suspect him of the murder of a dear friend and thinks he plans to kill her. The end reaches a crescendo in a well-paced scene when, sick with fear, Lina is brought a glass of milk by Johnny. She is sure the milk is poisoned, but it is not. In a frightening ride along the rocky coastline of England she almost jumps from the car to avoid being thrown out by Johnny. He stops the car to save her and she learns the truth.

In the original ending of the film, Johnny does kill Lina with poisoned milk. However, before she drinks it, she asks him to post a letter for her.

In it, he does not realize, are her thoughts and evidence about her murder. He smirkingly deposits the letter in the mailbox.

Joan Fontaine's understated performance, similar to the one she gave in *Rebecca,* earned her an Academy Award as Best Actress in 1941. Cary Grant's convincing portrayal of the "cad as hero, who pawns his wife's heirlooms to pay his gambling debts and filches money from his cousin," deserves acclaim as well.

"In *Suspicion,*" said the New York *Herald Tribune* the day after the film opened at Radio Music Hall, "the threat of violence is almost always present. It is not often that one finds a master of horror drama being equally perceptive in the field of subjective personal experience."

Saboteur
1942

Robert Cummings quiets Priscilla Lane.

Production: Universal; *Producers:* Frank Lloyd and Jack H. Skirball; *Screenplay:* Peter Viertel, Joan Harrison, and Dorothy Parker, from an original subject by Alfred Hitchcock; *Director of Photography:* Joseph Valentine, A.S.C.; *Sets:* Jack Otterson; *Music:* Charles Prévin and Frank Skinner; *Editing:* Otto Ludwig; *Studio:* Universal; *Distributor:* Universal; *Principal Actors:* Robert Cummings (*Barry Kane*), Priscilla Lane (*Patricia Martin: "Pat"*), Otto Kruger (*Charles Tobin*), Alan Baxter (*Mr. Freeman*), Alma Kruger (*Mrs. Van Sutton*), and Vaughan Glazer, Dorothy Peterson, Ian Wolfe, Anita Bolster, Jeanne and Lynn Roher, Norman Lloyd, Oliver Blake, Anita Le Deaux, Pedro de Cordoba, Kathryn Adams, Murray Alper, Frances Carson, Billy Curtis; *Running Time:* 108 minutes; *16mm Rental Source:* Universal Pictures.

Saboteur was ostensibly Hitchcock's contribution to wartime patriotic propaganda. But its sweeping panorama of the United States and its solid and absorbing story rose above its "Buy War Bonds" dialogue which tended to creep intermittently into the screenplay.

The film needed over 1,000 scenes and 4,500 camera setups to tell its intriguing story. Principal photography was shot at the Universal Studios in Hollywood, but Hitchcock also took cameras and cast to New York. Photography of actors was purposely shot in some scenes from a mile to a mile and a half away. Using a telephoto lens, Hitchcock was then able to create the impression of America's vastness. Yet when he couldn't find the exact desert he wanted, he had one built in the studio. A stickler for detail, Hitchcock ordered the Fifth Avenue mansion in the film to be built, at a cost of $45,000. "It's what strikes the eye that leaves the most lasting impression on moviegoers," Hitchcock noted about the extravagance of the settings.

The picture had many more things going for it than just expensive sets. Contributing to the screenplay was Dorothy Parker, whose wry humor is evident throughout, but especially in a scene with circus freaks that Robert Cummings and Priscilla Lane happen upon along their journey east. There are a pair of Siamese twin girls who aren't on speaking terms with each other and one of them complains that the other should do something about her insomnia: "*I do nothing but toss and turn all night.*" Then there is a bearded lady whose beard is in curlers for the night. Later in the film one of the saboteurs is talking about the blowing up of a new Navy ship. The explosives are hooked to a switch in a camera truck. "*It's a shame we'll have to lose a good camera,*" the spy says glumly.

110

Priscilla Lane tries to free herself from Robert Cummings, who she believes is a traitor.

Robert Cummings and Priscilla Lane find an occupied shack in a ghost town.

Robert Cummings hints that Priscilla Lane should escape by pointing to a book with the title *Escape.*

Otto Kruger.

Robert Cummings is given shelter by a blindman.

The picture was subtitled in its advertising as "The Man Behind Your Back" which played on the fear of all Americans that during a war you could trust very few people, that you had to stick together. But this was just part of the Allied propaganda that pervaded the film. Another Buy War Bonds line, from Robert Cummings to a menacing and smug Otto Kruger: "The world's choosing up sides, and I know which side I'm on."

Saboteur was a forerunner of Hitchcock's grand-slam hit *North by Northwest*. The same themes are found in both: the hero falsely accused of a crime, who cannot go to the police because he needs time to clear himself, and the cross-country chase that ensues.

The plot of *Saboteur* is about an aircraft mechanic Barry Kane (Robert Cummings), who is falsely accused of sabotaging the aircraft plant at which he works. Kane knows that only one man can clear him: the saboteur himself, Frank Fry (Norman Lloyd). He narrowly escapes a police dragnet and heads to a ranch where Fry may be. Instead he discovers an insidious Charles Tobin

Norman Lloyd ·holds Robert Cummings at gunpoint as his comrades hold him down.

Virgil Summers and Robert Cummings return money that was dropped by Norman Lloyd.

(Otto Kruger). Again he just barely escapes, and this time, ends up in the cabin of a blind man and his niece Patricia Martin (Priscilla Lane). At first Pat wants to turn Barry in, but finally she is shamed into believing his innocence when a troupe of circus freaks trustingly put them up for a night in their trailer. The pair next come to a deserted mining town which they discover has one room in use. The saboteurs return to it and Barry pretends to be one of them. Pat hightails it back to the police, who happened to be friendly with the saboteurs. The pair unknowingly come together again in the home of a wealthy socialite, Mrs. Van Sutton (Alma Kruger). When the police arrest Kane, after a spectacular shootout in Radio City Music Hall, he tells Pat to follow Fry. This, after Kane has managed to prevent a new Navy ship from being blown up by the spies. The end comes atop the Statue of Liberty. The shootout scene in Radio City Music Hall proved to be exciting and original (it has been copied many times since) when it was released—especially since almost every new Hitchcock film in the forties and fifties opened at the Music Hall.

Another part of the film was edited out in some parts of the country because of the Navy's displeasure with it. Hitchcock was filming the New York sequence of Fry's getaway from the Music Hall. As he is riding in the cab, the camera pans to stock newsreel shot of the capsized *Normandie,* then back to a smile on Fry's face. The Navy thought that this made it look like the ship's misfortune was linked to sabotage, which it was not. Hitchcock has said that the ship just happened to be there during shooting, so he conveniently included it.

While all the actors gave competent performances, Hitchcock was displeased with having to use the two leads. Robert Cummings, Hitchcock thought, had a comic face, so that his dramatic scenes were not convincing enough. Priscilla Lane was foisted upon Hitchcock by the studio, which had a contract for the actress, who was to appear in only three more films in what was to be her short seven-year film career. She was a good actress,

but not a "Hitchcock woman"; she was a girl-next-door type, hardly the sophisticate Hitchcock needed and wanted. Otto Kruger's conventional heavy was venal and evil enough for audiences to hate. He was to be a harbinger for James Mason's stunning performance in *North By Northwest* in 1959.

Saboteur is not considered by critics, or by Hitchcock, to be one of the director's better films. It certainly does contain some of his most ingenious moments. The movie seems, with the exception of the Dorothy Parker–Hitchcock humor, to be quite naïve today, its age rather evident. But for plot and pace it still holds up well. Probably one of the reasons it remains absorbing today is that the characters are all black-and-white—the good guys against the bad guys, with each side clearly drawn. While artificial, it is never self-consciously so. But that's what Hollywood escapism is like, and if accepted as that, it is appealing, if not intoxicating.

Priscilla Lane and Robert Cummings are befriended by a troupe of circus freaks.

Shadow of a Doubt

1943

Patricia Collinge with Joseph Cotten.

Production: Universal; *Producer:* Jack H. Skirball; *Screenplay:* Thornton Wilder, Alma Reville, and Sally Benson, from a story by Gordon McDonnell; *Director of Photography:* Joseph Valentine, A.S.C.; *Sets:* John B. Goodman, Robert Boyle, A. Gausman, and L. R. Robinson; *Costumes:* Adrian and Vera West; *Music:* Dimitri Tiomkin, directed by Charles Prévin; *Editing:* Milton Carruth; *Studio:* Universal; also shot at Santa Rosa; *Distributor:* Universal; *Principal Actors:* Joseph Cotten (*Charlie Oakley, the uncle*), Teresa Wright (*Charlie Newton*), MacDonald Carey (*Jack Graham*), Patricia Collinge (*Emma Newton*), Henry Travers (*Joseph Newton*), Hume Cronyn (*Herbie Hawkins*), Wallace Ford (*Fred Saunders*), and Janet Shaw, Estelle Jewell, Eily Malyon, Ethel Griffies, Clarence Muse, Frances Carson, Charlie Bates, Edna May Wonacott; *Running Time:* 108 minutes; *16mm Rental Source:* Universal Pictures.

Teresa Wright, Joseph Cotten, and Henry Travers.

One of Hitchcock's personal favorites, *Shadow of a Doubt* brought murder and violence "back into the home where it rightfully belongs." After all, he notes, it is in the home that most bad habits are formed. From murder, one may even progress to deceit, drunkenness, or smoking.

Shadow of a Doubt remains one of Hitchcock's little gems, a completely unpretentious, well-scripted, and well-characterized film which holds up well today. It was his second Universal picture and offered slick production values with much of the footage shot on location in the sleepy town of Santa Rosa, California, where the film takes place. Perhaps it is because the film is purposely slow and analytical that there is time to get to really know the characters. Usually people in a thriller are mere cardboard vehicles to carry the storyline. The literate script was written by Thornton Wilder with some additional flourishes supplied by Sally Benson, better known for *Meet Me in St. Louis* and other upbeat films. Hitchcock's wife, Alma Reville, also worked on the script, which was based on a short story idea by the husband of the woman who headed Selznick's story department.

The plot is simple and clean: Charles Cokley (Joseph Cotton) comes to Santa Rosa to visit his sister's family and elude two detectives on his trail. His sister Emma (Patricia Collinge) is married to Joseph Newton (Henry Travers) and is the mother of a family of precocious young children, including "Charlie" Newton, Cokley's adoring teenage niece. Through a series of incidents, "Charlie" begins to suspect that her uncle may be the "Merry Widow Killer" hunted by the police. Jack Graham (MacDonald Carey), one of the trailing detectives, convinces her even more that he is probably the

Joseph Cotten gives Teresa Wright a stolen ring which she later uses against him.

MacDonald Carey and Wallace Ford, as detectives, get the trust of Teresa Wright.

Joseph Cotten and Teresa Wright.

Joseph Cotten demands exposed film back from Wallace Ford as MacDonald Carey and Teresa Wright look on.

Joseph Cotten, feigning illness, is helped off the train at Santa Rosa by fellow passengers.

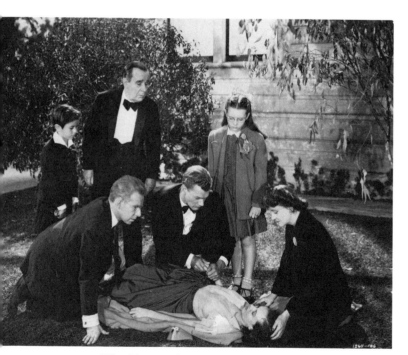

The Newton family and neighbor Hume Cronyn care for Teresa Wright after she's been trapped in a gas-filled garage.

man. When another suspect is accidentally killed by police in the East, the inquiry is officially closed. But Uncle Charlie, now aware of his niece's suspicions, attempts to kill her three times, all unsuccessful. The last attempt comes when he boards the train which will take him home. He tries to push her off the platform but in the struggle is himself thrown and crushed to death by a passing train. A funeral in Santa Rosa is held, and the detective and "Charlie" know that only they hold the truth about the dead man.

There is a realism to *Shadow of a Doubt* that is not found in most other Hitchcock pictures. The people are real and the town they live in is real. The motivations aren't contrived, but natural and believable. The on-location filming in Santa Rosa helps here, adding an authenticity not to be found in a studio. But towards the end of the film—when it becomes an out-and-out thriller—the graceful and controlled progression of characterization, which made the first part of the film so successful, ceases. There is no surprise left to scare the audience. Hitchcock creates a mood in *Shadow of a Doubt,* a psychological atmosphere. And as young Charlie begins to suspect her uncle of foul play, the audience does also. Even though we really know that Cotten is the killer, we are somehow rooting for him. Hitchcock manipulates the audience—his favorite pastime—into sympathizing with a man he has already shown as reprehensible.

Shadow of a Doubt has an Orson Welles texture to it, not only from the appearance of Joseph Cotten, an original Welles Mercury Player, but from the use of the lifelike speech patterns found in Welles's films. Normally, in a motion picture or a play one character waits for the other to finish his lines before commencing with his own. This is not the way people talk in real life; lines of dialogue overlap each other. Much talk is in incompleted sentences. And so this actual-speech approach was used in *Shadow of a Doubt,* as Welles had used it in *Citizen Kane.*

Several nonprofessionals were cast into the picture, with one of the largest roles going to Edna May Wonacott, who played the Newtons' younger daughter. She was discovered in Santa Rosa, where her father ran the local grocery. Another small detail that gives the film its sharpness is that Joseph Newton (Henry Travers) and his crony, Herbie Hawkins—played by Hume Cronyn—continually discuss various means of murder and crime—all for play—while a murderer sits at their dinner table. The humor is subtle and provides yet another dimension to the roles, which makes them all the more palpable.

Clues are constantly provided in advance. The audience, if perceptive, is always aware of what will eventually happen. They know that Uncle Charlie is the man who robs and kills rich widows because the motif of the "Merry Widow Waltz" and couples dancing to it haunt us throughout. We know that when both Charlies are inside the garage and the door jams, Uncle Charlie will later use it as a means of killing the niece who knows too much.

Hitchcock shows his eye for pictorial content and atmosphere in several shots in the film. As young Charlie first realizes that her uncle is probably the "Merry Widow Killer," she is at the library finding the article that her uncle cut from the newspaper. We go from a shot of Charlie with an expression of shock on her face to an extreme close up of a news column headed "Where is Merry Widow Killer?" The camera slowly moves down the column as the waltz is heard on the track.

Joseph Cotten tears out incriminating evidence from the newspaper and then pretends to be showing Edna May Wonacott a trick.

When the news arrives that the other possible killer was chopped up into little pieces by an airplane propeller as he ran from the police in Maine, Uncle Charlie relaxes. All is well. He walks past his niece and up to the second floor of the house. We feel that something is wrong. Cotten turns and finds young Charlie staring at him from the bottom of the stairs. We know that he now realizes that she must be done away with.

In one of the final sequences, when young Charlie is trapped in the garage, Hitchcock uses the standard suspense technique of the audience knowing more than the actors as the family slowly readies itself to leave for a speech. We know that Charlie may not have much more time to live as her father goes upstairs one more time to get his overcoat.

The acting by all is excellent, but certainly Joseph Cotten and Teresa Wright as the two Charlies carry the show with their responsive and perceptive performances.

Shadow of a Doubt is Hitchcock's full house (you can see him in his cameo playing poker on the train that brings Uncle Charles to Santa Rosa). In 1959 a remake of the film was produced with the title, *Step Down to Terror.* It was a *large* step down.

Lifeboat

1943

Hume Cronyn, Tallulah Bankhead, and John Hodiak.

Production: Kenneth MacGowan, 20th Century-Fox; *Screenplay:* Jo Swerling, from a story by John Steinbeck; *Director of Photography:* Glen MacWilliams; *Special Effects:* Fred Sersen; *Sets:* James Basevi and Maurice Ransford; *Music:* Hugo Friedhofer, directed by Emil Newman; *Costumes:* René Hubert; *Editing:* Dorothy Spencer; *Sound Engineers:* Bernard Fredericks and Roger Heman; *Studio:* 20th Century-Fox; *Distributor:* 20th Century-Fox; *Principal Actors:* Tallulah Bankhead (*Constance Porter: "Connie"*), William Bendix (*Gus Smith*), Walter Slezak (*Willy, captain of the submarine*), Mary Anderson (*Alice MacKenzie*), John Hodiak (*John Kovac*), Henry Hull (*Charles S. Rittenhouse*), Heather Angel (*Mrs. Higgins*), Hume Cronyn (*Stanley Garett*), Canada Lee (*George Spencer: "Joe," the steward*); *Running Time:* 96 minutes; *16mm Rental Source:* Films, Incorporated.

Walter Slezak

Hitchcock was continually fascinated with the challenge of shooting an entire picture within a confined setting. *The Lady Vanishes* was filmed on a ninety-foot set, but that was because of a meager budget. The first voluntary experiment with a single-set film was *Lifeboat*. (*Rope* and *Rear Window* followed.) Twentieth Century–Fox had purchased the services of Hitchcock from Selznick for two films. Asked if he had any particular ideas in mind, Hitchcock replied that he did—a film requiring only one set, a lifeboat. John Steinbeck, the novelist, was signed to write a treatment incorporating the director's ideas with a few of the writer's own. Jo Swerling then wrote the screenplay in collaboration with Hitchcock. It succeeded in depicting the war in microcosm without overworking the symbolism.

The film is a sharp allegory of democracy's all-but-suicidal acquiescences to Hitler's bullying in the thirties and wartime forties. In the mid-Atlantic fog a wailing horn echoes against the wreckage of a passenger ship as its smokestack gives a final moan and sinks below the oily waves. The camera travels along the surface of débris until it comes upon a perfectly coiffed Constance Porter (Tallulah Bankhead), who appears ready for an evening at the opera more than a voyage in a lifeboat. Hitchcock remarked that Tallulah "was the most oblique, incongruous bit of casting I could think of. Isn't a lifeboat in the middle of the Atlantic the last place one would expect Tallulah? For the sake of realism and suspense I am partial to people whose faces are not too familiar to the movie audience. Imagine reaching over the side of a lifeboat to haul someone out of the oily, debris-littered water and having that someone turn out to be last year's box office champion or a favorite pinup girl."

Tallulah Bankhead, bedecked in fur and jewels, shoots some newsreel footage while John Hodiak sneers.

William Bendix, John Hodiak, Walter Slezak, Tallulah Bankhead, Heather Angel, Mary Anderson, Henry Hull, and Canada Lee.

Tallulah Bankhead makes Canada Lee an offering while the other survivors look on.

Connie Porter soon picks up many other survivors, including Gus Smith (William Bendix), a sailor whose leg is eventually amputated on the swaying boat; a black steward named Joe (Canada Lee); a young Army nurse; a millionaire; a left-wing crew member (John Hodiak); and Willy (Walter Slezak), the captain of a German U-boat also wrecked in the shelling.

The passengers discuss whether they should throw Willy to the sharks, but he saves the boat from capsizing and is allowed to assume command. The survivors get hungrier and thirstier as days and nights on the high sea pass by. Somehow, only the German remains cool. When Gus discovers that Willy is withholding water from the others, Willy pushes him overboard. Eventually the others piece together what has happened and they attack and kill the German. It all seems in vain as the German supply ship is seen in the distance. But fortune is on their side, for an Allied ship sinks the German boat and rescues the survivors.

Lifeboat was shot entirely on a restricted set in which the boat was secured in a large studio tank. *Mal de mer* hit the entire cast at one point or another. Hitchcock, always striving for realism, insisted that the boat never remain stationary and that there always be an added touch of ocean mist and fog compounded of oil forced through dry ice. Hume Cronyn, who portrayed Stanley Garett, almost drowned when he got caught under a large metal water-activator, used for making waves. A lifeguard, hired especially for the production, saved him in the nick of time.

The film was received with highly partisan reviews. Either the critics thought it was a masterpiece or, as Dorothy Thompson stated, "I'll give the film three days to get out of town." Some called the film, which had become a cause célèbre, Communist propaganda. Others thought it was a brilliant piece of flag-waving. Hitchcock thought of it as more of the latter, it being the third in his trilogy of wartime-oriented efforts.

Because of its starkness, though, it is a film that has endured the ravages of time. Remarkably, it is still the powerful drama it was when it was first released. And as it happens, it was the only film Hitchcock made for Twentieth Century–Fox.

Spellbound

1945

Ingrid Bergman discovers the truth about Gregory Peck.

Gregory Peck suffers another one of his dizzy spells as Ingrid Bergman attempts to steady him.

Gregory Peck and Ingrid Bergman

Production: Selznick International; *Producer:* David O. Selznick; *Screenplay:* Ben Hecht, from the novel THE HOUSE OF DR. EDWARDES by Francis Beeding (Hilary St. George Saunders and John Palmer); *Adaptation:* Angus McPhail; *Director of Photography:* George Barnes, A.S.C.; *Special Photographic Effects:* Jack Cosgrove; *Sets:* James Basevi and John Ewing; *Music:* Miklos Rozsa; *Costumes:* Howard Greer; *Editing:* William Ziegler and Hal C. Kern; *Dream Sequence:* Salvador Dali; *Psychiatric Consultant:* May E. Romm; *Studio:* Selznick International; *Distributor:* United Artists; *Principal Actors:* Ingrid Bergman (*Doctor Constance Petersen*), Gregory Peck (*John Ballantine*), Jean Acker (*The Directress*), Rhonda Fleming (*Mary Carmichel*), Donald Curtis (*Harry*), John Emery (*Dr. Fleurot*), Leo G. Carroll (*Dr. Murchison*), Norman Lloyd (*Garmes*), and Steven Geray, Paul Harvey, Erskine Sandford, Janet Scott, Victor Killian, Bill Goodwin, Art Baker, Wallace Ford, Regis Toomey, Teddy Infuhr, Addison Richards, Dave Willock, George Meader, Matt Morre, Harry Brown, Clarence Straight, Joel Davis, Edward Fielding, Richard Bartell, Michael Chekov; *Running Time:* 111 minutes; *16mm Rental Source:* Audio/Brandon.

If Hitchcock dealt with psychological themes in *Shadow of a Doubt* and *Suspicion*, with *Spellbound* he was to fully confront the affairs of the mind. As Freudian as *Spellbound* is, it is also lushly romantic, with the haunting Academy Award Miklos Rozsa score and the pairing of Gregory Peck and Ingrid Bergman.

This was Hitchcock's second Selznick outing. The producer so fully trusted his director that he may have come to the set twice during production, highly unusual for Selznick who was known in Hollywood as a producer who wanted to know what was happening with his projects at every step. That doesn't mean that Hitchcock's ideas weren't tampered with. When it came to financial issues, he was invariably defeated. Although Selznick granted Hitchcock's wish for obtaining surrealist artist Salvador Dali to create the dream sequences, he would not allow the expense of filming them outside the studio. Hitchcock wanted them to be stark, and full of mysterious shadows, as are found in many of the surrealistic paintings of Dali and Chirico. Filming in bright sunlight would have achieved this effect. The producer vetoed the idea as too expensive and the now-famous dream sequences of the film were made in the studio along with the rest of the picture. The film was brought in on a two million dollar budget and after its opening at Radio City Music Hall grossed $8 million.

The story, which maintains its pace, is fraught

Ingrid Bergman is afraid that Leo G. Carroll will read the message he is giving her.

Leo G. Carroll introduces Gregory Peck to the doctors at the clinic.

with complications and, for all the mystique provided by the oblique Freudian associations, it is the suspense Hitchcock supplies that saves the picture. Based on a novel by Francis Beeding (pen name for Hilary St. George Saunders and John Palmer), *The House of Dr. Edwardes,* the Ben Hecht screenplay begins as the staff of a mental hospital awaits its new director, Dr. Edwardes (Gregory Peck), who takes over for the resigned Dr. Murchison (Leo G. Carroll). Dr. Constance Peterson (Ingrid Bergman) takes immediately to the new doctor and falls in love with him. Soon after, though, she realizes that he is really a mental patient who has assumed the role of Dr. Edwardes. Her lover now becomes her patient, and he finally is convinced that he must have killed the real Dr. Edwardes, with the amnesia as the result of the shock of his violent act. She hides him from the police with her former professor (Michael Chekhov —nephew of the Russian playwright) who immediately analyzes "Dr. Edwardes's" dreams. The reason for his guilt complex is revealed and quickly after, it becomes evident that the real killer is Dr. Murchison, who did it to save his job. Murchison, confronted by Constance, kills himself.

Casting problems still plagued Hitchcock. He felt, and rightly so, that Gregory Peck was not a Hitchcockian actor, but he was in Selznick's stable so Peck was more or less forced upon him. No one, however, had to beg him to take Ingrid Bergman,

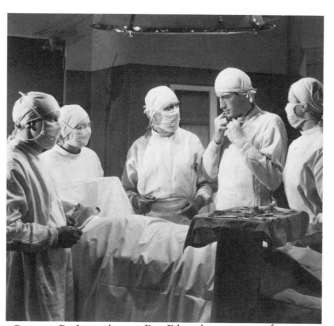

Gregory Peck, posing as Dr. Edwardes, prepares for an operation.

Leo G. Carroll is visited by detectives when he discovers that Gregory Peck is an imposter.

whom he recognized as a fine actress, perfect for his type of film. Cool, seductive, aloof, and alluring, Bergman was radiant in front of the camera. Rhonda Fleming made her debut in *Spellbound*, and Norman Lloyd, last seen as he fell from the Statue of Liberty in *Saboteur,* made a brief appearance as a patient.

Critics were not particularly fond of Peck's performance and as *Time* magazine sarcastically noted, "By flexing his jaw muscles and narrowing his eyes, Peck does his best to register the fact that all is not well with him." For Bosley Crowther of *The New York Times,* "Lovely Miss Bergman is both the doctor and prescription in this film. She is the single stimulation of dramatic logic and audience belief. The story is a rather obvious and often told tale. It depends, despite its truly expert telling, upon the illusion of the lady in the leading role."

The recurrent chase motif which plays such large parts of many Hitchcock films is used again. The chase here, though, is more implied than seen. For

although Peck as Dr. Edwardes/John Ballantine is indeed running from the police, he is more immediately running from his subconscious. It is *this* chase that becomes the crux of the film.

Hitchcock employed, in addition to the clever use of Dali dream sequences, two other cinematic gimmicks which surprised the audience. Both occur in the scene at the end of the film in which Constance confronts Dr. Murchison with the truth. He points a gun at her after she tells him that she knows he is the killer. The gun is seen from his eyes. To get the proper perspective an oversized gun was used. Constance talks herself out of Murchison's office, and the gun then turns to the audience. When he shoots to kill himself—and the audience—a red Technicolor clip of the film, no more than $1/12$th of a second, is interposed. The result is that the audience actually sees the gunshot and blood in a flash. Because we have been viewing black-and-white film for more than one hundred minutes, the red is devastating.

124

Notorious
1946

Ingrid Bergman, Cary Crant and Claude Rains.

Ingrid Bergman with Cary Grant.

Cary Grant holds Ingrid Bergman after saving her from Claude Rains, who has been slowly poisoning her.

Production: Alfred Hitchcock, R.K.O.; *Associate Producer:* Barbara Keon; *Screenplay:* Ben Hecht, from a theme by Alfred Hitchcock; *Director of Photography:* Ted Tetzlaff, A.S.C.; *Special Effects:* Vernon L. Walker and Paul Eagler, A.S.C.; *Sets:* Albert S. D'Agostino, Carrol Clark, Darrell Silvera, and Claude Carpenter; *Costumes:* Edith Head; *Music:* Roy Webb, conducted by Constantin Balaleinikoff; *Editing:* Theron Warth; *Sound Engineers:* John Tribly and Clem Portman; *Assistant Director:* William Dorfman; *Studio:* R.K.O.; *Distributor:* R.K.O.; *Principal Actors:* Ingrid Bergman (*Alicia Huberman*), Cary Grant (*Devlin*), Claude Rains (*Alexander Sebastian*), Louis Calhern (*Paul Prescott*), Leopoldine Konstantin (*Mrs. Sebastian*), Reinhold Schünzel (*Dr. Anderson*), and Moroni Olsen, Ivan Triesault, Alexis Minotis, Eberhardt Krumschmidt, Fay Baker, Ricardo Costa, Lenore Ulric, Ramon Nomar, Peter von Zerneck, Sir Charels Mandl, Wally Brown; *Running Time:* 101 minutes; *16mm Rental Source:* Images.

Since Alfred Hitchcock was the contractual "property" of David O. Selznick, the noted producer of *Gone with the Wind* and *Rebecca* could select the scripts he wished. In 1944 he sold a package of script, stars, and director to RKO for $800,000, plus 50 percent of the profits. The film was *Notorious* and was produced on a budget of $2 million. The world premiere was held where most other Hitchcock pictures had been held, Radio City Music Hall. Its spectacularly profitable run was duplicated across the country, and *Notorious* grossed a quick $9 million.

The reason for its immense popularity was aptly summed up by Bosley Crowther in his review in *The New York Times:* "Ben Hecht has written and Mr. Hitchcock has directed in brilliant style, a romantic melodrama which is just about as thrilling as they come—velvet smooth in dramatic action, sharp and sure in its character and heavily charged with the intensity of warm emotional appeal. As a matter of fact, the distinction of *Notorious* as a film is the remarkable blend of a love story with expert 'thriller' that it represents."

Always the audience-manipulator, Hitchcock toyed with the viewers' sympathies in *Notorious.* Claude Rains, master villain, is duped into falling in love with Ingrid Bergman. The audience despises what Rains stands for, yet cannot help feeling sorry that it is his 'love' that is being used against him. Of course, Hitchcock's reply to this is simply, "All's fair in love and war."

Notorious is about love and war. At the end of the war a Nazi agent is sentenced to prison. His

Ingrid Bergman begins to feel the effect of the poison she's been given.

Cary Grant and Ingrid Bergman discover the uranium in the fake wine bottles.

Reinhold Schunzel and Ivan Triesault censure Claude Rains for holding a large party in his home, which is the German underground headquarters.

daughter, Alicia Huberman (Ingrid Bergman), never involved with his activities, leads a jet set life until she is approached by an FBI man named Devlin (Cary Grant) with a request that she undertake a secret mission. She accepts and they both go to Rio. Devlin falls in love with Alicia, but her past reputation and her present assignment keeps him at a distance. Her job is to establish contact with Alexander Sebastian (Claude Rains), a former associate of her father's who is sheltering Nazi refugees in Brazil. Eventually, she is forced to marry him. As mistress of the house, she learns about Sebastian's covert activities. At a large party the couple holds, she and Devlin explore a curious wine cellar and discover that some of the bottles of fine wine contain not the precious liquid but uranium ore—what Cary Grant calls "vintage sand." Sebastian becomes aware that Alicia is an American agent and to conceal the mistake, he and his mother (Leopoldine Konstantin) poison her slowly with arsenic. Eventually, not hearing from the ailing Alicia, Devlin breaks his way into Sebastian's house and saves her. Sebastian, his compatriots hovering near, returns to face the consequences of love for Alicia.

Leopoldine Konstantin and Claude Rains look in on their captive, Ingrid Bergman.

"The Hitchcock 'touch' is apparent in several scenes, notably at a party where suspense is built magnificently as the champagne slowly disappears. The American agent in the wine cellar is working against the thirst of the celebrants," the *Herald Tribune* reviewer noted. The party sequence is probably the highlight of the film. Alicia has just secured the key to the wine cellar. The camera, mounted on an enormous crane, at first sees an extreme wide-angle shot of the festivities, then glides in to an extreme closeup of the key tightly clenched in Alicia's hand. We have gone from the most general to the most specific and have been let in on a secret. It is a scene very much like the one in the earlier film, *Young and Innocent,* in which the camera tracks across a ballroom, into the blinking eyes of the murderer, although the shot from the earlier English film is more difficult technically and a much more stylish and exciting experience.

Hitchcock knows now that he was ahead of his time when he and Ben Hecht decided that there would be uranium inside the fake bottles. This was a year before Hiroshima and no one was supposed to know about its powers or that it would be used in an atom bomb. It seemed like such a preposterous idea for a movie at the time that rather than produce it himself, Selznick sold the entire package to RKO. Hitchcock says that apparently the government was quite alarmed that he should be even using the term *uranium* in the script. He was followed by the FBI for three months.

The acting by all was exceptionally convincing, but it was the magnetic duo of Bergman and Grant that captured audiences and still does. "There is rich and real emotion expressed by Miss Bergman in her role and the integrity of her nature as she portrays it is the prop that holds the show," *The New York Times* said.

Notorious was Cary Grant's second Hitchcock vehicle, and he was all the more seasoned in executing the director's conception of the role. He adds sensitivity to the role of a man torn between love and duty. We feel his frustration and we share his determination to be able to perform both. Pitted against the equally suave and debonair Claude Rains, Grant has to work harder but his performance, like Rain's, seems effortless.

Notorious is a lush, romantic thriller with glamorous movie stars. Its element of suspense is hinged on the romantic interests, not on the ulterior motives of espionage. Hitchcock is again toying with our emotions.

Before they set out to the secret wine cellar, Cary Grant and Ingrid Bergman check the bar to see how much wine is left before the servants will have to come down to the cellar to get more.

The Paradine Case
1947

Louis Jourdan, in the witness stand of Old Bailey, is questioned by Gregory Peck.

Production: Selznick International; *Producer:* David O. Selznick; *Screenplay:* David O. Selznick, from the novel by Robert Hichens; *Adaptation:* Alma Reville; *Director of Photography:* Lee Garmes; *Sets:* J. MacMillian Johnson and Thomas Morahan; *Costumes:* Travis Banton; *Music:* Franz Waxman; *Editing:* Hal C. Kern and John Faure; *Studio:* Selznick International; *Distributor:* United Artists; *Principal Actors:* Gregory Peck (*Anthony Keane*), Anne Todd (*Gay Keane*), Charles Laughton (*Judge Horfield*), Ethel Barrymore (*Lady Sophie Horfield*), Charles Coburn (*Sir Simon Flaquer, the lawyer*), Louis Jourdan (*André Latour*), Alida Valli (*Maddalena, Anna Paradine*), and Leo G. Carroll, John Goldsworthy, Isobel Elsom, Lester Matthews, Pat Aherne, Colin Hunter, John Williams; *Running Time:* 112 minutes; *16mm Rental Source:* Audio/Brandon.

On November 22, 1946, tired and worried, David O. Selznick sent a memo to his chief aide, Daniel O'Shea. In it he confessed, "I am certain that *The Paradine Case* has tremendous flaws, and it looks to me as though it is going to have to go into work, willy nilly. I simply will have to hope that somehow we will be able to get together the cast for what will inevitably be costly retakes. . . ."

When *The Paradine Case* was completed, its budget came in over three million dollars, but cost was the least of the picture's or Selznick's problems. The point was that even after many script rewrites and elaborate set construction, the film was nothing more than an overlong, overproduced, talky whodunit—in short, the very type of film that Hitchcock always said he liked to avoid making.

Why Selznick proceeded with the project is difficult to understand. He saw from the start that it was going to be a troublesome affair. Probably the only reason for his continued support was Hitchcock. Even that faith diminished somewhat as filming got underway. Shooting fell hopelessly behind schedule right from the start. Selznick confided to his aide that he sensed Hitchcock had slowed down "unaccountably" and was aware of the director's "seeming indifference to cost, and the lack of the firm hand which I at least once applied with him."

Selznick was positive that Hitchcock was purposely doing this to point out that he himself would be much more efficient when filming was in his own operation. Hitchcock complained to Selznick on a number of occasions that he thought it was "disgraceful" that he should film a picture with a production whose technology was "twenty years behind the times." Such were the woes of the independent producer. Selznick himself adapted the

Valli as Mrs. Paradine.

Ann Todd is repelled by Charles Laughton's lecherous advances.

Valli, charged with murder, is readied for her stay in prison.

Louis Jourdan and Gregory Peck.

Ethel Barrymore and Charles Laughton.

final screenplay from the Robert Hichens novel of the same name, but Hitchcock didn't like his method of rewriting. The producer would write one scene at a time and send it down to the set immediately before it was to be shot.

If Hitchcock had had casting problems for his films previous to this, *The Paradine Case* was a cornucopia of·miscast actors and actresses. The only name star was Gregory Peck. Of course, Charles Laughton and Ethel Barrymore were part of the cast, but they were not box-office pulls. Hitchcock wanted Laurence Olivier for the Peck role and he tried to get Greta Garbo to make her comeback in the lead role of Mrs. Paradine. He had to settle for Alida Valli, an Italian actress whom Selznick had signed in hopes of transforming her into the new Ingrid Bergman. Mrs. Paradine's lover was supposed to be a rough-looking character, but since contract actors were the rule, Hitchcock was given the smooth-looking Louis Jourdan, not a man who looked like a manure-smelling groom.

The plot was another flaw—it was rambling and confusing. It tells of Mrs. Paradine (Alida Valli), who was accused of murdering her blind, rich husband. Her lawyer, Anthony Keane (Gregory Peck), married to a beautiful woman himself (Ann Todd), falls in love with his client and thus convinces himself of her innocence. Immediately before the trial is ready to begin, he learns that she had been the mistress of the groom, André Latour (Louis Jourdan). The trial judge is Harnfield (Charles Laughton) who, resentful after his fruitless attempt to seduce Mrs. Keane, is openly hostile to Peck in court. The trial culminates as Peck slowly loses control of Mrs. Paradine. He realizes that she does not want him as a lover and does not want him implicating Latour in any way. Latour is brought to the stand and is shown to have been Mrs. Paradine's lover. He has let his master down and, disgraced, he later kills himself. A highlight of the trial comes when Peck attempts to establish that someone other than Mrs. Paradine could have washed the wine glass which held the fatal dose of poison.

Peck, trying not to bring Latour's name back into the trial, asks Mrs. Paradine generally about the washing of the glass. However, Mrs. Paradine does not like the tone of the question and says that she washed it.

She then openly admits to the stunned Peck that she is the murderess and she blames Keane for her lover's death.

Keane walks from the courtroom with the camera looking straight down as his figure wends its way past the rows of benches. His career is at an ebb and his emotions shell-shocked. His wife stands behind him, a sign of hope.

Mrs. Keane (Ann Todd) gives one of the finest supporting performances in the film, or for that matter in any Hitchcock film. She is totally believable in the role.

Although only a third of the film is in court, it is the courtroom scenes that are the highlights of the otherwise pedestrian affair. The Old Bailey courtroom was recreated in Hollywood at a cost of seventy thousand dollars and seventeen hundred man-hours. To create tension in what amounts to verbal football, multiple cameras were used. While not a new approach, it was the first time that eight cameramen with four cameras were ever used for single scenes.

Each camera focused on different characters; the various complete takes were edited together in the cutting room. Of course, this extravagant approach left much waste on the cutting-room floor, but the final product is exciting to watch.

Charles Laughton and Ethel Barrymore were probably the two most interesting character studies in the film. They were an odd couple but typical of Hitchcock's approach to casting. The famous Barrymore profile was taken advantage of and appears as often as she does, which unfortunately is not very often.

One of Hitchcock's childhood-based fears, jail cells, is handled so that the entire audience shudders. Mrs. Paradine is thrown into prison, and when the door to her cell is closed, the slamming resounds in a thundering echo.

The Paradine Case was Selznick's project, not Hitchcock's, and the result on screen is obvious. For as many reasons as it was originally done, it was recreated again on television in 1962. Richard Basehart, Viveca Lindfors, and Boris Karloff starred in the special, which was unanimously panned by reviewers.

This was the last of Hitchcock's four productions under his contract with Selznick. It was an amicable parting, but one is led to believe that Hitchcock was happier about it than Selznick.

Ann Todd, Charles Coburn and Gregory Peck.

The Technicolor, Vistavision, 3-D Years

1948-1959

Robert Walker and Laura Elliott in *Strangers on a Train*.

On the set of *The Man Who Knew Too Much*

he Paradine Case may have been a failure, financially and critically, but its completion marked a new era for Alfred Hitchcock. Finally, he had enough capital and prestige to form his own production company. Together with his old friend, Sidney Bernstein, Hitchcock produced and directed films for the new company, Transatlantic Pictures. Distribution was handled by Hitchcock's next studio, Warner Brothers. The new company's name signified that films would be made in the United States as well as in Great Britain.

The first was *Rope,* which manifests many experiments with the cinematic medium that Hitchcock had been itching to try. *Rope* was the director's first film, after thirty-four features in black and white, to be shot in color. It was the first feature film in the history of Hollywood that was also edited "in the can" as it was shot, each take being the length of a full camera load of ten minutes. Although Hitchcock had previously directed film adaptations of stage plays, *Rope* was the first to be a filmed stage play: a movie which was nothing more than pictures of people talking.

After *Rope,* Hitchcock journeyed to England to prepare *Under Capricorn.* In *Rope,* he had attained the services of a big name, James Stewart, for $300,000. For *Under Capricorn,* Hitchcock spent a small fortune to get the then very popular Ingrid Bergman. Since the film was not a typical "Hitchcock" suspense thriller, audiences expecting one were disappointed, and the second production of Transatlantic Films was a failure. But it did give Hitchcock a further opportunity to experiment freely. *Under Capricorn* was in splendid color, which was appropriate for a costume drama.

His feelings about the use of color were simple; it should begin with the closest equivalent to black-and-white. In an interview, he defined this to mean "the muted color is black and white, and the screams are every psychedelic color you can think of, starting of course, with red."

The late forties and fifties in the career of Alfred Hitchcock could be broken into two distinct parts. From 1948 to 1954 was his Warner Bros. period, which was definitely weaker than the late fifties spent at Paramount and concluding with a one-shot at M-G-M. The Warners period was a low point in his career, with one successive mediocre picture after another. The exceptions, of course, are the expert and exciting *Strangers on a Train,* and the well-

paced *Dial M for Murder.* In between were *Stage Fright, I Confess, The Wrong Man,* and the earlier *Rope* and *Under Capricorn.*

Though he was able to pick and choose the material he wanted to put on the screen, Hitchcock made a number of errors in judgment, both in selection and in the actual direction. From the deceptive flashback of *Stage Fright* to the deadly seriousness of *I Confess,* there were a collection of reasons why each production did not click. It was at times like these, in which his creative juices did not flow smoothly, that Hitchcock stated, "my batteries need a charge." Running for cover, he took on any convenient vehicle that remotely interested him. *Dial "M" for Murder* was one such project in the early fifties. Produced in Warner Color, it was also shot in Naturalvision, or 3-D, another experiment for Hitchcock. There wasn't much you could do with a stage play in the way of gimmicky 3-D shots, but Hitchcock engineered them, and the critics who did see the few released 3-D prints, said that it was the most successful use of the ill-fated, goggle-eyed process.

The next four pictures for Paramount were all critical successes. Three of them were well received at the box office. Unsurprisingly, the one unprofitable film was also the most personal—the misunderstood black comedy, *The Trouble with Harry.* *Rear Window, To Catch a Thief,* and *The Man Who Knew Too Much* were as diverse in subject as they were in original design. It was evident that Hitchcock's batteries were fully charged. Each of the four films was re-released in various double Hitchcock bills and, because of his new TV program and subsequent rising popularity, they were well-greeted.

They represented the beginning of the master's most creative period in America. *Rear Window* was an expertly crafted piece of film, using all the cinematic components to involve the audience. *To Catch a Thief* was a sleek and glossy romantic caper on the glamorous Riviera with the equally sleek and glossy Grace Kelly and Cary Grant. Equally lightweight was *The Trouble with Harry,* probably Hitchcock's most unappreciated film, yet one of his personal favorites. A human comedy, it picks at our foibles and plays with a subject that customarily is given a heavy treatment—death. *The Man Who Knew Too Much,* a remake of his 1934 success, this time included touches Hitchcock wanted to add the first time around but missed. It was a spectacle of nerves and Hitchcock's first "family picture."

139

Kim Novak getting directions on the set of *Vertigo*.

Directing Montgomery Clift and Anne Baxter in *I Confess*.

Inspecting Grace Kelly on set of *To Catch a Thief*.

With Ingrid Bergman during the filming of *Under Capricorn*.

The Wrong Man was another experiment for Hitchcock. This time, he dealt with his recurring innocent-man theme with a factual background. It was a quasi-documentary which only failed when it digressed from the real story at hand. It was made in black-and-white for Warner Bros. because the property was conveniently available. Following that was his bizarre *Vertigo,* with its inventive use of wide screen and Technicolor. *Vertigo* was also one of the strangest stories Hitchcock ever tackled. Its slow exposition was fraught more with mystery than suspense—a film imbued more with intellectual labyrinths and psychological implications than with straightforward plot development. It was also Hitchcock at his best. In a special agreement with Paramount, the rights to all these Paramount features save *To Catch A Thief* reverted to Hitchcock. Except for limited TV showings, he has kept them out of circulation for a number of years.

Hitchcock's sole effort for M-G-M, *North by Northwest,* manifested every facet of his style and personality at the end of the fifties. An insouciant fantasy in modern dress, a cross-country Cook's tour that was at once suspenseful and funny, *North by Northwest* was as Hitchcock noted, "the epitome of all my American films."

Like many of the films that preceded it, *North by Northwest* also revealed how Hitchcock toyed with sexual implications. From the fireworks in *To Catch a Thief* to phallic imagery of the train shooting into the tunnel at the end of *North by Northwest,* Hitchcock preferred the use of understatement. Give the audience all the information it needs to know and then let it sweat it out.

Whether it is coincidental or not is not the point, but his highest artistic plateau was reached at the same time that his popularity was at its zenith. Now people expected more from him than ever and when he failed, as he would in the sixties, he was not forgiven or excused.

With cast on the set of *Rope*.

On the set of *Dial M for Murder*.

To Catch a Thief and the Riviera.

Cameo appearance in *I Confess*.

Cameo appearance in
Strangers on a Train.

With Cary Grant on the set of *To Catch a Thief*.

Rope
1948

James Stewart, John Dall, and Farley Granger.

Production: Transatlantic Pictures, Warner Brothers; *Producers:* Sidney Bernstein and Alfred Hitchcock; *Screenplay:* Arthur Laurents, from the play by Patrick Hamilton; *Adaptation:* Hume Cronyn; *Directors of Photography:* Joseph Valentine and William V. Skall, A.S.C.; *Color by Technicolor:* Consultant, Natalie Kalmus; *Sets:* Perry Ferguson; *Music:* Leo F. Forbstein, based on the theme "Perpetual Movement No. 1" by Francis Poulenc; *Costumes:* Adrian; *Editing:* William H. Ziegler; *Studio:* Warner Bros.; *Distributor:* Warner Bros.; *Principal Actors:* James Stewart (*Rupert Cadell*), John Dall (*Shaw Brandon*), Joan Chandler (*Janet Walker*), Sir Cedric Hardwicke (*Mr. Kentley, David's father*), Constance Collier (*Mrs. Atwater*), Edith Evanson (*Mrs. Wilson, the governess*), Douglas Dick (*Kenneth Lawrence*), Dick Hogan (*David Kentley*), Farley Granger (*Philip*); *Running Time:* 80 minutes; *16mm Rental Source:* Unavailable.

The filming of *Rope* was a turning point in the career of Alfred Hitchcock. It was his first Technicolor film, his first as an independent producer, his first released by Warner Bros., his first with actor James Stewart, and the first film in which he could experiment with new creative techniques.

Since it is the technical aspects of filming a picture, the behind-the-scenes gadgetry and ingenuity for making the filmed illusion work on the screen, which interest Hitchcock, *Rope* was an understandable choice for his first feature as an independent producer-director. It represented a challenge, something he always welcomed. The stage play upon which the film is based occurs in the actual time it takes to perform it, continuous from curtain-up to curtain-down. To achieve this clocklike effect on the screen, Hitchcock decided to go against his principles of the cinema and precut pictures. He shot *Rope* with no actual cuts and instead filmed ten-minute takes, the maximum amount of film (one thousand feet) that a camera will hold. Planning was necessary in defining just how the camera would move and how to create the effect of no cuts. The latter was obtained by closing and opening each ten-minute take in closeup behind an actor or object so that they would create a solid texture on the screen. The total effect of *Rope* was of one continuous shot, the length of the film being the actual time of the action in the story.

The single setting for the production had walls and furniture with silent wheels which could be moved away quietly while the camera was moving from place to place. A color backdrop skyline of New York was realistic. Clouds, made of spun glass, would move and the sky turned from the orange of sunset to the black and twinkling lights of night.

Color was a new medium to Hitchcock and he learned an expensive lesson when he discovered that the sunset was an unreal postcard orange. He reshot five reels with the adjusted backdrop. The film itself cost about $1.5 million to produce, although it certainly doesn't look it. The high budget is blamed on the experimental nature of the project—many technical operations were performed for the first time—and on James Stewart's whopping $300,000 salary. However, it recouped its costs and made a modest profit.

The Patrick Hamilton play, based on the Leopold-Loeb murder case, was adapted for the screen by Arthur Laurents and two-time Hitchcock actor Hume Cronyn. It is the grim story of two homosexual college men, Shaw (John Dall) and Philip (Farley Granger), who kill a third man, David, for the intellectual thrill of it. They hide the body in a large chest in the same room in which his parents and fiancée are expected for a cocktail party. One of the guests is Professor Rupert Cadell (James Stewart), a former instructor of theirs who actually taught them the philosophical concept for which they rationalize the killing. To continue their fun, they feed him academic hints about what they've done, trying to see if he'll figure out their foul play. They even give Mr. Kentley, David's father (Sir Cedric Hardwicke), some books tied with the very rope with which they have strangled his son. Eventually Cadell realizes what the two men have done. He finds the body and reports them to the police.

The play is a parlor drama and the film version remains faithful. Accordingly, with the new ten-minute-take approach, the actors learned their lines as if they were preparing for live theater. There were about ten days of rehearsal and then eighteen days of shooting, half of which were devoted to retakes with the adjusted sun coloring in the background.

If *Rope* was an ambitious experiment, it was not entirely a successful one and, as Howard Barnes wrote in the New York *Herald Tribune*, *Rope* is ". . . not one of his best, but it is the work of a master. Hitchcock has composed individual scenes with infinite care and craft in *Rope*, particularly in his use of color. One wishes that he had taken greater advantage of the motion picture form."

The acting was nothing but, then again, the actors were limited by their material. Although *Rope* is very uncinematic, without cutting or montage, it is an example of technical brilliance of which, more than any other director, Hitchcock was the master. Despite its staginess, *Rope*, by the nature of its story, is a suspenseful tale.

James Stewart, with Farley Granger and John Dall.

James Stewart, Sir Cedric Hardwicke, and Farley Granger with the rope.

Farley Granger, James Stewart, and John Dall.

Farley Granger, James Stewart, and John Dall.

John Dall, Edith Evanson, and Farley Granger.

The unmotivated crime is at once so heinous that its perpetrators become hateful. Yet we don't want the crime to be discovered. James Stewart is a likable, though lightweight, character, and we hope that he will figure out what the murderers have done. The situation is contradictory, a quagmire of mixed emotions producing tension in the audience until the characters on the screen absolve it for us.

144

M-G-M purchased the rights to *Rope* a number of years back but never made any use of them. Currently the film has been the object of intense legal battles.

James Stewart, Douglas Dick, Joan Chandler, Sir Cedric Hardwicke, Constance Collier, John Dall, and Farley Granger.

Hitchcock directing his first color film.

Under Capricorn
1949

Joseph Cotten, Ingrid Bergman and Michael Wilding

Production: Transatlantic Pictures, Warner Bros., G.B.; *Producers:* Sidney Bernstein and Alfred Hitchcock; *Managing Producers:* John Palmer and Fred Ahern; *Screenplay:* James Bridie, from the novel by Helen Simpson; *Adaptation:* Hume Cronyn; *Director of Photography:* Jack Cardiff, A.S.C., and Paul Beeson, Ian Craig, David McNeilly, Jack Haste; *Sets:* Tom Morahan; *Music:* Richard Addinsell; conducted by Louis Levy; *Editing:* A. S. Bates; *Costumes:* Roger Furse; *Color by Technicolor:* Consultants, Natalie Kalmus and Joan Bridge; *Studio:* M-G-M, at Elstree; *Distributor:* Warner Bros.; *Principal Actors:* Ingrid Bergman (*Lady Henrietta Flusky*), Joseph Cotten (*Sam Flusky*), Michael Wilding (*Charles Adare*), Margaret Leighton (*Milly*), Jack Watting (*Winter, Flusky's secretary*), Cecil Parker (*Sir Richard, the tutor*), Dennis O'Dea (*Corrigan, the attorney general*), and Olive Sloan, John Ruddock, Bill Shine, Victor Lucas, Ronald Adam, G. H. Mulcaster, Maureen Delaney, Julia Lang, Betty McDermot, Roderick Lovell, Francis de Wolff; *Running Time:* 117 minutes; *16mm Rental Source:* Audio/Brandon.

Joseph Cotten quiets a disturbed Ingrid Bergman.

Notorious had been Hitchcock's last big hit and *Under Capricorn* was the third film he had made since the 1946 romance thriller. If this, the third of the trio, proved anything, it was that Hitchcock was literally making "talkies." Ostensibly *Under Capricorn* is a costume epic with a suspenseful side story. It was Hitchcock in a terrain in which he did not belong. It was, however, his first film produced in England since he left in 1939 after finishing, his only other costume drama, *Jamaica Inn*. The plot of the film was as uninspiring as its nearly two hours of dialogue.

As the New York *Herald Tribune* tried to explain the story: "A titled Irish girl elopes with her father's groom, kills her outraged brother and follows her self sacrificial husband to a penal colony. A childhood friend (Michael Wilding) of the heroine, attempts to regenerate her from dipsomania, after an ex-convict maid has nearly crazed her with drink, shrunken skulls and poisonous gossip to her husband. You could never tell that the original novel from which this was taken was actually a comedy. The film is anything but. Its locale was Australia, and the lushness of the countryside settings and magnificent costuming blended in Jack Cardiff's sumptuous flowing photography, which showed that Hitchcock had become an expert cinematic craftsman.

Hitchcock has said the only reason he took on *Under Capricorn* was because it was a project that lured Ingrid Bergman, a star then in demand by every studio. Hitchcock thought it would be a coup if he could sign her up. It ended being a Pyrrhic victory because he spent some $2.5 million on the picture. The making of *Under Capricorn* was a caravan of mistakes. Heady with success and fame, Hitchcock became intoxicated with the idea of being the center of attention with his star as he returned to London after so long an absence. It was the only time Hitchcock publicly allowed his emotions to interfere with his craft. Before and after, he has remained the sober gentleman with the saturnine poker-face.

Another error lay in his allowing Hume Cronyn, the actor, and novelist James Bridie to assist in the scenario. The result was a "talking" picture, and a total financial and critical flop. After all the trouble Hitchcock had spent to get Ingrid Bergman, his star proved to have the petulant disposition of a prima donna, which, of course, she was at the time. Hitchcock was still hooked on his experiments with long takes, using whole magazines of film with no cuts. One sequence at a dinner table, just before Miss Bergman's entrance, ran more than seven minutes without a cut. What worked in the filming of a stage play (*Rope*) was not as successful in *Under Capricorn*. Bergman complained to her director about the stress caused by such long takes. Hitchcock, never the director to argue with his cast, simply walked off. Bergman continued her temperamental outburst long after she realized Hitchcock was no longer an audience to it.

Margaret Leighton stands accused by Ingrid Bergman and Joseph Cotten.

Ingrid Bergman and Joseph Cotten.

Joseph Cotten, Michael Wilding and Ingrid Bergman.

One of the chief reasons for the film's failure had nothing to do with its quality; it was simply because it was a costume picture. Although Hitchcock was billed as the Master of Suspense, there was little here. This was his second film with his own production company and he was eager to show Hollywood what he could do if left on his own.

Although he was always a stickler for extensive preproduction planning, Hitchcock learned his lesson the hard way from *Rope* and *Under Capricorn* and after them made sure he knew what he was doing *before* a frame was shot.

The acting was generally frowned upon by critics, although most felt that the actors were saddled with weighty material. Harold Barnes in the New York *Herald Tribune* summed it up: "As a past master of melodrama, Hitchcock has stumbled. It has taken all of Ingrid Bergman's nervous intensity, Joseph Cotten's suppressed violence, Margaret Leighton's malignance, and Michael Wilding's debonair intruding to keep *Under Capricorn* fluent and cumulative. Hitchcock may be remembered for this piece of direction, but only for snatches of it."

In the end, the film lost money and was repossessed by the bank that financed it. *Under Capricorn* also marked the collapse of Transatlantic Pictures.

Joseph Cotten, Ingrid Bergman and Michael Wilding

Michael Wilding is shot by Joseph Cotten as Ingrid Bergman looks on.

Stage Fright
1950

Todd with Marlene Dietrich.

Richard Todd.

Jane Wyman, Richard Todd, Alastair Sim, and Dame Sybil Thorndike.

Jane Wyman pretends to be Marlene Dietrich's maid to get past police guards.

Production: Alfred Hitchcock, Warner Bros., G.B.; *Screenplay:* Whitfield Cook, from two stories by Selwyn Jepson: "Man Running" and "Outrun the Constable"; *Adaptation:* Alma Reville; *Additional Dialogue:* James Bridie; *Director of Photography:* Wilkie Cooper; *Sets:* Terence Verity; *Music:* Leighton Lucas, conducted by Louis Levy; *Editing:* Edward Jarvis; *Sound Engineer:* Harold King; *Studio:* Elstree, G.B.; *Distributor:* Warner Bros.; *Principal Actors:* Marlene Dietrich (*Charlotte Inwood*), Jane Wyman (*Eve Gill*), Michael Wilding (*Inspector Wilfred Smith*), Richard Todd (*Jonathan Cooper*), Alastair Sim (*Commodore Gill*), Dame Sybil Thorndike (*Mrs. Gill*), and Kay Walsh, Miles Malleson, André Morell, Patricia Hitchcock, Hector MacGregor, Joyce Grenfell; *Running Time:* 110 minutes; *16mm Rental Source:* Warner Bros. Film Gallery.

Stage Fright is an excellent title for a film that does not really live up to its name. It was the second movie made during Hitchcock's return to England. He would not produce another in his home country for twenty-two years (although he did shoot some scenes of *The Man Who Knew Too Much* in London in 1956.)

The director has stated that one important quality of his films is their ability to withstand a second and third viewing. *Stage Fright* is one of a handful of Hitchcock's films that does not succeed.

Hitchcock fell prey to the advice of public pressure: first, in acquiring the rights to the story, simply because the reviewers said that it would make a good Hitchcock vehicle; then in listening to the English casting people when they told him that because Alistair Sim was one of the best actors around, Hitchcock should use him whether he fit the part or not.

Probably his biggest mistake, and he is the first to admit it, was lying to the audience. Almost as soon as the title credits are over, we are treated to a flashback which, by the end of the picture, we see was a deception. One of the cardinal rules in movies is that flashbacks should not lie. The audience is deceived and the result is a letdown by the director.

The story is your basic English whodunit with the touches that Hitchcock was fond of. But because of the deceptive flashback at the beginning, we are led to believe that the protagonist is innocent, which he is not.

Jonathan Cooper (Richard Todd), suspected of murdering the husband of his mistress, musical comedy star Charlotte Inwood (Marlene Dietrich), enlists the aid of another friend, Eve Gill (Jane Wyman), to help prove his innocence. Eve hides him aboard the boat of her father (Alastair Sim).

Jane Wyman.

Marlene Dietrich in musical number, "The Laziest Gal in Town."

Marlene Dietrich and Jane Wyman.

She then poses as Charlotte's housekeeper and meets Inspector Wilfred Smith (Michael Wilding), a Scotland Yard detective on the case. When Cooper shows up at Charlotte's theater, Eve helps him escape from the police. He tells Eve that Charlotte is the guilty one. Eve tries to get Charlotte to confess. Cooper shows up again only this time, under arrest. She helps him escape but soon learns that

Cooper really is the murderer and in fact has murdered before. After a chase through the theater, Cooper is caught. Eve, realizing she has fallen in love with Smith, returns to him.

If Alistair Sim was not Hitchcock's cup of tea, Jane Wyman was pure aggravation to the director. Besides receiving top billing over Marlene Dietrich, Wyman emphatically refused to follow Hitchcock's directions. Wyman was more a star than an actress. Her performance was not in character and she emerged looking more like Nancy Drew, amateur detective, than Eve Gill, aspiring actress.

Marlene Dietrich played Marlene Dietrich, singing a few songs and acting glamorous throughout. Richard Todd does a convincing job but, as a number of critics pointed out, there is really no motivation behind his character.

This was the first picture in which Hitchcock used his daughter, Patricia, who doubled for Jane Wyman in a few scenes. Patricia Hitchcock would appear in two more of her father's films, most successfully in the one that followed *Stage Fright*, *Strangers on a Train*.

Stage Fright has a subordinate theme that spans the entire film: the pretense of the stage and the roles people hide behind, on stage and off. Jane Wyman plays a character who wants to be an actress on stage, yet she is forced into circumstances where she must act convincingly in real life. Richard Todd must maintain an image of innocence so that Wyman will help keep him from the police. Marlene Dietrich plays an actress, and one is never sure when she is acting her ordinary self offstage or putting on an act. Although Alistair Sim as the Commodore is unpretentious and perceptively spots the human frailties in people, he also reveals that he occasionally wears an invisible mask.

There is really just one suspenseful scene in the entire movie, and it comes at the very end. Until then, no one is ever in any real danger and that is the main reason the viewer does not care about the people.

The sprinkling of humor in *Stage Fright* is probably its one saving grace. It comes from the four sideline performers who are all so-terribly-English and deftly amusing: Alistair Sim, Sybil Thorndike, Kay Walsh, and the marvelous Joyce Grenfell, who does a funny bit in a shooting gallery ("Lovely ducks").

We know from the beginning that we are not going to be scared by Hitchcock in this film, so we might as well laugh when we get the opportunity. The most hilarious moments in *Stage Fright* are when it is very English.

Strangers On A Train

1951

Robert Walker follows an intrigued Laura Elliot at the amusement park.

Robert Walker and Farley Granger: Strangers on a train.

Farley Granger toasts Pat Hitchcock as his future sister-in-law.

Robert Walker with Ruth Roman.

Production: Alfred Hitchcock, Warner Bros., U.S.A.; *Screenplay:* Raymond Chandler and Czenzi Ormonde, from the novel by Patricia Highsmith; *Adaptation:* Whitfield Cook; *Director of Photography:* Robert Burks, A.S.C.; *Special Photographic Effects:* H. F. Koene Kamp; *Sets:* Ted Hawortt and George James Hopkins; *Music:* Dimitri Tiomkin, conducted by Ray Heindorf; *Costumes:* Leah Rhodes; *Editing:* William H. Ziegler; *Sound Engineer:* Dolph Thomas; *Studio:* Warner Bros.; *Distributor:* Warner Bros.; *Principal Actors:* Farley Granger (*Guy Haines*), Ruth Roman (*Ann Morton*), Robert Walker (*Bruno Anthony*), Leo G. Carroll (*Senator Morton*), Patricia Hitchcock (*Barbara Morton*), Laura Elliot (*Miriam Haines*), Marion Lorne (*Mrs. Anthony*), Jonathan Hale (*Mr. Anthony*), and Howard St. John, John Brown, Norma Warden, Robert Gist, John Doucette, Charles Meredith, Murray Alper, Robert B. Williams, Roy Engel; *Running Time:* 101 minutes; *16mm Rental Source:* Warner Bros. Film Gallery.

Despite the reputation of *Strangers on a Train* as one of Hitchcock's top thrillers, he realized that it lacked certain elements which injured the film. The basic story is faithfully adapted from Patricia Highsmith's novel, but the actual dialogue in parts is insipid and unreal. The problem was finding a writer who could fashion some bright dialogue. After the director had prepared his treatment of the novel for the screen, he gave it to the head of Warner Bros. to give to a writer. Eight writers turned the project down for different reasons, the most common being their inability to visualize the treatment. Hitchcock handed the project to mystery writer Raymond Chandler, who had personal ideas of his own which didn't agree with the director's. The dialogue wasn't suitable, so Czenzi Ormonde, one of Ben Hecht's assistants, was brought in to sharpen the script. The final screenplay was only adequate, but this was only one of other problems that Hitchcock encountered, such as studio interference with casting. Farley Granger, who did a competent job with *Rope,* was "supplied" by Warners, with whom he was under contract. The part of Guy, the tennis champ, needed a stronger-looking actor, and Hitchcock wanted William Holden. Ruth Roman was their leading lady at the time, so she, too, was given to Hitchcock.

The story, which many critics found "thin and unconvincing," is nevertheless fraught with so much tension and action that it becomes subordinate to character motivations, which are followed closely throughout. Aboard a Washington–New York train, a brash society playboy, Bruno Anthony (Robert Walker), strikes up a conversation with Guy Haines

(Farley Granger), a tennis champ who is estranged from his wife Miriam (Laura Elliot) and is now in love with Anne Morton (Ruth Roman). Bruno comments on how much he hates his father and suggests that since Guy's wife won't give him a divorce, why doesn't he kill Bruno's father and Bruno will, in turn, murder Guy's wife, two motiveless murders. Guy, assuming Bruno is in jest, tells him laughingly to forget it. Bruno, used to having things his way, follows Guy's wife one night and kills her in an amusement park. When Guy cannot supply an alibi to the police, they keep the famous sports star under observation. Bruno confronts Guy and threatens to frame him if he doesn't live up to the deal. Realizing that Guy will expose him, Bruno sets out to plant Guy's cigarette

Farley Granger with Ruth Roman at the tennis match.

Farley Granger and Robert Walker on the carousel.

Robert Walker demonstrates how to commit a murder on a society matron.

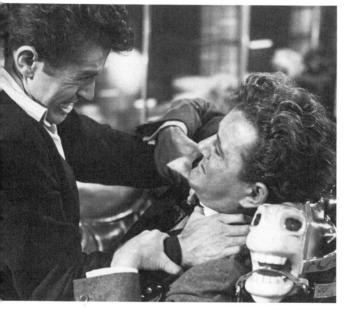

Leo G. Carroll tells Farley Granger to see that Robert Walker leaves his house.

Robert Walker murders Laura Elliot.

Robert Walker with Marion Lorne and Jonathan Hale in background.

Robert Walker tries to retrieve a lost cigarette lighter.

lighter at the scene of the crime. Guy is aware of this and wants to stop Bruno, but he can't—he has a crucial tennis match that day. Finally, after a race against the clock, Guy gets to the amusement park and chases Bruno on a merry-go-round which goes out of control because of their fighting. Bruno is crushed to death by the carousel but an alert concessionaire reveals to the police that it was the dead man whom he recognized as Miriam's killer.

The film made use of extensive location photography. The exposition of characters in *Strangers on a Train* begins with nothing but a closeup of shoes. We see only shoes as they move from a taxi to a train. Guy's shoes are a conservative monochrome and Bruno's are a gaudy brown and white. The audience does not learn which pair belong to which character until after they are on the train and the two pairs collide with each other. Before we know the characters, though, we have learned their style of dress and their manner of gait. It has been clearly established that we have two totally opposite personalities but that a similar link will be found. By the end of the film we realize that Bruno was the personification of Guy's sublimated alter ego. For everything Bruno did, Guy would like to have done but couldn't because of his sense of responsibility. Each of the men have patronizing, independent women in their lives. Bruno's mother (Marion Lorne), as disturbed as her son, is the adoring soul in his life. For Guy Haines, it is Anne Morton, the daughter of a senator (Leo G. Carroll), who views him as upright and pure. The double characters in the film extend beyond Bruno and Guy. Hitchcock cast his daughter, Patricia, in the role of Anne Morton's inquisitive sister, Barbara. At a party which Bruno crashes, it is Barbara's strong resemblance to Miriam, the woman he has just killed, that causes him to momentarily relive the murder. He begins to strangle a society matron whom he was charming before spying Barbara.

Although *Strangers on a Train* was not a masterpiece, it was, nevertheless, brilliant film-making and a gripping suspense film of the type people had come to expect from Hitchcock. After his past four flops with critics and at the box-office, the success of *Strangers on a Train* was that much more exhilarating. Although the dialogue was not as strong as it could have been and characters were consequently not as defined as they might have been, *Strangers on a Train* was pure cinematic storytelling, spinning a web so diabolical and absorbing that within five minutes we become ensnared for the next one hundred. The psychological implications of Bruno's behavior are not elaborated but

Robert Walker presents evidence that Farley Granger's wife has been murdered.

merely exposed. Here again, Hitchcock created a brilliant murder sequence. When Miriam meets Bruno in the amusement park, it is her eyeglasses which fall to the ground, reflecting her demise.

Strangers on a Train was to be the pinnacle of Hitchcock's career at Warner Bros. He says that he was running for cover after his last few bombs and that Patricia Highsmith's novel seemed like appropriate material with which he could work.

Robert Walker's performance as the deranged playboy was probably one of the best of his career. Limited by studio pressure to roles beneath his ability, Walker was finally cast against type, and excelled. Unfortunately he would make only one more film, *My Son John,* before his untimely death later in 1951.

Farley Granger, although not the image of the tennis player Hitchcock had in mind, carried the role of Guy believably, and our sympathy for him remains constant. Ruth Roman is a letdown, however. Her delivery sounds insincere and her acting was studied. The character actress Marion Lorne is perfect as Bruno's loony mother. And Leo G. Carroll as Senator Morton makes his almost regular Hitchcock picture appearance in the dapper style that Hitchcock had come to rely on. *Strangers on a Train* was re-released by Warners in 1957, when it again fared well at the box-office.

I Confess
1952

Brian Aherne questions Montgomery Clift at his trial.

Production: Alfred Hitchcock, Warner Brothers; *Associate Producer:* Barbara Keon; *Supervisory Producer:* Sherry Shourdes; *Screenplay:* George Tabori and William Archibald, from the play OUR TWO CONSCIENCES by Paul Anthelme; *Director of Photography:* Robert Burks, A.S.C.; *Sets:* Edward S. Haworth and George James Hopkins; *Music:* Dimitri Tiomkin, conducted by Ray Heindorf; *Editing:* Rudi Fehr, A.C.E.; *Costumes:* Orry-Kelly; *Sound Engineer:* Oliver S. Garretson; *Technical Consultant:* Father Paul la Couline; *Police Consultant:* Inspector Oscar Tangvay; *Studio:* Warner Bros., *Location Work:* Quebec; *Assistant Director:* Don Page; *Distributor:* Warner Bros.; *Principal Actors:* Montgomery Clift *(Father Michael Logan)*, Anne Baxter *(Ruth Grandfort)*, Karl Malden *(Inspector Larrue)*, Brian Aherne *(the attorney Willy Robertson)*, O. E. Hasse *(Otto Keller)*, Dolly Haas *(Alma Keller, his wife)*, Roger Dann *(Pierre Grandfort)*, Charles André *(Father Millais)*, Judson Pratt *(Murphy, a policeman)*, Ovila Legare *(Vilette, the lawyer)*, Giles Pelletier *(Father Benoit)*; *Running Time:* 95 minutes; *16mm Rental Source:* Warner Bros. Film Gallery.

If transference of guilt was an underlying theme in *Strangers on a Train,* it became the provocative key to *I Confess,* Hitchcock's next production. Similar to *Strangers on a Train,* it was filmed on location, this time in Canada with picturesque Quebec adding to the dramatic effect of the film.

Hitchcock had reached a respected prominence in the film industry and could pick and choose the projects he wanted to direct. On only a few rare occasions did he select a story that was more of personal interest than commercial feasibility. *I Confess* reflects his Jesuit upbringing and the strong grip the Church had on him as a growing boy. It questions the role of duty to society and God, to State and Church and of course, the consequences of transference of guilt. A religious theme limited the film to a select audience.

The story is taken from a 1902 drama, *Nos Deux Conscienses* ("Our Two Consciences"), by Paul Anthelme. The screenplay adaptation was somber and lacked the subtle humor found in most Hitchcock films. The result is that the story is both frustrating and tedious. Otter Keller (Otto E. Hasse) confesses to Father Michael Logan (Montgomery Clift) that he has committed murder. Keller had worn a priest's cassock during the crime, obtaining it at Father Michael's church in Quebec where Keller was the sexton. Father Michael was being blackmailed by the victim about a love affair he had had with a married woman, prior to his ordination as a priest. Father Michael cannot come up with an alibi nor reveal the identity of the murderer because of the confession.

Roger Dann, Brian Aherne, and Anne Baxter.

Montgomery Clift, Anne Baxter, in a flashback memory sequence.

Because he cannot reveal the facts even to his lawyer, Willy Robertson (Brian Aherne), Father Michael appears guilty from the circumstantial evidence. He is acquitted by a doubtful jury but is shunned by the crowd in the courtroom. Finally, Otto Keller's wife tells the truth and when he tries to escape, the police shoot him. As he lies on the street, he makes his final confession to Father Michael. Anne Baxter portrays Michael's former lover and Karl Malden is the intense prosecutor, Inspector Larrue.

Of course, the entire premise upon which the film rests is that a priest's first obligation is to God and the holy vows of the Church. It is precisely this concept that annoyed non-Catholic viewers. "Why wouldn't he just speak up to save his life?" is the question. As Hitchcock has said, "If the basic

idea is not acceptable to the public, it compromises the whole picture." *I Confess* was compromised. The transference-of-guilt idea still looms large as a concurrent question. Michael Logan feels guilty because Otto has killed a man he himself would have liked to kill. Even if Otto didn't confess, Michael feels guilty for having such thoughts and consequently wants the punishment of the state.

Montgomery Clift seemed perfectly cast in the role of the conscience-ridden priest, with his brooding looks and dignified air. Hitchcock confesses that he didn't enjoy Clift's Method acting approach, which made him too elusive and obscure. The only reason Anne Baxter was cast was because the actress Hitchcock had imported from Sweden, Anita Bjork, supposedly arrived in Quebec with an illegitimate baby and a lover. The last thing Warners needed on a pious production was a scandal. Bjork was shipped back and Baxter brought in, totally miscast as a member of Quebec society.

The lynch mob outside the courthouse echoes *The Lodger* but is somewhat anticlimactic in a slow, solemn film. The question of the moral structure of Church and State was perhaps a bit too heavy and as a result, weighs down the entire drama. The convenient coincidence that the victim should be the very person that was blackmailing the priest was asking too much from the already put-upon audience. Although Hitchcock eschews the necessity of plausibility, the lack of it cannot be excused in so serious an outing. The failure of the film was again the fault of the screenplay. *The New York Times* stated, "It takes a long, meandering time for Alfred Hitchcock to set suspense simmering. Only toward the end in a culminative splash of melodrama does this curious picture begin to vibrate interestingly. There are always those surprising Hitchcock trimmings along the way, but the scenario is cumbersome, padded development that moves ponderously to an expected resolution."

Even with the director's name featured in the advertising, *I Confess* was a disaster at the box-office, and it sent Hitchcock scurrying for cover in his next film, *Dial M for Murder*.

O. E. Hasse and Dolly Haas as the murderer sexton and wife.

Montgomery Clift and Karl Malden in the manhunt at the end.

Montgomery Clift is questioned by Karl Malden.

Dial M For Murder
1954

The fatal phone call

Production: Alfred Hitchcock, Warner Bros.; *Screenplay:* Frederick Knott, adapted from his stage play. *Director of Photography:* Robert Burks, A.S.C.; *Film:* Naturalvision (3-D); *Color:* Warner Color; *Sets:* Edward Carrère and George James Hopkins; *Music:* Dimitri Tiomkin, conducted by composer; *Costumes:* Moss Mabry; *Sound Engineer:* Oliver S. Garretson; *Editing:* Rudi Fehr; *Studio:* Warner Bros.; *Distributor:* Warner Bros.; *Principal Actors:* Ray Milland (*Tom Wendice*), Grace Kelly (*Margot Wendice*), Robert Cummings (*Mark Halliday*), John Williams (*Chief Inspector Hubbard*), Anthony Dawson (*Captain Swan Lesgate*), Leo Britt (*the narrator*), Patrick Allen (*Pearson*), George Leigh (*William*), George Alderson (*The Detective*), Robin Hughes (*Police Sergeant*); *Running Time:* 88 minutes; *16mm Rental Source:* Audio/Brandon.

Based on a Broadway play, this was yet another film which Hitchcock decided to direct merely to complete contractual obligations to a movie studio. Another reason for its selection was that his "creative juices" weren't flowing and this was the perfect vehicle to take while his batteries recharged.

Hitchcock insists that *Dial M for Murder* is a film he could have "phoned in." But it seems improbable that any other director could have conceived some of its more terrifying moments.

Although photographed in Naturalvision, Warner Bros.' version of the 3-D craze of the time, the picture was unfortunately released as the fad's novelty had worn off. Most theaters opted for a regular 2-D version after audiences complained of the awkwardness of the cardboard glasses that came with the 3-D movies. But critics agreed that if 3-D was ever a worthwhile gimmick, it was successful in Hitchcock's film.

Most of the three-dimensional pictures of the time went to extremes to find setups for camera angles that emphasized the process. Hitchcock devised a murder sequence which played on the process and made it the high point of the film in the regular version as well.

The murder scene comes halfway through the film, which concerns a society playboy, Tony Wendice (Ray Milland), who plots the death of his wealthy wife, Margot (Grace Kelly). Tony fears divorce and disinheritance from Margot because of her affection for American writer Mark Halliday (Robert Cummings). He contacts Captain Lesgate (Anthony Dawson), an old school chum operating illegal ventures, to whom Tony outlines his murder scheme and then blackmails into carrying it out. The murder is set up but backfires as Margot in self-defense stabs Lesgate with a pair of scissors. The 3-D process is particularly effective

Anthony Dawson lies dead, as Ray Milland realizes that his murder plans for his wife, Grace Kelly, have gone awry.

John Williams and Robert Cummings go over the evidence of the murder.

here as Margot, her outstretched arm grasping for the scissors, seems to thrust her arm out of the screen almost pleading with the audience to place the scissors in her hand.

Undaunted, Tony leads Scotland Yard into believing his wife is guilty of deliberate murder. Mark joins inspector Hubbard (John Williams) to clear Margot; together they invent one final trick which makes Tony admit to the crime.

Dial M for Murder was Grace Kelly's fourth film and her first of three for Hitchcock. She begins her role dressed in bright crimson reds but as the film progresses and she finds herself accused, her outfits become dull greys and blacks. Kelly's performance was poised, if not exciting, and most critics were generous in their praise.

Robert Cummings, whom Hitchcock objected to using in *Saboteur* because of his comical face, proved again that despite this he was a highly competent actor. The film, however, belonged to the sinister portrayal by Ray Milland of the easy-talking playboy husband. If ever there was a demonstration of venality, Milland's Tony Wendice was it.

Dial M for Murder was shot in thirty-six days, highly unusual for a feature-length film. And keeping to his belief that a stage play should not be opened up for the screen, Hitchcock had only a half-dozen shots that occur outside the apartment of Tony and Margot. Despite the single set, the proceedings are kept brisk, never becoming a parlor melodrama. However, this essentially one-set film was only a preview of the director's next production, in which the camera never left the single setting.

Robert Cummings with Grace Kelly.

Robert Cummings, Ray Milland, and Grace Kelly in a rare happy moment.

Rear Window
1954

The single setting as viewed from the rear window of James Stewarts' apartment.

James Stewart and Thelma Ritter.

James Stewart, Thelma Ritter, and Grace Kelly.

James Stewart and Grace Kelly.

Production: Alfred Hitchcock, Paramount; *Screenplay:* John Michael Hayes, from a novelette by Cornell Woolrich; *Director of Photography:* Robert Burks, A.S.C., *Color:* Technicolor; *Consultant:* Richard Mueller; *Special Effects:* John P. Fulton; *Sets:* Hal Pereira, Joseph McMillan Johnson, Sam Comer, Ray Mayer; *Music:* Franz Waxman; *Editing:* George Tomasini; *Costumes:* Edith Head; *Assistant Director:* Herbert Coleman; *Sound Engineers:* Harry Lindgren and John Cope; *Distributor:* Paramount; *Principal Actors:* James Stewart (*L. B. Jeffries, called "Jeff"*), Grace Kelly (*Lisa Fremont*), Wendell Corey (*Thomas J. Doyle, the detective*), Thelma Ritter (*Stella, the nurse*), Raymond Burr (*Lars Thorwald*), Judith Evelyn (*Miss Lonelyheart*), Ross Bagdasarian (*The Composer*), Georgine Darcy (*Miss Torse, the dancer*), Jesslyn Fax (*the lady sculptor*), Rand Harper (*honeymooner*), Irene Winston (*Mrs. Thorwald*), and Denny Bartlett, Len Hendry, Mike Mahoney, Alan Lee, Anthony Warde, Harry Landers, Dick Simmons, Fred Graham, Edwin Parker, M. English, Kathryn Grandstaff, Havis Davenport; *Running Time:* 112 minutes; *16mm Rental Source:* Unavailable.

One of Hitchcock's greatest films is also a voyeur's delight. Hitchcock has always been the voyeur, his camera the Peeping Tom, the audience's eyes. With *Rear Window* he exploited our weakness for wanting to know our neighbors' business. The story, which is confined to one setting for the entire film, is so contained that it becomes the archetypal classical drama, but it is also fully cinematic.

L. B. Jeffries, nicknamed Jeff, is a news photographer (James Stewart) who has been confined to a wheelchair by a broken leg. A man of action and adventure, Jeff finds he can best pass the time by watching the behavior of the neighbors in the courtyard of his Greenwich Village apartment complex He becomes fascinated by one particular window until it slowly dawns on him that the man across the way, Lars Thorwald (Raymond Burr), has murdered his wife. Jeff's fiancée, Lisa Fremont (Grace Kelly), at first is disbelieving and scoffs that he has to look into other people's windows for excitement. Soon, however, she becomes interested, and when she finds incriminating evidence she too believes that Lars has killed his wife. Together, Lisa and Jeff try to convince Tom Doyle, a detective friend (Wendell Corey), but in the true tradition of Hitchcock policemen, he proves to be pigheaded. Stella, Jeff's nurse (Thelma Ritter), warns the invalid to watch out by relating grisly stories about other murders. Lars finds out he is being watched and comes into Jeff's apartment to kill him. In a cliffhanging climax, Jeff is saved just in time, but not before his other leg is broken.

The ending no doubt is just one manifestation of the Hitchcock humor. It is a sadistic humor which the audience shares with Hitchcock. What is obviously a piece of bad luck and painful to the victim is funny to us. It is very much like someone slipping on a banana peel. They have probably hurt themselves but the manner of the injury provides humor.

The humor in *Rear Window* is diverse, from the wisecracks of Thelma Ritter, who makes them even more amusing with her wry delivery, to the less obvious theme of the whole film, a man who spies on his neighbors and gets a broken leg for sticking his nose where it does not belong.

Hitchcock places us in James Stewart's shoes and we become just as much a voyeur as he. We relish it. The sharp reality that we are all voyeurs stings us when we realize what we have done. Hitchcock manipulated our emotions, making us sympathize with Stewart and designing the film so that his eyes are our eyes.

Because the entire film is compacted into a few days and a single setting, it becomes more universal in its message. As Peeping Toms, we witness different aspects of life into each window we peer. In less than two hours, we see life, death, love, loneliness, happiness, sadness—the whole gamut of human experience. If at moments we feel slightly squeamish about spying on intimacies, our curiosity quashes that anxiety soon enough.

As the master of suspense, Hitchcock sways our emotions without the use of hypnotism. While the entire film is seen subjectively from Stewart's eyes, a heightened dramatic moment takes us for an instant out of his apartment into the courtyard as objective observers. After the death of a dog belonging to a childless couple, the camera shoots to every window in the complex. Everyone comes out to see why the woman is hysterical—everyone except Lars Thorwald. In the recesses of the only darkened apartment, we see a single sign of life: the tiny burning tip of a cigarette. We have our suspicions that Lars is the man who killed the dog, and this confirms them.

It is the technique and technical aspects of the cinema that fascinate Hitchcock, and he was able to employ all of his craft in *Rear Window*. Because it is a single-set production, he had to keep interest alive and prevent the film from settling into staginess. The opening sequence exploited the camera as a narrator. The camera continuously and smoothly tours the scene and then pulls into Stewart's apartment where it takes in facts that let us know who he is, what he does for a living, and just

Thelma Ritter and James Stewart.

James Stewart, Grace Kelly, and Wendell Cory.

how it is that he is in a cast. Later in the film when Stewart becomes more and more aroused at the possibility of a murder, he uses a pair of binoculars and then we see even closer again through his telephoto lens. His occupation is conveniently a photographer, which makes him a sort of professional voyeur and thus well equipped to look out his rear window.

As Stewart's anxiety grows, ours builds accordingly. When Grace Kelly is caught by Burr, the murderer, in his apartment as she is hunting for clues, she is saved by the police who arrest her as a burglar. Burr knows that someone is on to his

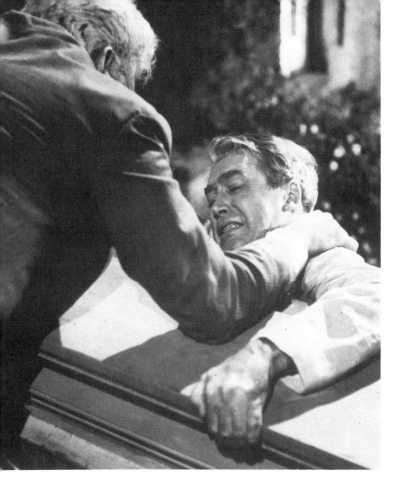

Stewart forced from his window by killer Raymond Burr.

Stewart is rescued after being pushed from his window by Raymond Burr.

Grace Kelly makes a hasty retreat, as Raymond Burr searches for the person that was just in his apartment.

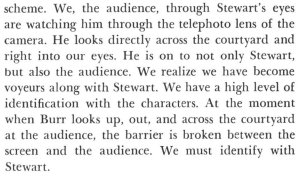

scheme. We, the audience, through Stewart's eyes are watching him through the telephoto lens of the camera. He looks directly across the courtyard and right into our eyes. He is on to not only Stewart, but also the audience. We realize we have become voyeurs along with Stewart. We have a high level of identification with the characters. At the moment when Burr looks up, out, and across the courtyard at the audience, the barrier is broken between the screen and the audience. We must identify with Stewart.

Each character has been assigned a role in the story and stands for one human foible or ideology. Grace Kelly portrays a jet-setter with rich tastes, empty ideals and, underneath, simple human desires. Stewart represents the crusader, the person who helps even if he has to force his help upon you, and Thelma Ritter is the down-to-earth, unpretentious woman who isn't afraid to bluntly talk truths but is afraid to face them. Each of the people we view from the rear window is playing out their fantasy rituals after being clobbered by the naked truth.

168

Raymond Burr is seen wrapping butcher knives in newspaper.

Publicity shot of Grace Kelly and James Stewart.

Because of the tight physical limitations of the action and camera, Hitchcock worked with a perceptive screenplay by John Michael Hayes. Grace Kelly was already a favorite Hitchcock actress and James Stewart had proven to be a Hitchcock trouper in *Rope.* In fact, the entire ensemble had been expertly cast. Hitchcock opened up the Cornell Woolrich story and created a "revealing, touching, and sometimes amusing kaleidoscope of pantomime and vignettes illustrating both the loneliness of city life and the impulse of morbid curiosity."

The advertising campaign for the re-release of the film in 1968 employed some of Hitchcock's black humor but ironically was truthful also. Hitchcock suggested that *"Rear Window* is such a frightening picture that one should never see it unless accompanied by an audience." And, "If you do not experience delicious terror when you see *Rear Window,* then pinch yourself—you are most probably dead."

To Catch A Thief
1955

Cary Grant trapped on the roof of a Riviera mansion.

Production: Alfred Hitchcock, Paramount; *Second Unit Direction:* Herbert Coleman; *Screenplay:* John Michael Hayes, from the novel by David Dodge; *Director of Photography:* Robert Burks, A.S.C. (VistaVision); *Photography Second Unit:* Wallace Kelley; *Color:* Technicolor; *Consultant:* Richard Mueller; *Special Effects:* John P. Fulton; *Process Photo:* Farciot Edouart, A.S.C.; *Sets:* Hal Pereira, Joseph MacMillan Johnson, Sam Comer, and Arthur Krams; *Music:* Lynn Murray; *Editing:* George Tomasini; *Costumes:* Edith Head; *Assistant Director:* Daniel McCauley; *Sound Engineers:* Lewis and John Cope; *Studio:* Paramount; *Principal Actors:* Cary Grant (*John Robie, "The Cat"*), Grace Kelly (*Frances Stevens*), Charles Vanel (*Bertrani*), Jessie Royce Landis (*Mrs. Stevens*), Brigitte Auber (*Danielle Foussard*), René Blancard (*Commissioner Lepic*), and John Williams, Georgette Anys, Roland LeSaffre, Jean Hebey, Dominique Davray, Russel Gaige, Marie Stoddard, Frank Chellano, Otto F. Schulze, Guy de Vestel, Bela Kovacs, John Alderson, Don McGowan, W. Willie Davis, Edward Manouk, Jean Martinelli, Martha Bamattre, Aimee Torriani, Paul "Tiny" Newlan, Lewis Charles; *Running Time:* 97 minutes; *16mm Rental Source:* Films, Incorporated.

Even though *To Catch a Thief* was expertly crafted and called "Hitchcock Champagne," it is a film that is seldom acclaimed. To the surprise of most first-time viewers, Hitchcock's VistaVision production is a "fine bubble-bright and sleekly machined suspense and romance with Cary Grant and Grace Kelly handsomely and coolly rivaling a stunning expanse of mouthwatering French Riviera scenery" (*The New Yorker*).

The film opens with a series of shots of a black cat casually slinking along rooftops, and then screams from women who find their jewels have been stolen. We now quickly move to an estate high above the city. A cat sits on a sofa next to a newspaper with claw marks slashed through an Art Buchwald article: "The Cat Prowls Again." The camera smoothly glides to a view out of the window. We meet a disturbed John Robie (Cary Grant), ex-jewel thief ("The Cat") and resistance worker in France during World War II. Someone is stealing his way across the glittering French Riviera in the exact manner that Robie had done twenty years earlier. The police would like to prove Robie guilty of the current rash of robberies and put him away once and for all. Robie has a limited amount of time to keep away from the police and find the real thief. The plot is again the typical Hitchcock situation of the double chase with the hero chasing and being chased simultaneously. The film was shot on location and in the studio by

Cary Grant and Grace Kelly on the beach at Nice.

Grace Kelly and Cary Grant before the fireworks.

Grace Kelly and Cary Grant with Jesse Royce Landis.

Cary Grant behind an egg-splattered window.

Cary Grant gets a goodnight kiss from Grace Kelly.

John Williams, Jesse Royce Landis, and a saturnine Grace Kelly.

Robert Burks, who earned an Academy Award for his high-gloss Technicolor photography. Indeed, the way Burks captured the Côte d'Azur scenery helps make *To Catch a Thief* even more lively and sparkling. His graceful rooftop photography with its catlike moments added a disquieting atmosphere to the silky blue-green night sky.

In the first third of the story, Grace Kelly plays the expected frigid Hitchcock blonde, meticulously coiffed, usually shown standing perfectly erect in profile and dressed in an ice-blue gown. By the middle third of the film, the real Francie Stevens (Grace Kelly) comes to the surface. Robie escorts Francie and her mother (Jessie Royce Landis) to their rooms. After Mrs. Stevens has been left, Robie takes Francie to her suite at which point she takes the initiative and kisses the startled John Robie.

From then on the match slowly ignites until the classic fireworks scene in which their amorous adventure reaches a climax as fireworks explode outside. Kisses are intercut with vibrant explosions of Technicolor.

Another display of Hitchcock's pictorial imagery comes when Jessie Royce Landis, portraying the earthy millionairess mother unaffected by her wealth, extinguishes her cigarette in the unblemished yolk of a fried egg. Besides the coarse humor of the shot, it also depicts Hitchcock's private displeasure with eggs.

The remainder of the film has Robie enlisting the support of Mrs. Stevens and Francie to lure the "cat" burglar. A lavish costume ball is to be given and Robie, in disguise, accompanies the two ladies to the affair. The camera introduces us to an army of guests in their resplendent costumes, with closeups of their glittering jewels. As the gala gets under way, each of the police is identified for us with repeated high crane shots, which then swoop down to flowing closeups of each gendarme.

The cat is finally caught by the tail on the roof of the mansion in which the party is held. Robie's suspicions have proven to be correct. The thief is the daughter of his best friend. The climactic rooftop chase is reminiscent of a number of Hitchcock's other films, notably the chase across Mount Rushmore in *North by Northwest*, also with Cary Grant; *Vertigo*, and *Saboteur*.

John Michael Hayes's script is literate and witty, which makes this an unusually whimsical chase film. Hitchcock, for a change, was able to cast his film perfectly and get balanced as well as urbane performances from all the principals. Of course, it was not a very difficult chore to do this: Grant was a senior member in Hitchcock's "stock company,"

Cary Grant and John Williams in the chase through the flower market.

and Kelly's two previous pictures were Hitchcock's as well. The remainder of the cast, especially Jessie Royce Landis and John Williams, played their character roles with a polished flair.

Grace Kelly projected the cool and sensual woman with sex appeal that wasn't advertised, the way Hitchcock thinks it should be. Her role in *To Catch a Thief* brought her to the French Riviera where she met her future husband, Prince Rainier of Monaco. After completing two more films, she left Hollywood and films, to become Princess Grace, a role for which she looks typecast.

To Catch a Thief is not great Hitchcock, but it is Hitchcock, and that is why it transcends its genre to become an exquisitely crafted film which many other directors have tried to duplicate. A whole parade of frothy thriller romances in the early sixties are indicative of this. Stanley Donen's *Charade* and *Arabesque* are formidable examples of imitations of *To Catch a Thief.*

Hitchcock was able to control the audience completely, making them scream and shudder on cue and be misled by a general assortment of his expected red herrings. Critics found it a superficial entertainment at the time it was released but many have changed their opinions since. Audiences apparently did not care all that much about what the critics thought, and it netted $4.5 million in North America alone.

Cary Grant and Grace Kelly, who is amused that she is driving with John Robie, "The Cat."

Cary Grant and Grace Kelly.

The Trouble With Harry
1956

John Forsythe and Edmund Gwenn discuss Harry's burial.

Production: Alfred Hitchcock, Paramount; *Screenplay:* John Michael Hayes, from the novel by John Trevor Story; *Director of Photography:* Robert Burks, A.S.C. (VistaVision); *Special Effects:* John P. Fulton; *Color:* Technicolor; *Consultant:* Richard Mueller; *Sets:* Hal Pereira, John Goodman, Sam Comer, Emile Kuri; *Music:* Bernard Herrmann; *Song:* "Flaggin' the Train to Tuscaloosa"; *Lyrics:* Mack David; *Music:* Raymond Scott; *Editing:* Alma Macrorie; *Costumes:* Edith Head; *Studio:* Paramount; *Distributor:* Paramount; *Principal Actors:* Edmund Gwenn (*Captain Albert Wiles*), John Forsythe (*Sam Marlowe, the painter*), Shirley MacLaine (*Jennifer, Harry's wife*), Mildred Natwick (*Miss Gravely*), Jerry Mathers (*Tony, Harry's son*), Mildred Dunnock (*Mrs. Wiggs*), Royal Dano (*Alfred Wiggs*), and Parker Fennelly, Barry Macollum, Dwight Marfield, Leslie Wolff, Philip Truex, Ernest Curt Bach; *Running Time:* 99 minutes; *16mm Rental Source:* Unavailable.

Jerry Mathers brings his mother, Shirley MacLaine, to see what he's found in the woods.

The trouble with Harry is that he is dead. Everybody seems to feel responsible for his death. The Hitchcock humor is at its most macabre in this black comedy as guilt-ridden townspeople bury and dig up Harry's body four times. To counterpoint the droll proceedings, the entire story takes place amid the spectacular autumnal beauty of Vermont. The stark photography of the multicolored natural hues almost makes the crispness of the New England season leap off the screen.

Based on the novel of the same name by John Trevor Story, the Hitchcock film stayed loyal to the original. It begins with three shots echoing through a wooded area. A little boy, Tony (Jerry Mathers), finds the body and brings his mother to it. It is Harry, Jennifer's (Shirley MacLaine) former husband. She feels responsible for his death, having clobbered him too hard with a bottle. So does Captain Wiles (Edmund Gwenn) who, while hunting rabbits in the area, mistakes Harry, already dead, for the object of one of his stray shots. Then there's an abstract painter, Sam Marlowe (John Forsythe) who has a blasé attitude about the body. Lastly there's an old woman, Miss Gravely (Mildred Natwick), who thinks that she's the culprit.

Harry doesn't stay dead and buried for very long before he reappears at precisely the wrong time and place, the last of which is a bathtub. Finally it is discovered that Harry died of natural causes. The commotion has brought Sam and Jennifer together. The captain and Miss Gravely find each other as well.

If the plot relies on one joke, it is only Hitchcock's inventiveness with the situation which keeps our interest sustained for an hour and a half. The humor is not a belly-laugh variety, but more under-

John Forsythe, Jerry Mathers, and Shirley MacLaine.

Harry in tub, Jerry Mathers, and Shirley MacLaine, with Royal Dano.

stated, sly and intellectual. Perhaps it was too personal because, despite *The Trouble with Harry* being Hitchcock's labor of love; it did not garner the audience response the director expected and so very much wanted.

Hitchcock is amused by understatement itself and the effect is that the characters discuss the body with complete nonchalance—as if it were a loaf of bread. For a director who knows that he has to practically hit people over the head with information to make them understand, this attempt at sophisticated humor was bound to fail. Hitchcock has noted repeatedly that he can't even expect everyone in the audience to know the locale of the scene, so he always provides a conspicuous title frame or other clue. In *The Trouble with Harry* he is working with the same audience but assuming they will accept more. Although the critics enjoyed the film and found it deftly amusing, the small-budget picture was a bomb at the box-office, despite Hitchcock's popularity on television with his new series.

Screenwriter John Michael Hayes remained faithful to the novel, a brilliant satiric observation of

Back from the burial.

Playing cards nonchalantly to get Royal Dano off the track.

176

Shirley MacLaine, Mildred Natwick, Edmund Gwenn, and John Forsythe at yet another funeral for Harry.

Edmund Gwenn was an old favorite of Hitchcock, having worked with him as far back as *The Skin Game* in 1931. Mildred Natwick was the type of character actress that Hitchcock relished but Jessie Royce Landis was to be the ideal for him.

When Hitchcock began his TV series, writers of his introductions had to view *The Trouble with Harry* to find the type of diabolically devilish monologues he wanted.

People expected a Hitchcock picture, and even the advertising played up the deadness of the body, but not the liveliness of those around it. This was no thriller and Hitchcock learned that making personal pictures may not be profitable. The film business is compromise.

John Forsythe is confronted by Royal Dano with the evidence.

human behavior, and even used some of the novel's dialogue. Also helping to capture the tone and understatement of the film was the perceptive music composed by Bernard Herrmann. This was the first of many films in which Herrmann partnered his genius with Hitchcock. It was after his rejected score for *Marnie* that studio executives talked Hitchcock out of using Herrmann any longer because he was not a commercial composer—that is, he did not write scores that could be made into soundtrack recordings. Hitchcock was to regret having listened to the money men.

The Trouble with Harry also introduced Shirley MacLaine in her first film role. Hitchcock thought she was very good, as did the critics, and her career rocketed. John Forsythe had appeared in a number of Hitchcock's TV films and established himself as a competent TV actor after *The Trouble with Harry*. He would rejoin Hitchcock in *Topaz* thirteen years later.

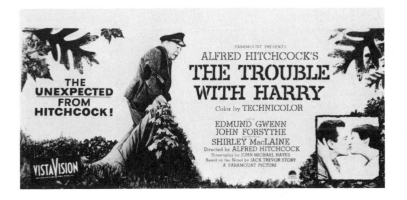

THE UNEXPECTED FROM HITCHCOCK!

PARAMOUNT PRESENTS
ALFRED HITCHCOCK'S
THE TROUBLE WITH HARRY
Color by TECHNICOLOR

EDMUND GWENN
JOHN FORSYTHE
SHIRLEY MacLAINE
Directed by ALFRED HITCHCOCK
Screenplay by JOHN MICHAEL HAYES
Based on the Novel by JACK TREVOR STORY
A PARAMOUNT PICTURE

VISTAVISION

The Man Who Knew Too Much
(Second Version)   1956

In the Marrakesh marketplace, an "Arab" is knifed in the back under the eyes of Doris Day and James Stewart.

Production: Alfred Hitchcock, Paramount, Filmwite Prod.; *Associate Producer:* Herbert Coleman; *Screenplay:* John Michael Hayes and Angus McPhail, from a story by Charles Bennett and D. B. Wyndham-Lewis; *Director of Photography:* Robert Burks, A.S.C. (VistaVision); *Color:* Technicolor; *Consultant:* Richard Mueller; *Special Effects:* John P. Fulton, A.S.C.; *Sets:* Hal Pereira, Henry Bumstead, Sam Comer, Arthur Krams; *Music:* Bernard Herrmann; *Lyrics:* Jay Livingston and Ray Evans: "Que Sera, Sera" ("Whatever Will Be"); "We'll Love Again"; Cantata "Storm Cloud" by Arthur Benjamin and D. B. Wyndham-Lewis, performed by the London Symphony Orchestra, under the direction of Bernard Herrmann; *Editing:* George Tomasini, A.C.E.; *Costumes:* Edith Head; *Sound Engineers:* Franz Paul and Gene Garvin, Western Electric; *Assistant Director:* Howard Joslin; *Studio:* Paramount; *Location Work:* Morocco, London; *Distributor:* Paramount; *Principal Actors:* James Stewart (*Doctor Ben MacKenna*), Doris Day (*Jo, his wife*), Daniel Gélin (*Louis Bernard*), Brenda de Banzie (*Mrs. Drayton*), Bernard Miles (*Mr. Drayton*), Ralph Truman (*Inspector Buchanan*), Mogens Wieth (*The Ambassador*), Alan Mowbray (*Val Parnell*), Hilary Brooke (*Jan Peterson*), Christopher Olsen (*little Hank MacKenna*), Reggie Malder (*Rien, the assassin*), and Yves Brainville, Richard Wattis, Alix Talton, Noel Willman, Caroline Jones, Leo Gordon, Abdelhaq Chraibi, Betty Baskomb, Patrick Aherne, Louis Mercier, Anthony Warde, Lewis Martin, Richard Wordsworth; *Running Time:* 120 minutes; *16mm Rental Source:* Unavailable.

Apparently, Hitchcock was convinced that his excellent 1934 version of *The Man Who Knew Too Much* could have been better. And now, more than twenty years later, still under the delusion of the if-at-first-you-don't-succeed-try-try-again syndrome, he decide to give the film another whirl. He had everything going for its success, too: a cast headed by James Stewart and the popular Doris Day; Technicolor and VistaVision photography by his favorite cameraman, Robert Burks; a tingling musical score by Bernard Herrmann; and more than twenty years' further experience with the medium he loved.

The new *Man Who Knew Too Much* did not excite critics but did win popular favor with audiences. When both versions are compared, most people find that while the later version holds up, the earlier one, because of its compactness, is more exciting.

The scenario was rewritten by John Michael Hayes and Angus McPhail from the old story by Charles Bennett and D. B. Wyndham-Lewis. This time, instead of beginning in St. Moritz, the story opens in Morocco—decidedly more exotic and dangerous. Leslie Banks was replaced with James Stewart and Edna Best's role was taken over by singer-actress Doris Day who instead of being a markswoman was a retired musical star. The fact that Doris Day was a singer was worked convincingly into the script with her singing "Que Sera Sera" to save her little boy at the shrill climax. (The song won the Academy Award for Best Song in 1956.)

Location photography was shot in Morocco, but most of the action was filmed in the studios in Hollywood and London. In this version Hitchcock actually filmed the crucial assassination attempt sequence in Albert Hall—still, however, with a fake audience. This time, enhanced with the rich sound of the Bernard Herrmann orchestration of the "Storm Cloud" Cantata, the scene continues for almost the duration of the entire movement, and for many minutes we hear nothing but the music and see staccato shots of a petrified Doris Day, the box of the assassin, and the box of the diplomat. When the assassin receives his instructions and hears the section of the Cantata in which to fire the gun, we, like him, await the decisive note and the crash of the cymbal which will drown out the sound of the gunfire. The music takes on new meaning as we listen attentively but helplessly. We do not want the music to stop yet; we want our tension relieved. The chase up to this scene has built up the suspense. Hitchcock, aware of every nuance—when to use sound, when to not let us hear what the actors are saying, when to use different colors to get our attention—has set up our emotions exactly as he wants them, like a ticking timebomb with a faulty alarm.

The new storyline follows the 1934 film plot but changes various aspects so that Hitchcock could employ certain personal touches he missed the first time around. Dr. Ben MacKenna (James Stewart) and his wife Jo, a former musical star (Doris Day), are vacationing in Morocco with their son, Hank (Christopher Olsen), when they meet Mr. and Mrs. Drayton, a British couple (Brenda de Banzie and Bernard Miles). They are also befriended by a Frenchman, Louis Bernard (Daniel Gélin), who invites them to dinner but then cancels at the last minute. The MacKennas go to a restaurant and end up having their meal with the Draytons, when they spot Louis Bernard. The next day in the market place, they watch an Arab get stabbed in the back. He falls near them and Ben discovers it is Louis Bernard in disguise; Bernard whispers secret information to Ben. Later, on returning to the hotel he finds that the Draytons have kid-

Stewart removes the knife from Daniel Gelin's back.

The crash of cymbals in Albert Hall.

James Stewart confronts the wrong "Ambrose Chapel" in his taxidermy shop.

The clerks in the shop, believing Stewart insane, hold him down.

Dinner . . . Morrocan style.

The police are finally convinced that Stewart is telling the truth when they see the would-be assassin fall to his death in Albert Hall.

napped Hank and have headed back to England. Ben and Jo rush to England and look for the name Bernard told them to look up: Ambrose Chapel. After mistaking a taxidermist named Ambrose Chapel for one of the conspirators, Ben and Jo realize that it is not a *person* but an *address* and go to a small church, where they find the Draytons. Jo tries to locate a helpful Scotland Yard inspector and is told he is at Albert Hall for a Royal performance. In the concert hall, she is approached by the assassin who tells her not to foil his plans if she wants her son alive. She screams at the last minute, saving the diplomat's life. The climax comes at the embassy where the diplomat thanks Jo and asks her to sing one of her songs. She sings "Que Sera Sera," a song that Hank knows, hoping to smoke him out—which, with the help of a contrite Mrs. Drayton, she does.

If the choice of Doris Day, of all people, seemed unusual for Hitchcock, it wasn't, and the specially prepared ending which relies on her singing ability works, even if it is a little soapy. The director had seen her in a nonsinging role in *Storm Warning* in which she gave a good performance. Her portrayal of the nerve-racked mother in *The Man Who Knew Too Much* was moving and believable, if slightly overacted. Dwight MacDonald noted that Miss Day has two basic and possibly favorite expressions. She has a slightly loving look and also opens her eyes wide in times of stress. One wonders which Hitchcock preferred.

James Stewart was charged with emotion as the Midwestern doctor, accidentally embroiled in political intrigue. His perceptive facial expressions and indignant delivery made him convincingly human—a person we could easily identify with. It is his temperament that actually sets the pace for the entire film. The casting of character actor Reggie Malder as Rein, the assassin, was brilliant. The man looks like a menace and his unctuous portrayal radiates evil.

It is obvious that Hitchcock made concessions to Paramount to keep *The Man Who Knew Too Much* a family picture. The picture is full of twists and setup devices. It is a superficial film or, as Hitchcock would prefer to think, "a piece of cake." But he has us eating it out of his hands—and we want more.

Bernard Miles and Brenda de Banzie plan the murder of a diplomat. Reggie Maldar will be the man who pulls the trigger.

The dying Daniel Gelin tells Stewart an important secret.

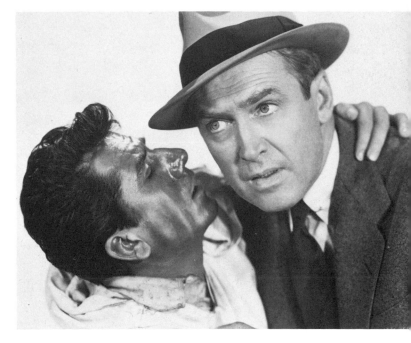

The Wrong Man
1957

Fonda is picked up by New York policemen Harold Stone and Charles Cooper.

Henry Fonda, bass player at the Stork Club.

Production: Alfred Hitchcock, Warner Brothers; *Associate Producer:* Herbert Coleman; *Screenplay:* Maxwell Anderson and Angus McPhail, from "The True Story of Christopher Emmanuel Balestrero" by Maxwell Anderson; *Director of Photography:* Robert Burks, A.S.C.; *Sets:* Paul Sylbert and William L. Kuchl; *Music:* Bernard Herrmann; *Editing:* George Tomasini; *Assistant Director:* Daniel J. McCauley; *Studio:* Warner Bros.; *Location Work:* New York; *Technical Consultants:* Frank O'Connor (Police Magistrate to the District Attorney, Queens County, New York); *Sound Engineer:* Earl Crain, Sr.; *Distributor:* Warner Bros.; *Principal Actors:* Henry Fonda (*Christopher Emmanuel Balestrero, called "Manny"*), Vera Miles (*Rose, his wife*), Anthony Quayle (*O'Connor*), Harold J. Stone (*Lieutenant Bowers*), Charles Cooper (*Matthews, a detective*), John Heldabrant (*Tomasini*), Richard Robbins (*Daniel, the guilty man*) and Esther Minciotti, Doreen Lang, Laurinda Barrett, Norma Connolly, Nehemiah Persoff, Lola D'Annunzio, Kippy Campbell, Robert Essen, Dayton Lummis, Frances Reid, Peggy Webber; *Running Time:* 105 minutes; *16mm Rental Source:* Warner Bros. Film Gallery.

Like *I Confess, The Wrong Man* was a personal film which Hitchcock enjoyed making, despite its dim commercial possibilities. In 1957 the American motion picture industry was in financial straits. Warners had slowed production on features and had made an abrupt switch to join "the enemy"—television—with *77 Sunset Strip, Maverick,* and similar popular fare. Although Hitchcock's contract had been fulfilled, he directed *The Wrong Man,* a Warner Brothers property, without salary. The reason he liked the project was because it was a factual version of his favorite theme of the innocent person accused of something he did not do. As filmed, *The Wrong Man* is a semidocumentary with the factual part being the most interesting. The audience could sense the director's intrinsic fear of police by the atmosphere he creates on the screen. However, the fictitious part of the film is an intrusion on an otherwise flawlessly structured story.

Produced on location in New York, the story concerns Christopher Emmanuel "Manny" Balestrero (Henry Fonda), a nightclub musician and family man, who is accused of an armed robbery he did not commit. The evidence is against him because the actual criminal looks almost identical to him. Manny's wife, Rose (Vera Miles), slowly loses her sanity while he awaits trial. In minute detail we watch Manny being humiliated by the process of justice that is supposed to protect him. From his arrest to his fingerprinting, handcuffing,

Henry Fonda reading about the crime of which he will falsely be accused by the police.

and jailing, we watch as he is intimidated and depersonalized. Finally, at the end the real man is caught robbing another store and Manny is freed. He goes to the sanatorium where his wife has been committed. He tells her the good news but all she can do is say, "Good for you, Manny," and he leaves without her.

The Wrong Man has a newsreel quality to it, with starkly lit black-and-white photography and real-life details that give it authenticity. When Hitchcock switches gears and no longer emphasizes Christopher Balestrero's story, turning instead to his wife's, he loses the audience's interest. The intensity of the drama, horrifying because of its reality, diminishes because the chief focal point has been complicated with more details than the audience wants to consider.

183

Henry Fonda is identified by an insurance clerk as the man who looks like the holdup man of a Queens robbery.

Fonda is booked with other common criminals.

Fonda and his attorney Anthony Quayle concerned about Vera Miles' depression.

Fonda in court.

It is precisely because of this twist in the plot, the focusing on Rose's mental breakdown, that explains why Manny turns to prayer at the end. He prays for a miracle and gets it as the real culprit commits another holdup and gets caught. Hitchcock treats this incident, based on fact, as if it really was a miracle. With double exposure, he superimposes the holdup man's face over Manny's as he is praying. The documentary flavor of the film has been lost and religious motifs, harking back to *I Confess,* take over. The Kafkaesque nightmare of reality that Hitchcock has maintained has turned into a moralistic question.

The fact that Henry Fonda was a well-known and popular star and not an unknown as the part seemed to call for did not hurt the plausibility of the role and his performance transcends his recognizability. Vera Miles, who appeared on a number of Hitchcock's TV shows, was well cast as the disturbed wife. Her slow transformation from an outraged citizen into an apathetic mental case is handled sensitively.

Critical reception to *The Wrong Man* was mixed, and the capsule review from *The New York Times* summarizes what most critics felt: "Substituting fact for fiction and certainly fright, Alfred Hitchcock has elected to recreate in clinical detail the actual case of a New York musician, identified (by positive witness) as a thief, but innocent, and more or less martyrized legally until at long last, vindication. The Maxwell Anderson–Angus McPhail scenario ticks off and stretches out the sad, jolting stoicism by Henry Fonda. As his wife whose mind snaps, Vera Miles conveys real anguish and Anthony Quayle is excellent as Fonda's attorney. Here the master is being factually lucid, with little concern for the hearts and dramas of those involved."

This was Hitchcock's experimenting again, with a narrative genre he had never before attempted. If his overriding fear of the police is manifested here, it serves as a testament of all of us. For if the picture points out anything, it is that justice can be vindictive and cruel and that *anyone* could become the wrong man.

Fonda outside the courthouse with Vera Miles and Nehemiah Persoff.

Vertigo
1958

James Stewart and Kim Novak.

James Stewart clings to a rooftop gutter.

Production: Alfred Hitchcock, Paramount; *Associate Producer:* Herbert Coleman; *Screenplay:* Alec Coppel and Samuel Taylor, from the novel D'ENTRE LES MORTS by Pierre Boileau and Thomas Narcejac; *Director of Photography:* Robert Burks, A.S.C. (VistaVision); *Special Effects:* John Fulton; *Sets:* Hal Pereira, Henry Bumstead, Sam Comer, Frank McKelvey; *Color:* Technicolor; *Consultant:* Richard Mueller; *Music:* Bernard Herrmann; conducted by Muir Mathieson; *Editing:* George Tomasini; *Costumes:* Edith Head; *Assistant Director:* Daniel McCauley; *Sound Engineers:* Harold Lewis and Winston Leverett; *Titles:* Saul Bass; *Special Sequence:* Designed by John Ferren; *Studio:* Paramount; *Location Work:* San Francisco; *Distributor:* Paramount; *Principal Actors:* James Stewart (*John "Scottie" Ferguson*), Kim Novak (*Madeleine Elster, Judy Barton*), Barbara Bel Geddes (*Midge*), Henry Jones (*The Coroner*), Tom Helmore (*Gavin Elster*), Raymond Bailey (*The Doctor*), and Ellen Corby, Konstantin Shayne, Lee Patrick; *Running Time:* 120 minutes; *16mm Rental Source:* Unavailable.

Vertigo is a sensation of dizziness or a confused, disoriented state of mind. It is also the name of one of Alfred Hitchcock's finest films. The title refers to the result of the fear of heights, or *acrophobia,* of the hero, played by James Stewart.

Based on a novel by Pierre Boileau and Thomas Narcejac, *D'entre les morts,* written supposedly with Hitchcock in mind, *Vertigo* became a Hitchcock project when Paramount purchased the rights and made them available to the director.

It has certainly become one of Hitchcock's most analyzed films, probably because critics love studying masterpieces under the microscope. Nevertheless, *Vertigo* fares best on the screen and not in discussions on paper.

The story takes place in picturesque San Francisco where John "Scottie" Ferguson leaves the police force because of his acrophobia. Gavin Elster (Tom Helmore), an old college buddy, comes to him and asks that he shadow his wife, Madeleine, who believes she is possessed by the spirit of her great-grandmother—a woman who committed suicide after going mad. Scottie follows Madeleine around San Francisco and when she tries to drown herself in the bay directly underneath the Golden Gate Bridge, he rescues her and falls in love with her. She has a vision of the Mission at San Juan Batista and Scottie takes her there, hoping he can erase her delusion. But she impulsively climbs to the top of the lofty Mission tower, where Scottie, because of his fear, cannot follow her. He then helplessly watches as she plunges to her death. His loyal girlfriend Midge (Barbara Bel Geddes) helps

him to recover from his feelings of guilt and remorse. Soon after he meets a woman named Judy Barton who is the living image of Madeleine. We soon learn that Judy really is Madeleine, who was at the time of their first encounter Elster's mistress, not wife. Her faked death (the real Madeleine was thrown from the roof) was a carefully planned ruse to get Scottie as an unimpeachable witness to Mrs. Elster's suicide. When Scottie notices that Judy has an heirloom locket which originally belonged to her great-grandmother Carlotta (seen earlier in a portrait), he realizes what has happened. To make July confess, he takes her to the tower. She loses her balance and falls to her death.

Only in retrospect did critics agree that this was one of Hitchcock's greatest, most deftly thought-out films. In truth, when the film opened its reception was less than gratifying. "The old master," *Time* noted, "has turned out another Hitchcock-and-bull story in which the mystery is not so much who done it as who cares. . . ." *Saturday Review* was less severe but equally disapproving: "Hitchcock's occasional bursts of slam-bang action, cinematic sleight of hand, and his inventive use of color cannot sustain interest through the long pull of his slender narrative."

186

James Stewart, with the help of Barbara Bel Geddes, tries to overcome his fear of heights.

James Stewart and Kim Novak.

Stewart with coroner (Henry Jones).

James Stewart listens to Tom Helmore explain the suicidal tendencies of his "wife" Madeleine.

Kim Novak attempts to prove to Stewart that she is not the original Madeleine.

Kim Novak as Judy Barton.

It is only on repeated viewings that the viewer can begin to comprehend that this is a film with a cumulative effect. The whole is greater than the sum of its parts. The entire film is expository.

If *Rear Window* explored the realm of the voyeur, *Vertigo* unravelled what essentially was a man obsessed with making love to a dead woman. Necrophilia is the psychological term and, as unpleasant as it may be, this is the unseemly subject of the last two-thirds of the film. Scottie tries to make Judy Barton into the living and walking image of the Madeleine he so dearly loved. When finally he persuades Judy to wear the type of clothes Madeleine did and fix her hair the same way, Scottie is expecting the living reincarnation of the dead Madeleine—he would make love to Judy but be thinking of Madeleine.

For the climactic scene in which Judy makes her final cosmetic transformation into Scottie's image of Madeleine, Hitchcock has her come out of the bathroom into the eerie green neon light reflected from the hotel sign outside the window. The green casts a ghostly translucent image similar to the one cast upon Madeleine when Scottie first observed *her*. For the scene, he had a special set constructed. So as the camera makes its 180-degree swing around the lovers, we see what James Stewart imagines he sees: the interior of the Mission from which Madeleine jumped. There are no fades, no double exposures, no trick photography to complicate the scene—just the clean movement of the camera in a smooth arc.

The added suspense comes when Hitchcock clues the audience that Judy really is Madeleine in disguise. Now we watch, hoping that Scottie will discover this also.

The final scene in the Mission and the earlier scenes are taken from Scottie's perspective and we see the effect the vertigo has on him. For these shots, Hitchcock tracked back and zoomed forward at the same time. The shot was prepared on a specially created miniature of the real set, since the mounting of a camera in the real set would have been overly expensive.

Kim Novak gave one of her best performances, something few thought was possible at all. James Stewart was earnestly emotional and carried off his role of the guilt-ridden cop engagingly. Bernard Herrmann's symphonic score has become today a collector's item, so perfectly did it fit the film as well as stand on its own played alone.

Kim Novak as Madeline during one of her flights of identity.

James Stewart and Kim Novak.

Stewart saves Kim Novak after she has jumped into San Francisco Bay.

189

North By Northwest

1959

Cary Grant struggles with Martin Landau, Adam Williams, and Robert Ellenstein.

Production: Alfred Hitchcock, M-G-M; *Associate Producer:* Herbert Coleman; *Original Screenplay:* Ernest Lehman; *Director of Photography:* Robert Burks, A.S.C. (VistaVision); *Color:* Technicolor; *Consultant:* Charles K. Hagedon; *Special Photographic Effects:* A. Arnold Gillespie and Lee Le Blanc; *Sets:* Robert Boyle, William A Horning, Merrill Pyle, Henry Grace, Frank McKelvey; *Music:* Bernard Herrmann; *Editing:* George Tomasini; *Title Design:* Saul Bass; *Sound Engineer:* Frank Milton; *Assistant Director:* Robert Saunders; *Studio:* M-G-M; *Location Work:* New York (Long Island), Chicago, Rapid City (Mount Rushmore), South Dakota (National Memorial); *Distributor:* Metro-Goldwyn-Mayer; *Principal Actors:* Cary Grant (*Roger Thornhill*), Eva Marie Saint (*Eve Kendall*), James Mason (*Phillip Vandamm*), Jessie Royce Landis (*Clara Thornhill*), Leo G. Carroll (The Professor), Philip Ober (*Lester Townsend*), Josephine Hutchinson (*Mrs. Townsend, the housekeeper*), Martin Landau (*Leonard*), Adam Williams (*Valerian*), and Carleton Young, Edward C. Platt, Philip Coolidge, Doreen Lang, Edward Binns, Robert Ellenstein, Lee Tremayne, Patrick McVey, Ken Lynch, Robert B. Williams, Larry Dobkin, Ned Glass, John Bernardino, Malcolm Atterbury; *Running Time:* 136 minutes; *16mm Rental Source:* Films, Incorporated.

Alfred Hitchcock has stated on a number of occasions that *North by Northwest* contains the essence of all his American films. Perhaps that explains in part its phenomenal success commercially and critically.

After its record-breaking engagement at Radio City Music Hall, the film went on to make a profit of $6.5 million in North America alone. The screenplay, Hitchcock concedes, took him and his writer Ernest Lehman well over a year to create, just a fraction of the intense planning that went into the picture—only this time his meticulous calculations caused some concern to M-G-M executives. Later in the production, as it was nearing final editing, executives attempted to tamper with the film by cutting sequences out. They thought that 136 minutes was too long a running time. Fortunately, Hitchcock's agents had negotiated an ironclad contract which gave him complete and final artistic control, something few directors are ever given. The director told the studio that the editing would remain as he wanted it.

The picture was completed on a budget of $4 million, which is conspicuous on the screen. In this quick-paced, tongue-in-cheek odyssey, Roger Thornhill (Cary Grant), a successful Madison Avenue advertising executive, is plunged into a world of crime and intrigue and hunted down by police

and ruthless spies alike. His attempts to clear himself of a murder he did not commit take him on a colorful and breathless cross-country adventure which has its cliff-hanger climax atop Mount Rushmore in South Dakota.

The fantastic plot twists and turns constantly starting as Thornhill is kidnapped by spies who mistake him for one George Kaplan, a fictitious person U.S. agents have concocted to draw the spies out into the open. After narrowly escaping death—and the spies—Thornhill goes to the police, who do not believe his story. Neither does his wise-cracking mother (Jessie Royce Landis), who gives her son advice now and then. In attempting to unravel the mystery of who George Kaplan is, Thornhill is mistaken as the killer of a U.N. diplomat. He escapes again, this time on a train to Chicago. On the train he is aided by Eve Kendall (Eva Marie Saint). When the train arrives in Chicago, Eve arranges a rendevous for Thornhill with Kaplan but it ends up being an ambush as a cropduster attacks him in a flat and very open corn field. He gets back to Chicago, though, and follows Eve to an auction where he finds her with her lover, Phillip Vandamm (James Mason). Thornhill creates a disturbance to bring police when he is threatened by Vandamm's henchmen. The police take Thornhill to the airport, where he is met by the professor (Leo G. Carroll), who explains that Kaplan is a decoy and Eve Kendall is a federal agent now endangered by Thornhill's actions. He agrees to go to Rapid City and play out the character he has inadvertently given flesh-and-blood status.

Vandamm agrees to meet Thornhill at the Mount Rushmore Monument cafeteria where Eve feigns killing Thornhill with a gun loaded with blanks. He eventually winds up trying to stop Eve from leaving the country with Vandamm. He reaches Vandamm's modernistic house, where he overhears that Leonard (Martin Landau), Vandamm's assistant, knows it was a fake shooting. Thornhill attempts to save Eve, but they are forced to climb down Mount Rushmore Monument. The police arrive just in time, and the picture closes as the couple, now married, are returning east on a train which at the last fade darts into a tunnel—Hitchcock's phallic imagery.

Whether quickly tracking through the dusty cornfield or slowly craning his camera above the heads of Grant and Mason at the Townsend mansion, the Technicolor, Vistavision cinematography of Robert Burks flawlessly heightened the suspense of the story.

Cary Grant finds a knife in his hands and is falsely accused of the murder of a U.N. diplomat.

Cary Grant is unamused by his mother's (Jesse Royce Landis) jokes to the two thugs (Adam Williams and Robert Ellenstein) who are trying to kill him.

The crane, which takes the camera above the scene, is used several times in the film. The first, at the mansion, gives us an idea of impending danger. Vandamm and his men are deadly serious. Later, at Vandamm's Mount Rushmore retreat Leonard is told by his employer that the problem of the now exposed agent (Saint) is "best disposed of from a great height, over water." The latter shot also foreshadows the coming chase, also at great heights down the side of the monument.

While everyone else was pleased with Hitchcock's production, the National Park Service was not amused one bit. Apparently, they had entered into agrement with M-G-M to allow scenes to be shot in the famous South Dakota landmark park so long as no violence was depicted there. But violence on Mount Rushmore was indeed present and the Service demanded that Metro remove the credit line. They wanted no responsibility for giving permission to the chase across the heads of the presidents.

Aside from this nitpicking, nothing could impede the brightness of the production. Producer-director Hitchcock again availed himself of the services of one of his favorite actors, Cary Grant (who made this his fourth and final appearance in a Hitchcock picture). As *The New Yorker*'s critic Pauline Kael noted, "Cary Grant is the perfect actor for the part." *Newsweek* was more emphatic: "If it does nothing else (but it does, it does), *North by Northwest* resoundingly reaffirms that Cary Grant and Alfred Hitchcock are two of the very slickest operators before and behind the Hollywood cameras. Together they can be unbeatable."

James Mason proved to be the incarnation of evil and nastiness and his mere presence in a scene was enough to emotionally unnerve the audience. Eva Marie Saint was another Hitchcock attempt at casting a cool-yet-fiery, seductive woman in the leagues of Ingrid Bergman, Grace Kelly, and Kim Novak. For Hitchcock, she was able to evoke the equivocal remoteness of a Hitchcock woman. Leo G. Carroll made his fifth Hitchcock picture appearance, something of a record for any actor. He would go on to star in a similar role for M-G-M television's *The Man from U.N.C.L.E.*

North by Northwest reflects many of Hitchcock's inovations with suspense and intrigue. Certainly motion pictures have given us innumerable car chases, but Hitch created one that was equally frightening and humorous, its intensity rivaling the San Francisco car chase in Peter Yate's *Bullitt*. The cropdusting sequence has been copied many times since, but never as effectively. The best mimic so far has been the helicopter chase in Terence Young's *From Russia with Love,* one of the James Bond epics. Working against cliché as he always did, Hitchcock figured that most murders occur on dark misty streetcorners lit by the single overhead beam of a streetlamp. This time he placed Grant, dressed neatly in a business suit, in bright sunlight in the open stretches of a cornfield. To make his victim-hero more vulnerable, he made the murder weapon a crop-dusting plane.

Means of escape have always been a prime point of interest with Hitchcock. One workable and at the same time humorous approach is that of disrupting a meeting crowd to provide temporary cover or means of exit.

Typical of this idea is the auction sequence in which, cornered by Vandamm's henchmen at all exits, Grant disrupts the very proper proceedings by questioning the authenticity of the art works being offered, making inappropriate bids and finally starting a fight when asked to leave. The police arrive to take him away for being "drunk and disorderly." He leaves safely, commenting to one of the henchmen, "Sorry old man, better luck next time!"

Similar scenes have played several times before, even in the same film, as Grant uses the people around him to escape from the elevator at the Plaza Hotel. In *Foreign Correspondent* Joel McCrea escapes his potential killers by making an exit through a bathroom window after leaving the water running. He arrives in Laraine Day's room in a bathrobe. In order to get his clothes, he summons all possible hotel services to his room at once, thereby covering the action of a porter sent to gather his needs. The scene cannot but remind one of the stateroom scene in the Marx Brothers' *Night at the Opera.* Another typical crowd escape was found in *Saboteur,* as Robert Cummings and Priscilla Lane again make their way from the second floor of the Van Sutton mansion to the ballroom where Cummings attempts to explain his plight and that of the nation. Unfortunately, that time it didn't quite work.

The witty and sophisticated script by Ernest Lehman provided the film with its insouciance and exuberance, and as Hollis Alpert remarked in his *Saturday Review* critique, "Mr. Lehman not only provided Hitchcock with exactly the right kind of story to take advantage of his skills, but he has written that rare thing these days—a screen original. It is no wonder that *North by Northwest* is all movie and a delightful treat as well."

The picture, as it turned out, was a harbinger

Cary Grant and Eva Marie Saint meet on the Twentieth Century Limited.

Cary Grant, aided by Eva Marie Saint, disguises himself as a porter to elude the police.

193

for a whole crop of allegedly tongue-in-cheek spy capers with fancy arts-and-craftsy photography and lots of running around, all very pretentious and clumsy after Hitchcock's work. If *North by Northwest* is to be compared to any films, they are Hitchcock's earlier productions as *The 39 Steps* and, more closely, his American *Saboteur*, where Robert Cummings and Priscilla Lane go north by north*east* from California to New York in the pursuit of spies. *Saboteur*, like *North by Northwest*, ends with a cliff-hanger, also on a National Monument—the Statue of Liberty.

The music provided by Bernard Herrman is an integral part of the wit and suspense and is scored to flow with the actor's movements and to counter-point the sometimes ludicrous spectacle on the screen. Cast against Saul Bass's splendid credits is a racing and mocking overture which provides the audience with a clue to the tempo of the next 136 minutes.

Hitchcock can be accused of relying on the same formula plots, but his unique style and ingenuity with his crafts always makes them appear to be original. In short, even though the film is fantasy, its maker projects class.

The title is taken from Hamlet's "I am but mad north-north-west; when the wind is southerly, I know a hawk from a handsaw." *North by Northwest* is the apt clue to the displaced geography and improbable plot. As Pauline Kael says, "The com-

Cary Grant runs for his life.

Grant, momentarily trapped under a truck which has just been struck by a cropduster.

Cary Grant with Eva Marie Saint, James Mason, Martin Landau at the Chicago auction house.

Cary Grant and The Professor, Leo G. Carroll.

A mock killing as Eva Marie Saint fires a gun loaded with blanks at Grant.

Grant and Eva Marie Saint rendezvous near Mt. Rushmore monument.

pass seems to be spinning as the action hops all over the country and the wrong people rush about in the wrong directions."

Even the greatest of the films have their technical flaws, and in *North by Northwest* they are found at the Mount Rushmore cafeteria as Grant is shot by Saint. Hitchcock always attempted to get around crowd situations by use of rear projections, and here is an excellent example of just what can occur when using a crowd. If you look just to Eva Marie Saint's right before she fires, you will see a young boy sitting with his back to the action, and in one shot, his fingers in his ears. He must have been tired of repeated takes of the gunfire.

Grant and Eva Marie Saint atop Mt. Rushmore.

Grant and Eva Marie Saint in the cliff-hanging ending.

Mr. and Mrs. Roger O. Thornhill (Cary Grant and Eva Marie Saint).

The Television Interlude

1955-1962

Breakdown: Joseph Cotten.

For more than 350 episodes, Alfred Hitchcock, director and producer, became Alfred Hitchcock, master of ceremonies. Each week his famous line and shadow profile, coupled with the now synonymous "Funeral March of a Marionette," welcomed the TV viewer to another taste of the macabre. More often than not, the entire play depended upon the last line of the dialogue, or one last action. If you happened to cough or sneeze or become otherwise distracted at that instant, you missed the entire joint of the tale.

The first show was the epitome of Hitchcock's black humor. He attempted to make all his stories "as meaty as the sponsor and the network would stand for." He remarked that "any tendency towards the macabre," he hoped would be offset with humor. "As I see it, that is a typically English form of humor, even a typically London type of humor. It's like the joke about the man who was being led to the gallows which was flimsily constructed, and he asked in some alarm, "I say, is that thing safe?" Another story he likes to tell also helps to illustrate the type of humor he presented on his program: English actor Charles Coburn (no relation to the American actor) attended the funeral of another comedian named Harry Tate. As the coffin was being lowered, a young comedian asked Charlie, "How old are you now?"

"Eighty-nine."

"Hardly seems worth while you going home," the young man replied.

If this type of humor was not rampant in the stories, it was conspicuous in Hitchcock's marvelously droll introductions and closings. Frequently, when the story was not up to par, it was Hitchcock's understated delivery that provided the best entertainment.

From the fall of 1955 to the spring of 1961, Hitchcock was the host and executive producer of the half-hour series *Alfred Hitchcock Presents*. For the single TV season 1961–1962, his show was lengthened to an hourly series and called *The Alfred Hitchcock Hour*. In 1957 he directed an hour-long television drama for another series called *Suspicion,* and in 1960 he was induced to direct an hour's production for *Ford Star Time*. On his own series, he directed seventeen half-hour and one-hour television plays.

His playful introductions were always fresh, sarcastic, and supercilious. He was always a cherubic ham on camera. If Hitchcock manifested a chilling soberness to the crimes he introduced, he was more irreverent to his advertising sponsor. His philosophy toward his sponsor was that "A knock is as good as a boost." In a *Saturday Evening Post* interview with Pete Martin in 1957, Hitchcock explained: "My guess is that my sponsor enjoys my lack of obsequiousness but in the beginning had difficulty in getting used to my approach and they took umbrage at my less than worshipful remarks. However, the moment they became aware of the commercial effects of my belittling, they stopped questioning the propriety of my cracks. The tradition is that the sponsor must be coddled. In such an atmosphere I was a novelty." And for television, so were the little dramas he and his ex-secretary-turned-producer, Joan Harrison, selected. The particular episodes that Hitchcock himself directed, he says, were simply taken as they cropped up. It seems that of the nineteen programs, all possessed the understated comic qualities that Hitchcock so enjoyed.

Alfred Hitchcock enjoyed the challenge of being restricted so that he could find methods to overcome his newly encountered encumbrances. Television, by its nature, was restrictive and Hitchcock shot his thirty-minute shows in three days and the hour programs in five. He met the challenge easily and, in fact, put it to its most profitable use when he filmed *Psycho* in 1960 with his TV crew, maintaining TV series' low-budget methods.

His first production for the tube was *Breakdown* (CBS, November 13, 1955)* and starred Joseph Cotten in his first reunion with the master since *Under Capricorn.* The story concerns a wealthy businessman played by Cotten, who is so cold-hearted that he sneers at a twenty-five-year employee who literally cries after being fired. Cotten cannot understand how a man could lose control of his emotions. On a trip back to New York from Miami, he is detoured by a prison road crew and then hit by a tractor. Pinned behind the wheel, he is taken for dead, robbed of his possessions, and then left overnight in a mortuary. The next morning, the coroner is about to pronounce Cotten dead when he notices a tear in his eye. His released emotions save his life. In twenty-three minutes, Hitchcock plays with the ironies of the man. He starts with power and ends with none—he begins with disdain for open emotions and in the end saves himself by displaying them. Clever use of subjec-

* In parenthesis is the original air date and network; dates of actual shooting do not necessarily correspond to the order of play dates.

tive camera and still photography made this premiere an example of what was to come in the next seven years from Shamley Productions.

The second Hitchcock-directed play was *Revenge* (CBS, October 2, 1955) with one of the director's favorite actresses, Vera Miles, and Ralph Meeker. Miles portrayed the wife of an aircraft worker. She has just returned from the hospital after a nervous collapse. When Meeker returns home after work one day, he finds his wife unconscious and upon reviving her learns that she had been attacked by a man. The doctor tells Meeker that the shock could give her a total relapse, unless they get away for a while. On leaving, they are riding in the car when Miles spots the assailant: "That's the man, that's the man." Meeker, seeking revenge, follows the man to his hotel room and clubs him to death. Back on the road, he assures her everything will be all right when she exclaims, "That's the man, that's the man," as she points to another one on the street. Meeker realizes what has happened as we hear the police siren in the background. Hitchcock obviously reveled in the sublime but horrifying irony of the situation even though it was a one-joke plot, complete with a final punchline. His introduction and closing took it for all it was worth: "As you can see, crime does not pay—even on television. You must have a sponsor. Here's ours, after which I shall return." After the commercial he closed with: ". . . very well put. In fact so well, there is nothing more for me to say. Until next week then . . ."

The Case of Mr. Pelham (CBS, December 4, 1955) is a tale of madness but with no respite from black comedy. Tom Ewell played Mr. Pelham, a businessman who becomes disturbed when he finds a double duplicating his daily routine. To outsmart his double, Pelham wears outrageous clothes and acts differently than he usually does. When finally the twain meet, it is the real Mr. Pelham that is called the impostor because of his erratic behavior. The "new" Mr. Pelham takes over as the real one is carted off to the funny farm.

John Williams who last worked with Hitchcock in *To Catch a Thief* appeared in *Back for Christmas* (CBS, March 4, 1956) which tells of a man who murders his wife and buries her in the cellar of their home. He leaves on their planned vacation to the West and discovers that she was going to surprise him with a wine cellar to be excavated while they were on their vacation. Again, it was that backstabbing twist that piqued Hitchcock's interest.

Williams returned in the next Hitchcock stint in *Wet Saturday* (CBS, September 30, 1956), which

202

also starred Sir Cedric Hardwicke, who hadn't appeared in a Hitchcock production since *Suspicion*. Here he plays the wealthy father of a daughter who kills her boyfriend with a shovel. Daddy tries to protect his child by attempting to frame a neighbor for the slaying. He is almost successful, yet he doesn't account for one thing—the irrationality of his daughter which finally does him and her in. Harking back to Hitchcock's interest of the transference-of-guilt theme from *Strangers on a Train* and *I Confess,* this story is less serious and enjoyable for its inherent comedy.

The twist in *Mr. Blanchard's Secret* is that there isn't any. This program (CBS, December 23, 1956), while based on a different story, was a copy of the director's *Rear Window*. It was about a busybody housewife-cum-mystery-writer who thinks that Mr. Blanchard has murdered his wife. Just as the audience believes she's right, we—and she—find out she's wrong. The secret, of course, is that there is none, which as a result was a half-hour practical joke by Hitchcock on all of us.

David Wayne starred in *One More to Go* (CBS, April 7, 1957), which begins with his killing his

Lamb to the Slaughter: Barbara Bel Geddes.

Bang! You're Dead: Billy Mumy.

wife with an andiron. He secrets her body in the trunk of his car and drives down what he thinks is a deserted country road. A cop stops him because one of his tail lights isn't functioning. Hitchcock plays with the suspense of the situation. We know, but the cop doesn't, about the corpse in the trunk. Just as it is about to be pried open so a mechanic can fix the light, it flickers back on. Wayne drives on with the policeman not far behind. The light goes out again, and this time the policeman is insistent that Wayne drive to headquarters where the light will be fixed once and for all—even if it means prying the trunk open. Comparisons of this show to some sequences from *Psycho* made three years later point out the shots in which Wayne drags the body to the trunk (Anthony Perkins does the same in *Psycho*) and the patrolman's stopping Wayne on the highway (Janet Leigh also gets tailed by a cop in *Psycho*).

Hitchcock's first hour-length film for television was not for his own show but for another series, called *Suspicion*. He still used the same crew that worked on his program, including the prolific script-writer Francis Cockrell, who wrote a majority of the AHP teleplays. *Four O'Clock* (NBC, September 30, 1957) starred E. G. Marshall and Nancy Kelly in a traditional Hitchcockian web of suspense. Marshall portrayed a watchmaker who imagines his wife is cheating on him. To get revenge he plants a bomb in the basement of their house. Some hoodlum-type teenagers break in just as he's leaving and tie him up so he can't escape. The bomb is set to go off at four o'clock, and we sit and sweat with Marshall as he thinks how he can get out of the place. A gas meter man comes and a little boy chasing a bug, but because Marshall is gagged, he cannot scream for help. The detonation time arrives, but the bomb does not explode. The twist of fate is that the electricity is off but Marshall is practically dead from fright, waiting for the overdue explosion.

The next television film was *The Perfect Crime* (CBS, October 20, 1957), which concerned criminologist-sleuth Vincent Price who, upon learning from James Gregory that he was responsible for sending an innocent man to the gallows, successfully bakes Gregory in a pottery kiln.

What followed was probably his most well known, if not best, show, *Lamb to the Slaughter* (CBS, April 13, 1958). When her police-chief husband says he wants to leave her, wife Barbara Bel Geddes bludgeons him with a frozen leg of lamb. Slightly stunned at what she's done, she puts the lamb in the oven. When the investigating police come over, the chief's wife graciously invites them to the lamb dinner. As they are eating, they complain about not being able to find the murder weapon; "For all we know, it could be right under our very noses." Mrs. Maloney smiles. This was a whimsical Hitchcock demonstrating his acuity for understatement.

Keenan Wynn starred as a conniving chiseler-tourist in *Dip in the Pool* (CBS, September 14, 1958). On a vacation with "Aunt Jenny's $4,000," Wynn and his wife (Fay Wray) are watching their pennies when he fritters it away at a card game. He sees a way to get the money back by wagering with other passengers who during a midnight swim in the pool, bet how far the ship will travel the next day. To make sure it doesn't go far (he bet a low mileage), he jumps off the ship. The only problem is, the woman he chose as a witness is a mental patient who isn't believed when she tells what she saw. This is the only TV show in which Hitchcock appears during the play—as a cover picture on a magazine a passenger is reading.

Another 1958 production (CBS) was called, simply, *Poison* and starred James Donald as an alcoholic who explains to his doctor and anyone else he can get to listen that he's being attacked by a deadly snake. Of course, no one believes him—"he's only a rummy."

Hitchcock delved into tales of the supernatural —but with the obligatory droll twist—with *Banquo's Chair* (CBS, May 3, 1959). John Williams, duplicating a police inspector role he played in *Dial "M" for Murder,* is investigating the murder of a woman and decides to trick the murderer into confessing. He hires an actress to play the dead woman's ghost. All this is arranged in such a lighthearted, almost overtly humorous fashion that it seems Hitchcock himself is planning it, not the characters. The "ghost" appears and the killer, frightened half to death, confesses. Just then the hired actress rushes in, very apologetic for being late and not arriving for her job—a typical last-minute switch which closes, like many of the other shows Hitchcock directed, with the fixed, incredulous stare of the star. While the story has all the little details that maintain our interest, the entire play is a setup for the final line—a means to a grand ending.

In *Arthur* (CBS, September 27, 1959), Laurence Harvey plays the title role, a farmer who is annoyed by Helen (Hazel Court) continually, about their getting married. Arthur is the unmarrying kind and kills the nagging woman. To cover up the evidence, he chops her up and feeds her to his chickens and nobody's the wiser—except, perhaps, the chickens.

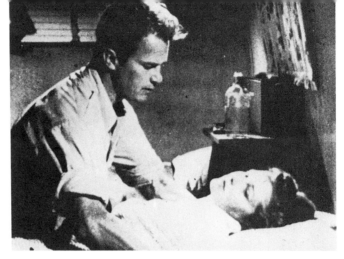

Revenge: Ralph Meeker and Vera Miles.

The Perfect Crime: Vincent Price and James Gregory.

The next Hitchcock-directed show was *The Crystal Trench* (CBS, October 4, 1959), a tale of a newly married couple·played by James Donald and Patricia Owens. When Donald falls down a cliff he's climbing into a deep glacier, the faithful bride says she will wait the expected forty years, by which time the glacier will have moved into a position where she can once again see her frozen husband. She feels guilty for his death and waits until the appointed day when she is able to view his frozen countenance. She also discovers that he was wearing a locket with a picture of another woman, obviously a secret lover of long ago. Here, again, was another little fable with a twist.

Incident at a Corner (NBC, April 5, 1960) was prepared by Hitchcock for *Ford Star Time* and was an hour drama about one incident repeated from different people's viewpoints: a seemingly innocuous reprimand from a school crossing guard to the PTA president for driving carelessly. Later the guard is fired from the job because of an anonymous note, claiming he is too chummy with the little schoolgirls. Although it appears that the PTA president sent the note to get even, it was actually sent by a woman living across the street from the corner. The guard knew her in another city and she was afraid he might disclose her sordid past. The entire episode was not the Hitchcock material we would expect.

Another lighthearted truffle of Hitchcock's was *Mrs. Bixby and the Colonel's Coat* (NBC, September 27, 1960), with Audrey Meadows playing the title role of a wife who cheats on her husband. She tells her boring husband that she is going to visit Aunty overnight as an excuse for her affair. Her lover, the Colonel gives her a luxurious mink as a parting gift. To get the coat past her husband, she pawns it and then tells him she found the ticket. He goes to get it out of hock but returns with a raggedy fur instead. When she goes to visit him at his office soon after, she finds the secretary wearing the Colonel's coat. There is nothing she can say or do to get it back without giving herself away.

The Horseplayer (NBC, March 14, 1961) saw Claude Rains and Hitchcock together again for the first time since *Notorious*. Rains is a priest who finds that a gambler is giving large donations to the church each Sunday. The man says it helps him to win at the horse races. To get even more money for the needy church, Rains gives the gambler three hundred dollars from the building fund to bet. After the man goes, Rains is plagued with guilt feelings about what he's done and prays for the horse not to "win." As it turns out, the gambler had put the church's money on "place," and his own on "win." His prayers are answered.

Bang! You're Dead! (NBC, October 17, 1961) was a half-hour sweat-it-out suspense about a little boy (Billy Mumy) who comes upon his visiting uncle's gun, which everyone who sees him with it things to be fake. Loaded with two bullets, little Jackie goes around the town and his house, pointing the gun at people and saying "Bang!" Every once in a while, he spins the chamber Russian roulette style and only at the end does he pull the trigger, but the bullet hits a wall. The suspense is kept taut throughout and the ending with no injuries is satisfying.

For his last outing in television direction, Hitchcock did a courtroom drama of sorts, starring John Forsythe. *I Saw the Whole Thing* (CBS, October 11, 1962) concerns a man, accused of a hit-and-run

accident, proving in court how unreliable witnesses can be. The switch here is that Forsythe's wife is the actual culprit. The beginning of the film has a *Rashomon* flavor to it as we see each of the witnesses in quick shots directly before it happens.

During this period of seven years, Hitchcock also directed *To Catch a Thief, The Trouble with Harry, The Man Who Knew Too Much, The Wrong Man, Vertigo, North by Northwest, Psycho,* and *The Birds*. For these theatrical releases, he employed some of the TV actors and actresses such as John Forsythe and Vera Miles. All TV films were released by Revue, a company which is part of Universal-MCA. The entire package of 350-plus programs has since gone into syndication on local stations and been repeated many times.

TELEVISION SHOW CREDITS

(All TV films were released by Revue and prepared by Shamley Productions, Joan Harrison, associate producer; John L. Russell, photography, except *The Crystal Trench* and *Dip in the Pool*, John F. Warren, photography.)

Revenge Script by A. I. Bezzerides and Francis Cockrell, from a short story by Samuel Blas—with Ralph Meeker, Vera Miles.

Breakdown Story and script by Francis Cockrell and Louis Pollack—with Joseph Cotten.

The Case of Mr. Pelham Script by Francis Cockrell, from a story by Anthony Armstrong (George Anthony Armstrong Willis)—with Tom Ewell.

Back for Christmas Script by Francis Cockrell, from a story by John Collier—with John Williams, Isobel Elsom, and A. E. Gould-Porter.

Wet Saturday Script by Marian Cockrell from a story by John Collier—with Sir Cedric Hardwicke and John Williams.

Mr. Blanchard's Secret Script by Sarett Rudley from a story by Emily Neff—with Mary Scott, Robert Horton.

One More Mile to Go Script by James P. Cavanaugh from a story by F. J. Smith—with David Wayne.

Four O'Clock Script by Francis Cockrell from the short story by Cornell Woolrich—with E. G. Marshall, Nancy Kelly, Richard Long.

The Perfect Crime Script by Stirling Silliphant from a short story by Ben Ray Redman—with Vincent Price and James Gregory.

Lamb to the Slaughter Script by Roald Dahl from his short story—with Barbara Bel Geddes, Allan Lane, and Harold J. Stone.

Dip in the Pool Script by Francis Cockrell from the story by Roald Dahl—with Keenan Wynn and Fay Wray.

Poison Script by Casey Robinson from Roald Dahl's story—with James Donald, Wendell Corey, Arnold Moss, and Weaver Levy.

Banquo's Chair Script by Francis Cockrell from the short story by Rupert Croft-Cooke—with John Williams, Kenneth Haigh, Reginald Gardiner, Max Adrian.

Arthur Script by James P. Cavanaugh from the short story by Arthur Williams—with Laurence Harvey and Hazel Court.

The Crystal Trench Script by Stirling Silliphant from the short story by Alfred Edward Woodley Mason—with James Donald and Patricia Owens.

Incident at a Corner Script and story by Charlotte Armstrong—with Vera Miles, Paul Hartman, and George Peppard.

Mrs. Bixby and the Colonel's Coat Script by Halsted Welles from the short story by Roald Dahl—with Audrey Meadows and Les Tremayne.

The Horseplayer Story and script by Henry Slesar—with Claude Rains.

Bang! You're Dead! Script by Harold Swanson from the story by Margery Vosper—with Billy Mumy.

I Saw the Whole Thing Script by Henry Cecil Leon and Henry Slesar from a story by Henry Slesar—with John Forsythe, Kent Smith, Evans Evans, John Fiedler, and Philip Ober.

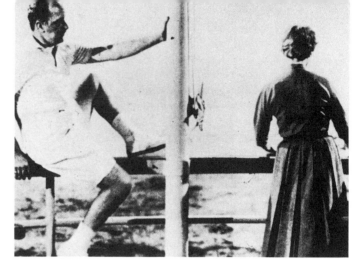

Dip in the Pool: Keenan Wynn.

Arthur: Laurence Harvey.

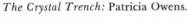

The Crystal Trench: Patricia Owens.

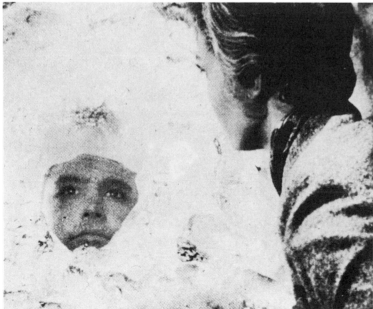

207

The
Mature Years

1960-1975

Anthony Perkins in *Psycho*.

In London for *Frenzy*.

Enter the tumultous sixties. For his first film in what would be our most violent decade of the twentieth century, Hitchcock devised his most adult film and, prophetically, one of his most violent. This was not so much a physical violence (although there was enough of that) as it was psychic assault. The film was *Psycho* and because it used the audience, it was attacked as a horror film, a nasty concoction of gore and madness. Gone was the featherweight irreverent humor of *North by Northwest*. Now it was hard, brash, and vicious. *Psycho* made us insecure because it destroyed traditions of the cinema, such as in killing the star one-third through the picture.

It was a film that fit well into our age of anxiety. Hitchcock played with our intrinsic fears and we were simultaneously titillated and unnerved. To top this masterpiece, Hitchcock told us, "*The Birds* is Coming." Here at least we knew where the danger was going to be coming from. *The Birds* was an outside force. Still, Hitchcock left us dangling with an ambiguous open ending.

The sixties marked Hitchcock's most ambitious efforts at perfection. Although he was always striving for immaculate productions, in the sixties his popularity pressured him to be even more exacting.

After Hitchcock and his wife, Alma, viewed the completed version of *Psycho*—a custom they followed with all his films—Alma exclaimed, "You simply can't ship it, Hitch." But why not? "After Janet Leigh has been killed in the shower, you can see her swallow." Hitchcock had the film rerun to the particular sequence and sure enough, you could see the actress swallow. The scene was fixed and the film was sent out on schedule.

The Birds posed more technical problems than Hitchcock had ever attacked but three years of perseverance brought us a horror so real we shuddered—not because of the immediate shock value, but because of the frightening possibility it posed.

Perhaps it was because these first two films of the sixties were so on target that the three that followed seemed worse than they otherwise might have been. *Marnie* looked—and was—too hurriedly made. It was an anachronistic psychodrama that was passé and unmoving. *Torn Curtain* followed, adorned with stars Paul Newman and Julie Andrews. A Cold War espionage story, it started with a cliché-ridden plot and continued with walk-through performances.

Topaz was released in 1969 to unanimous pans. Hitchcock, critics said, was letting his age dominate

Is Hitchcock going loco over *Psycho?*

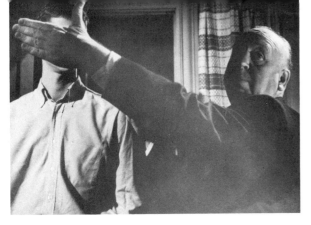

On the set of *Psycho*.

Mr. Hitchcock gets down to business.

With friend.

Directing *Marnie*.

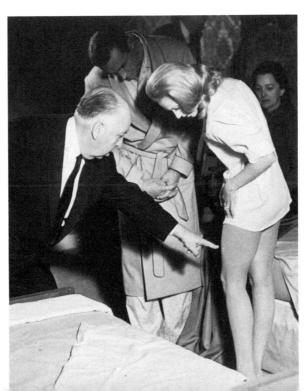

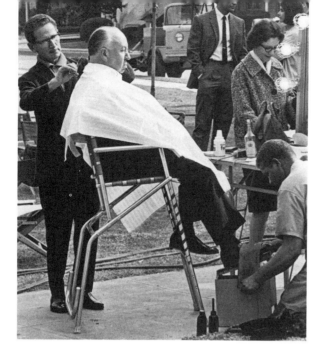

Directing *Marnie*.

Hitchcock tells Paul Newman how to play a scene in *Torn Curtain;* Newman tells Hitchcock how he *will* play the scene.

On the set of *Frenzy*.

During shooting of *Torn Curtain*.

During shooting of *Topaz*.

Cameo in *Marnie*.

Directing *Frenzy*.

him. With this second espionage hodgepodge, their assertions seemed like a very distinct possibility. He was seventy years old and seemed to be less discriminating in the projects he chose to produce and direct. *Topaz* had the expected Hitchcock production values but missed the sharp suspense with which his name had become synonymous.

He restored his stature by returning to England —after an absence of close to twenty years—to produce the dazzling *Frenzy*. A new age of reason, or liberality, had opened up what could be shown on the screen. Nudity was acceptable, and *Frenzy* was the first Hitchcock picture where any real trace of it appeared. Even so, Hitchcock, believing modesty to be the best policy, tried to keep it to a minimum. The film itself is a return to his favorite theme of innocent man accused by circumstantial evidence. This was a subject with which Hitchcock obviously had confidence and had control. It was evident on the screen, in the unique casting, and in the weaving of comedic relief with the more suspenseful moments, that Alfred Hitchcock's return to England was a propitious one.

For his fifty-fourth feature film, Hitchcock purchased the rights to *The Rainbird Pattern,* a novel by Victor Canning. Joining forces with Ernest Lehman, who wrote the original script for *North by Northwest,* Hitchcock retitled his film *One Plus One Equals One,* then *Deceit,* and finally *Family Plot.*

Cameo in *The Birds*.

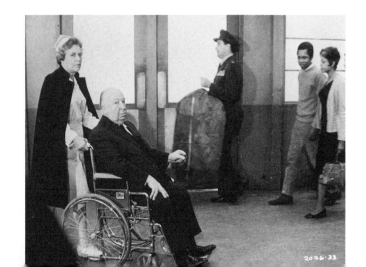

Cameo in *Topaz:* Many critics thought this was appropriate, considering how slow the film was.

Psycho
1960

Anthony Perkins.

Production: Alfred Hitchcock, Paramount; *Unit Manager:* Lew Leary; *Screenplay:* Joseph Stefano, from the novel by Robert Bloch; *Director of Photography:* John L. Russel, A.S.C., *Special Photographic Effects:* Clarence Champagne; *Sets:* Joseph Hurely, Robert Claworthy and George Milo; *Music:* Bernard Herrmann; *Sound Engineers:* Walden O. Watson and William Russell; *Title Design:* Saul Bass; *Editing:* George Tomasini; *Assistant Director:* Hilton A. Green; *Costumes:* Helen Colvig; *Studio:* Paramount; *Location Work:* Arizona and California; *Distributor:* Paramount; *Principal Actors:* Anthony Perkins (*Norman Bates*), Janet Leigh (*Marion Crane*), Vera Miles (*Lila Crane, Marion's sister*), John Gavin (*Sam Loomis*), Martin Balsam (*Milton Arbogast, detective*), John McIntire (*Chambers, the Sheriff*), Simon Oakland (*Doctor Richmond*), Frank Albertson (*the millionaire*), Patricia Hitchcock (*Marion*), and Vaughn Taylor, Lurene Tuttle, John Anderson, Mort Mills: *Running Time:* 109 minutes; *16mm Rental Source:* Universal 16.

After preparing his last dessert in the form of the delicious fantasy, *North by Northwest,* Hitchcock remained consistent by being inconsistent, and gave the audiences a shock from which many viewers have still not recovered fifteen years after its release. Ever since Janet Leigh got stabbed in the shower of Room One at the Bates Motel, moviegoers and Hollywood have never been the same. Because the grisly murder sequence was so effective, some people ever since witnessing it have been reluctant to take showers, even in their own homes.

Alfred Hitchcock is slightly nonplused by all the commotion caused by *Psycho,* but he is also completely delighted by the severe reaction. He just didn't expect people to take it so seriously, the only miscalculation for the most premeditated film he's ever produced and directed. Hitchcock says flatly that *Psycho* is a humorous film, the darkest of black comedies to be sure, yet humorous nonetheless. But it's his humor, not ours. The humor is derived from the ironic situation in the plot and in the psychological effect the film creates in the audience. With *Psycho* Hitchcock directs the audience more than the actors. And shot for shot, cut for cut, Hitchcock knows he was using pure cinema to arouse audience emotions. As far back as 1947, Hitchcock had espoused his philosophy of manipulating public emotions. In a press conference he declared, "I am to provide the public with beneficial shocks. Civilization has become so protective that we're no longer able to get our goose bumps instinctively. The only way to remove the numbness and revive our moral equilibrium is to use artificial means to bring about the shock. The best way to achieve that, it seems to me, is through a movie."

The entire rhythm of the film has been geared for exacting suspense and shock. The story seems to proceed at the start at an inordinately slow pace, and for forty minutes the film appears to be nothing more than a tale about a secretary who has absconded with forty thousand dollars in cash. The shock comes in the form of an unexpected and violent slaying. Janet Leigh, ostensibly the star, is killed off one-third through the film. First of all, we didn't expect the murder and are that much more surprised by it. Second, Hitchcock knows that audiences think that nothing can happen to her because she is the star. Hence, our sense of security is shattered. If we can't identify with the characters because they are so artificial and distorted, we can identify with the vulnerability of being attacked in a shower where we stand naked and defenseless. The violence of the scene, now cinema legend, keeps the audience so alert for more at any possible moment that we are not aware that there is less and less violence as the film continues; just the suspense of anticipating it is enough to keep our adrenalin flowing. The story is a flimsy vehicle on which Hitchcock can play with our emotions and our miscalculated expectations. Marion Crane (Janet Leigh) is a bored Phoenix, Arizona, secretary who wants to marry Sam Loomis (John Gavin), who also feels he is too poor to wed and divorce his present wife. When a brash millionaire (Frank Albertson) leaves forty thousand dollars in cash at the real estate office where Marion works, her boss tells her to deposit the money in the bank. Instead, she packs her bags and steals the money. She buys a new car and then heads toward San Francisco, where Sam runs a hardware store. After shaking off a suspicious state trooper, she drives on, but in a blinding rainstorm makes a wrong turn. She decides to get some sleep and checks into the Bates Motel, where she meets a strange young proprietor, Norman Bates (Anthony Perkins). They engage in some small talk and Marion learns of Norman's strong devotion to his irritable mother. Their talk convinces her to return the money and make good.

Later, as she is taking a shower in her room, she is suddenly attacked by a person who seems to be Mrs. Bates, the old woman. She is stabbed fourteen times. Norman comes in and, fearing the consequences, throws Marion in the trunk of her car, which he then pushes into quicksand in the back of the motel.

217

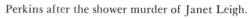
Janet Leigh and Patricia Hitchcock.

Perkins after the shower murder of Janet Leigh.

Anthony Perkins and Janet Leigh as the doomed Marion Crane.

Perkins interrogated by Martin Balsam.

Anthony Perkins and "Mother's House."

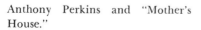

When Lila Crane (Vera Miles), Marion's sister, can't reach her, she goes to Sam Loomis for aid. The pair is approached by Milton Arbogast (Martin Balsam), a private detective hired by Marion's boss to recover the money. He comes upon the Bates Motel and becomes suspicious. Before sneaking back to the Bates mansion atop a hill near the motel, he calls Sam and Lila to tell them of his first break. Upon returning to the mansion, he is brutally and fatally attacked by Mrs. Bates.

When Arbogast doesn't report back, Sam and Lila go to Sheriff Chambers (John McIntire), who tells them that Mrs. Bates has been dead and buried for eight years. The pair head out to the Bates place and while Sam keeps Norman busy, Lila sneaks up to the house. Norman gets suspicious and knocks Sam over the head. Lila sees Norman coming and flees to the fruit cellar, where she finds Mrs. Bates is a stuffed skeleton. Norman, knife in hand, runs in dressed as his mother but is stopped in time by Sam. The psychiatrist (Simon Oakland) at the police station explains about Norman's psychosis. Induced by the murder of his mother and her lover, he became a schizophrenic with a multiple personality and homicidal rages.

Psycho was shot in black-and-white because Hitchcock felt the gore of the shower scene would be too much for the audience to take. It is rumored, though, that color material on *Psycho* does exist in Hitchcock's personal collection. Produced by Hitchcock with a television crew for expediency, *Psycho* was made on a budget of $800,000 and has proven to be the director's biggest hit, earning some $16 million in its original engagement and a re-release in 1966 when it was co-featured with his 1963 film *The Birds*.

One critic called *Psycho* "the most astounding, audacious and successful horror film ever made— a demagogic work." The praise is correct but the classification of *Psycho* as a horror film is not. *Psycho* is a film with two murders. Both are shocks because they are sudden and vicious. But the film is based on the Master's premise that heart-pounding suspense can be more terrifying than what the suspense is actually about. That is, the murders themselves shock us for a few moments, but the fear and anticipation resulting from not knowing when they will occur is what really scares us. Keeping ahead of the audience Hitchcock knows what they will be thinking. Audiences always like to think they have figured out what is going to happen next. *Psycho* deceives us because just when we think we've gotten ahead of the story, we find that our predictions are wrong. Not having the upper

Vera Miles and John Gavin ask Anthony Perkins about the whereabouts of Janet Leigh.

Janet Leigh.

John Gavin and Vera Miles go to sheriff John McIntire and his wife for help.

Janet Leigh is questioned by highway patrolman.

hand, becoming totally helpless in the hands of the director, we can only follow by covering our eyes but always managing to peek out to see what will occur next.

In an interview, Janet Leigh remarked that Hitchcock was a "very cool man." She attended several meetings before *Psycho* and was told by Hitch what he wanted from her for his picture. He said to her, "I'm not going to tell you how to act. If I didn't think you could act, I wouldn't have you in my picture. I'm telling you the qualities I need, where I need certain points, and I'll remind you as we do the scenes what the sequence is, and then you can do whatever you like. If you're not up, I'll tell you. If you're too up, I'll tell you. But as long as your concept of her doesn't interfere with what I need from her, do whatever you want."

Janet Leigh was fascinated that her role in the story was only a small part of the film. The film doesn't really begin until after the murder occurs. But once she is killed, you never stop thinking about her. The film was shot very quickly but the shower scene took one week alone, with special scaffolding built for the scene and more than seventy different setups for the forty-five seconds on the screen. Demonstrating the illusion of film, Hitchcock says that at no time does the knife ever touch the victim's body. The fast cutting of the montage makes it appear that Leigh has been stabbed repeatedly. We really only see the blood as it spatters on the wall and into the tub. In reality it was nothing more than chocolate sauce.

What satisfies Hitchcock about *Psycho* is that it was pure film that aroused the audiences around the world. There was no message to stir them, nor any great performance. *Psycho* was, to Hitchcock, "a film that belongs to the film-makers"—assembling all the elements of pieces of film, soundtrack, and technical arts to create a picture that would evoke viewers. The music by Bernard Herrmann played a huge part in terrifying the audience. The composer thought that he should complement the black-and-white film and black-and-white story with black-and-white sound. The result was the only film with a score played by an orchestra exclusively comprised of strings. The piercing and shrieking violin strings abetted Hitchcock's remarkably timed shower scene and magnified the tension throughout the rest of the film.

The acting is yeoman-class. These are drab peo-ple who take us where Hitchcock wants us to go. Released at the height of Hitchcock's popularity (his TV program was toprated and increased from a half-hour to an hour weekly series), *Psycho* had an advertising campaign built around the director's fame. First of all, it was shot on a restricted set, with no visitors allowed. Stills of important scenes were not released in advance, as is usually customary. Reviewers and theater owners were not permitted to view the film until opening day. Hitchcock, showman that he is, forced everyone to see the picture from the beginning. No one was allowed in the theater once the show had started. Hitchcock had Paramount enforce the policy by having it written in to the booking contract of all the theaters that exhibited it. Not only did this help the publicity by giving the movie a special aura, but it created long lines in front of theaters hours before the showing began.

Of course when *Psycho* started making the money that it did, a long parade of sleazy imitations poured out of Hollywood, none equaling the quality of *Psycho*.

Anthony Perkins comments: "Not many people know this, but I was in New York rehearsing for a play when the shower scene was filmed in Hollywood. It is rather strange to go through life being identified with this sequence knowing that it was my double. Actually, the first time I saw *Psycho* and that shower scene was at the studio. I found it really scary. I was just as frightened as anybody else. Working on the picture, though, was one of the happiest filming experiences of my life. We had fun making it—never realizing the impact it would have."

Janet Leigh comments: "Every time *Psycho* is shown on TV today I get piles of crank mail, some of it threatening real harm. Some of the letters demand money. But the ones that are really terrifying are those that threaten me with the horrid death I had in the shower scene. We used a stand-in for that scene as it happens. The crank letters didn't start until the film was put into TV distribution. Now *Psycho* is shown on local TV stations about 25 times a year—and every time I get those threatening letters. They are given over to the FBI. I should be used to the letters by now but I'm not. I didn't get scared by the shower scene, but these cranks could haunt me for the rest of my life."

The Birds
1963

Children running from birds (that were later added with special effects).

Production: Universal; *Producer:* Alfred Hitchcock; *Screenplay:* Evan Hunter, from the work by Daphne du Maurier; *Director of Photography:* Robert Burks, A.S.C.; *Color:* Technicolor; *Special Effects:* Lawrence A. Hampton; *Special Photographic Adviser:* Ub Iwerks; *Production Director:* Norman Deming; *Sets:* Robert Boyle and George Milo; *Sound Consultant:* Bernard Herrmann; *Composition and Production of Electronic Sound:* Remi Gassman and Oskar Sala; *Bird Trainer:* Ray Berwick; *Assistant Director:* James H. Brown; *Assistant to Hitchcock:* Peggy Robertson; *Illustrator:* Alfred Whitlock; *Credits:* James S. Pollak; *Editing:* George Tomasini; *Studio:* Universal; *Location Work:* Bodega Bay, California; San Francisco; *Distributor:* Universal; *Principal Actors:* Rod Taylor (*Mitch Brenner*), Tippi Hedren (*Melanie Daniels*), Jessica Tandy (*Mrs. Brenner*), Suzanne Pleshette (*Annie Hayworth*), Veronica Cartwright (*Cathy Brenner*), Ethel Griffies (*Mrs. Bundy*), Charles McGraw (*Sebastien Sholes*), Ruth McDevitt (*Mrs. MacGruder*), and Joe Mantell, Malcolm Atterbury, Karl Swenson, Elizabeth Wilson, Lonny Chapman, Doodles Weaver, John McGovern, Richard Deacon, Doreen Lang, Bill Quinn; *Running Time:* 120 minutes; *16mm Rental Source:* Universal 16.

Rod Taylor plays with bird in cage and a bird plays with Rod Taylor in a "cage" of his own.

After *Psycho,* Hitchcock undertook a project which, because of its demanding technical requirements and execution of special effects, took three years of preparation before its final release. *The Birds* was his third major film based on the writing of the prolific Daphne du Maurier.

Hitchcock realized that after *Psycho* people would be expecting him to top himself, and he did. There were some 370 trick shots in the film, and the last scene alone took 32 different pieces of film to create a scene in which thousands of birds sit as far as the eye could see.

Although Hitchcock employs music to enhance the cinematic effects he creates on screen; for *The Birds* he asked his favorite composer, Bernard Herrmann, not to write music but instead to be a sound consultant. Replacing the expected musical score is an electronic one, simulated sounds for bird cries and wing-flapping. Even the sounds with the opening credits are electronic duplications of bird noises.

The property appealed to Hitchcock because the birds who descend upon man in the story are not birds of prey but ordinary birds that, up until then, have lived in harmony with man. Of course the whole thing is a fantasy and the audience doesn't really believe that such a thing could happen, but Hitchcock has us almost convinced by the end that anything is possible. Daphne du Maurier based her short tale of horror on factual incidents and since

The Birds has been released, many similar occurrences have been reported throughout the country. If Hitchcock's film is farfetched, it is for dramatic effect.

The Birds was shot on location in Bodega Bay and San Francisco, with studio work completed at Universal City. In addition to the vast array of specially trained birds, Hitchcock also introduced his new discovery. Her name was Tippi Hedren, a former model who Hitchcock thought could be the new Grace Kelly. A statuesque blonde with a frozen expression, Ms. Hedren possessed the classic Hitchcockian beauty and lacked only the ability to act. Even Jessica Tandy, a fine actress, wasn't up to par. Fortunately the film relied more upon special effects than sheer acting for its success. The plot and dialogue were not demanding, though, and besides, it was the birds people came to see.

Evan Hunter prepared the screenplay. During shooting Hitchcock became aware that it was mediocre and some quick changes would have to be made. The story is about Melanie Daniels (Tippi Hedren), a carefree playgirl who meets a young lawyer, Mitch Brenner (Rod Taylor), in a San Francisco pet store. Despite his insolent manner towards her,

able to safely wait until the birds' fury is spent. They then continue down the hill into town to the safety of the restaurant. Soon the birds swoop down on the town, causing a fire and explosion in the gas station. Annie is discovered dead outside her house by Mitch and Melanie as they are returning to the Brenner house. That evening the Brenner house is boarded up, birds of all types madly attack and chop away at the shingles and doors. Melanie, investigating a noise upstairs, is brutally attacked by birds which have pecked their way through the roof. When the attack has quieted down, the Brenners and Melanie flee. Their car travels through thousands of birds as far as the horizon. The birds sit and wait.

The horror of the film is intensified with the aid of the slick location photography. The sleepy town of Bodega Bay where activity is slow and insignificant and people are involved in the trivial events of the day seems the most unlikely place for the wrath of the birds to be vented. Thus, when they do attack, it seems all the more vicious and malevolent.

Hitchcock "touches" abound in *The Birds*. The opening, in the bird department of a chic pet shop in San Francisco, with the tame birds in their cages and Mitch Brenner telling Melanie, "I'm putting you back in your gilded cage," seems ironic later when Melanie is trapped in the human cage of a telephone booth as the birds attack her from the outside. The seagull hitting the window of Annie Hayworth's house at night is another ominous sign. Annie says, "It probably couldn't see where it was going." Melanie replies, "But there's a full moon tonight." With these small lines Hitchcock is cluing us in to "be patient—the birds are coming." They create an air of tension that is not relieved until the birds actually do attack.

One of the themes that pervades the entire story is the failure of communication, witnessed in the scene in which Melanie and the patrons in the restaurant watch a man light a cigarette beside his car as gasoline is flowing past him on the ground. They all scream at him not to drop the match, but in their garbled unison entreaty he cannot understand them and drops the match, causing a fiery explosion.

The love interest of Melanie and Mitch starts because neither understands what the other is about. It is only the catastrophe that brings them together.

The ominous ending confused some people and was changed by Universal. The original ending has the Brenner car moving through the birds slowly

she follows him on a whim to Bodega Bay. Although she says she had come to deliver lovebirds to Mitch's sister Cathy (Veronica Cartwright) for her birthday, she has really come to the seaside town to see Mitch. But her fun is ruined when she is attacked by a seagull which gashes her forehead. While it doesn't hurt her seriously, she decides to stay the night with Annie Hayworth (Suzanne Pleshette), the local schoolteacher. The next day the seagulls attack the children at Cathy's outdoor birthday party. Later that night, dozens of sparrows come down the chimney of the Brenner house and cause much damage. The following morning Mitch's mother (Jessica Tandy) goes to see a neighboring farmer. She discovers his house wrecked by birds and his bloody body with his eyes gouged out. More events follow that same day when Melanie visits the schoolhouse and sees a crowd of crows waiting to attack. She warns Annie and the children run for their lives. Halfway down the hill into town, one of the children is attacked by the birds and falls, breaking her eyeglasses. Cathy goes to her aid and is also attacked. Seeing their predicament, Melanie manages to beat off the birds and drag the children into a nearby car, where they are

Tippi Hedren and bar patrons hear dire forecast of an old ornithologist played by Ethel Griffies.

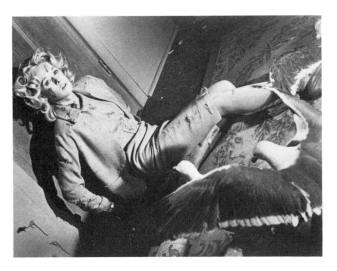

Tippi Hedren attacked by birds in attic.

Rod Taylor with friend.

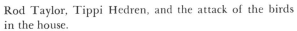

Rod Taylor, Tippi Hedren, and the attack of the birds in the house.

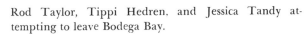

Rod Taylor, Tippi Hedren, and Jessica Tandy attempting to leave Bodega Bay.

Rod Taylor and Tippi Hedren walk through bird-ravaged town.

into the distance and then fading out with no credit of "The End." Universal thought this left the ending up in the air and added a credit line to signify that it was the end.

Again, as in *Psycho,* the beginning of the film tends to drag for audiences eager to get on with the horror. *Saturday Review*'s Arthur Knight noted accordingly, "The story gets off to an incredibly slow start, embellishing the introduction of the principals with all sorts of tedious and unnecessary details. Throughout the film while awaiting the next onslaught from the skies, we are asked to endure long patches of dull, expository dialogue heavily handled by Rod Taylor, Jessica Tandy, Suzanne Pleshette and by Hitchcock's newest 'find,' Tippi Hedren, a decidedly lovely, but utterly deadpan blonde. . . . But when the birds come wheeling back, clearly The Master is at work again. Ornithologists may not approve, but to the rest of us his message is obvious: Leave no tern unstoned."

For the most part, critics were uncomplimentary to Hitchcock for making *The Birds,* and *Variety,* which bends over backward to say something nice, declared that *The Birds* was "a Hitchcock-and-bull story that's essentially a fowl ball." Garnering the most uniform praise were the real stars of the film, the birds themselves. As *Time* magazine said, "They are utterly, terrifyingly believable as they go about their bloody business of murdering humanity."

The Birds was avant-garde Hitchcock, as outrageous and humorous as ever, making the hero squirm and the audience squeal.

The discovery of Susanne Pleshette's body.

Tippi Hedren with "Baldy."

Marnie
1964

Tippi Hedren and Sean Connery during a thunderstorm.

Production: Alfred Hitchcock, Universal; *Producer:* Albert Whitlock; *Screenplay:* Jay Presson Allen, from the novel by Winston Graham; *Director of Photography:* Robert Burks, A.S.C.; *Color:* Technicolor; *Sets:* Robert Boyle and George Milo; *Music:* Bernard Herrmann; *Editing:* George Tomasini; *Assistant Director:* James H. Brown; *Assistant to Hitchcock:* Peggy Robertson; *Sound Engineers:* Waldon O. Watson and William Green; *Distributor:* Universal; *Principal Actors:* Tippi Hedren (*Marnie Edgar*), Sean Connery (*Mark Rutland*), Diane Baker (*Lil Mainwaring*), Martin Gabel (*Sidney Strutt*), Louise Latham (*Bernice Edgar, Marnie's mother*), Bob Sweeney (*Cousin Bob*), Alan Napier (*Mr. Rutland*), S. John Launer (*Sam Ward*), Mariette Hartley (*Susan Clabon*), and Bruce Dern, Henry Beckman, Edith Evanson, Meg Wyllie; *Running Time:* 120 minutes; *16mm Rental Source:* Universal Pictures.

Marnie was a woman's picture, a shrill melodramatic tale of a woman's psychological problem and a man's love for her because of her illness. Unlike *Rebecca,* another woman's film, *Marnie* was lazy movie-making, technically and artistically.

Even if you excuse the cardboard sets that look like cardboard sets, even if you excuse the melodramatic camera angles, even if you excuse the film's many other inadequacies—you are still left with Tippi Hedren. Critic Judith Crist assayed Ms. Hedren with quiet dispassion and so noted, "Alfred Hitchcock has given us one Grace Kelly in our generation and seems intent on giving us another in the person of Tippi Hedren. She is described in studio literature as 'classically beautiful . . . a regally poised [sic] blonde with wide-set green eyes,' and made her debut in the director's *The Birds.* But in his new film, the studio fact sheet continues, 'she inherited one of the most challenging roles of recent time. The actress, who had no dramatic training prior to her discovery, approached the extremely difficult assignment with understandable concern. Hitchcock allayed her qualms when he pointed out that even the most complex role is played but one scene at a time—and that no single sequence lay beyond her talents.' We will avoid the irreverent insinuation that similarly a bright seven-year-old piano student could cope with Ives' Concord Sonata by playing one note at a time."

Complementing Hedren is brawny actor Sean Connery, who was enjoying a peak in popularity at the time because of his dashing performance as James Bond in the first two of the Ian Fleming series. But here he is restrained, or as Miss Hedren says to him at one point, "You Freud—Me Jane." All that he was missing was a beard and a Viennese accent. Diane Baker gives one of the most believable performances as the sister of Connery's late wife.

Perhaps Hitchcock was on the rebound from his last two shockers. Both were incredible horror stories and his image as the amiable spooksmith had changed more towards a purveyor of fine horror. *Marnie* was a property that would put his reputation into a more realistic perspective. What it did establish is that nobody, not even Alfred Hitchcock, is perfect. It was his first clunker since the early 1950s' *Stage Fright* and *I Confess.*

Remaining faithful to the Winston Graham novel, screenwriter Jay Bresson Allen writes Hollywoodish dialogue which thins the dynamics the plot provides. Marnie Edgar (Tippi Hedren) is a neurotic, frigid woman who loves only her lame mother. She sublimates her sexuality by staging successful robberies of her various employers. Her method is to become a secretary, establish an honest, reliable, hard-working reputation, and then help herself to the contents of the company's safe; she changes her name and appearance and moves from city to city. Her operation runs smoothly until her new employer, Mark Rutland (Sean Connery), falls in love with her, already aware that she is a thief. When he discovers her breaking into his safe, he offers her the choice of marriage or prison. On their honeymoon, her frigidity results in Mark's almost raping her and her resultant attempt at suicide. Marnie is continually in fear of bright red colors and thunderstorms. While riding her horse, the sight of a red coat causes Marnie to whip her horse into a dangerous gallop. The horse is seriously hurt on a bad jump over a brick wall and she is forced to kill it. Disturbed at the loss, she tries to rob Mark's safe again but finds that she can't. Mark makes her go with him to her mother's house where she relives the traumatic childhood experience that is causing her current problems. Marnie killed a sailor, played by Bruce Dern, to protect her prostitute mother. The phobias—men, the color red, and thunderstorms—are tied quickly together and explained as the film finally concludes.

Hitchcock declares that he is not concerned with the content of a film, which is quite obvious in *Marnie,* and it is how a film is put together which stands uppermost in his mind. *Marnie* was, or at least looks as if it were, manufactured hastily and cheaply. The very first shot of Mrs. Edgar's street has a painted backdrop which gives an ersatz effect to the whole scene. Later in the story there is a hunt on horseback, and the rear projections for these scenes are made so poorly they intrude on

Alan Napier, Diane Baker, Sean Connery, and Tippi Hedren.

Tippi Hedren.

Tippi Hedren in a hunt sequence that employed inferior rear projection.

228

any sense of reality established. Thunderstorms arrive at convenient moments to get Marnie appropriately upset. Hitchcock has conceded that he was pressed for time during the production and he was forced to accept faulty scenery and rear projections.

Marnie marked the final project in which three production people, involved in Hitchcock's films for a ten-year period, were to work together. This is the last we would see of Robert Burks's photography, George Tomasini's editing, and Bernard Herrmann's music. The three had worked separately on many of Hitchcock's films, and as a team on *Vertigo, The Birds,* and *North by Northwest.*

There are three interesting pieces of photographic design in the film. Whether these are directly attributable to Hitchcock or Burks or to the two in combination remains to be discovered. The first of the movements reverts to an idea used in *Vertigo.* Marnie is having a nightmare. We see her for the first time in a strange setting. She is lying on a couch, next to a window. A fist knocks ominously against the pane of glass. The camera pans, and we see a door as it opens, revealing Sean Connery. The camera then cuts back to a shot of Marnie, this time in her own bed, on the second floor of the Rutland house. A combination set seems to have been used here, as in the scene in Madeleine's bedroom/stable combination in *Vertigo.*

The second of the movements occurs at a party at the Rutlands', and echoes the famous camera crane from the balcony of Claude Rains home to the closeup of the "borrowed" key in *Notorious.* In the case of *Marnie* the shot starts again, at the second floor near the staircase. The camera moves down and forward slowly toward the front door. The bell continues to ring as guests arrive. Finally, as the camera is in a closeup at the door, the bell rings and the door is opened to reveal Sidney Strutt (Martin Gabel), who was Marnie's first victim at the beginning of the film.

The third shot is difficult to explain, but again is a repeat of former Hitchcock/Burks photography—this time returning again to *Vertigo* for the shot looking down the interior of the church tower. The shot—which would seem to be a combination of a zoom and a tracking shot as the camera moves closer physically to the subject and zooms out at the same time—occurs as Marnie remembers the situation in which she murders a sailor, whom she feels is hurting her mother. As it turns out, her mother took the blame for the killing but the impression was left on Marnie's mind. Her mother remarks that she wanted to make sure that she was brought up "decent." As Marnie finds after

Tippi Hedren killing her beloved horse after it has broken a leg in a fall.

she understands the impact of the incident, "I'm a cheat and a liar and a thief, but I *am* decent."

As Marnie and Mark walk out of Mrs. Edgar's apartment in Baltimore after all is explained, children nearby, including Marnie's mother's current favorite, are playing an old children's game as they recite "Doctor, doctor I am ill, send for the doctor, over the hill. . . ." An interesting comment on Marnie's former problem.

The ironic contradiction in character and audience emotions are what clearly interest Hitchcock. The audience roots for Marnie even though she is a thief (we don't want her to get caught). Her erratic behavior is analyzed, though in drawing-room fashion. *The New York Times* described it, "Curiously he (Hitchcock) has also settled for an inexplicably amateurish script, which reduces this potent material to instant psychiatry, complete with flashback 'explanation scene' harking back to vintage Joan Crawford and enough character exposition to stagger the most dedicated genealogist."

The script was originally the work of Evan Hunter, but when that didn't work, Jay Bresson Allen prepared another. Other changes included a cut of twenty minutes from the original running time. Even that sizable cut didn't help what *Saturday Review* called "the unpardonable sin for Hitchcock: it never stops talking."

In theme, *Marnie* is very much like Hitchcock's 1945 *Spellbound*. The latter, however, was skillfully calibrated suspense, despite its textbook psychology. The romantic situation of psychologist Ingrid Bergman falling for the helpless Gregory Peck, was enough to hold our attention and sway our emotions. Even Salvadore Dali's stark dream sequences dazzle us with their Freudian imagery and, for 1945, their provocative nature. *Spellbound*'s psychologizing is part of the story, but in *Marnie* it is an intrusion.

Perhaps *Time* magazine said it best when it concluded its review of *Marnie* by commenting, "When an unknown director turns out a suspense melodrama as dreary and unconvincing as this, moviegoers reveal in the thought of what it might have been if Hitchcock had done it. It is disconcerting to come away from *Marnie* feeling precisely the same way."

Tippi Hedren discovered by Sean Connery as she robs a safe.

Tippi Hedren and Sean Connery on a honeymoon cruise.

Tippi Hedren and Sean Connery.

Tippi Hedren.

Julie Andrews and Leipzig University scientists run to the aid of Paul Newman, who has just fallen down a flight of stairs.

Screenplay: Brian Moore; *Director of Photography:* John F. Warren, A.S.C.; *Sets:* Frank Arrigo; *Sound:* Walden O. Watson and William Russell; *Music:* John Addison; *Editing:* Bud Hoffman; *Assistant Director:* Donald Baer; *Principal Actors:* Paul Newman (*Professor Michael Armstrong*), Julie Andrews (*Sarah Sherman*), Lila Kedrova (*Countess Kuchinska*), Hans-jörg Felmy (*Heinrich Gerhard*), Tamara Toumanova (*Ballerina*), Wolfgang Kieling (*Hermann Gromek*), Gunter Strack (*Professor Karl Manfred*), Ludwig Donath (*Professor Gustav Lindt*), David Opatoshu (*Mr. Jacobi*), Gisela Fischer (*Dr. Koska*), Mort Mills (*Farmer*), Carolyn Conwell (*Farmer's wife*), Arthur Gould-Porter (*Freddy*); *Running Time:* 128 minutes; *16mm Rental Source:* Universal 16.

For his fiftieth production, Alfred Hitchcock directed and produced an original spy melodrama, a story of Cold War espionage. Besides reaching new technical vistas (shooting in natural light) and one of the most excruciatingly realistic murder sequences ever devised, the film offers little and was universally panned.

Brian Moore wrote an original screenplay based on an idea Hitchcock had on the defection of two British scientists. Unfortunately Moore, a Canadian novelist of high acclaim, created characters who were downright naïve, especially about scientific secrets. To add glamour to the incredible plot, Hitchcock cast two of the leading box-office stars, Paul Newman and Julie Andrews. No doubt he thought this was a coup of some sort (during shooting he was to regret casting Newman because of his hampering Method acting approach).

The New York Times assayed the problem of *Torn Curtain* when Bosley Crowther noted, "It is a pathetically undistinguished spy picture and the obvious reason is that the script is a collection of what Alfred Hitchcock most eschews—clichés . . . he is so badly burdened with a blah script and a hero and a heroine who seem to miss the point that he has come up with a film that plows through grimly, without any real surprises, suspense or fun."

Almost the entire film, set in East Germany, was actually filmed in Hollywood on Universal City sets. Location photography was made on a farm near Camarillo, California, at an airport in the San Fernando Valley, at the port of Long Beach, and on the campus of the University of Southern California. For the bus-ride escape sequence, a team of German photographers shot rear-projection footage which Hitchcock was unhappy with. Unfortunately his two leading stars cost so much that the budget was cut elsewhere and he could not send an American team who knew exactly what he wanted and needed.

The story centers around Professor Michael Armstrong (Paul Newman) who, while attending a physicist's convention in Copenhagen, publicly defects to the Communist side. His loyal assistant and fiancee Sarah Sherman (Julie Andrews) follows him and soon learns that Michael is only feigning defection in order to find out crucial information from Professor Gustav Lindt (Ludwig Donath), who is working on a similar project on which Michael has come to a dead end in America. Aided by the East German underground, Michael stays ahead of Heinrich Gerhard, the security chief, and tricks Lindt into divulging his formulas for the anti-missile defense system. Before their escape, Michael and Sarah are discovered and are quickly hustled out of Leipzig. Other underground members help the pair to East Berlin in a phony "off-schedule" bus, and a Countess Kuchinska (Lila Kedrova) aids them in escaping from the police. They are finally secreted aboard a ship taking a Russian ballet group to Sweden. The leading ballerina spots them as she did earlier in an East German theater and causes the basket they are supposedly in to be riddled with machine-gun fire. Michael and Sarah elude the Communists and make it safely to Stockholm.

The movie runs 128 minutes and would have run longer if Hitchcock had retained a sequence in which the twin brother of the Communist chaperone agent appears. The humor the scene was based on was the fact that Newman had just killed agent Gromek (Wolfgang Kieling) with a butcher knife and gas from a stove in a farmhouse. His brother, a look-alike, talks to Newman in the deleted scene while he cuts some sausage with a knife similar to the one that has killed his twin.

Even at its present length, though, the film is too long. *Time* magazine complained that, "Alas, good Hitchcock touches no longer make a good Hitchcock film and *Torn Curtain* falls, more redolent of mothballs than mystery."

Some of the "touches" he has added that are taken for granted include filming all the Communist country scenes in a muted grey and stark natural lighting with production design by Hein Heckroth, well known for his brilliant work for Michael Powell and Emeric Pressburger (The Archers), on *The Red Shoes* and *Tales of Hoffman,* and compacting the escape bus-ride into a short edge of the seat affair. By far the highlight of *Torn Curtain* is the murder sequence in the farmhouse. Newman's Communist party escort reveals he is aware that New-

Paul Newman and Julie Andrews.

Paul Newman and Julie Andrews with Lila Kedrova as the Countess Kuchinska.

Julie Andrews and Paul Newman.

man has not really defected and attempts to call the authorities. Newman and the woman in the farmhouse try to silence Gromek. She stabs him with a butcher knife, but the blade breaks. Newman tries to strangle him and then, after Gromek is knocked down with a shovel across the knees, Newman and the woman push his face into a gas oven after dragging him the length of the room. Hitchcock says benignly that he was only trying to show how difficult it can be to kill a person.

Again escape brings us back to a familiar Hitchcock situation—an escape by means of causing a disturbance or in this case a full scale panic. On stage, papier-mâché flames leap into the air while Tamara Toumanova, as the ballerina, recognizes Newman and Andrews seated in the audience. The shots of Toumanova as she spins and catches quick glimpses of the hunted couple are similar to shots in *The Red Shoes* in which we are shown extreme closeups of Moira Shearer with her eyes made up a bright red. As Newman realizes they have been spotted, he looks for a means of escape and **finds it** in the papier-mâché flames, screaming "fire" to panic the audience. The crowd not only keeps the police away from the couple but momentarily separates them from each other and escape as Andrews is swept away in a wave of people.

Hitchcock, known as a supreme technician of the cinema, seldon slips up with technical details. This is why one bit during the film seems all the more humorous. Paul Newman takes Julie Andrews to the top of a hill in East Germany, away from the Germans, in order to explain his real mission to her. The camera follows them but holds on a long shot of the couple on the hill. Unfortunately, this is one time when director Hitchcock should have bothered looking through the viewfinder of the camera, rather than leaving it to the cinematographer, as what we see at the upper portion of the scene is the top of the sky cyclorama and the lights hanging from the electrical fittings above the scene, both inside the studio. One of the only other instances of a technical failure may be found in *Saboteur*. Priscilla Lane throws a large card with a message requesting help out of the window of a skyscraper. Unfortunately, it is a different card that is found by taxi drivers on the ground.

Paul Newman and Julie Andrews, with Lyle Sudrow, who welcomes the wet pair back to the free world.

PAUL NEWMAN   JULIE ANDREWS

ALFRED HITCHCOCK'S   IT TEARS YOU APART WITH SUSPENSE!

'TORN CURTAIN'

TECHNICOLOR.

co-starring LILA KEDROVA · HANSJOERG FELMY · TAMARA TOUMANOVA
LUDWIG DONATH · DAVID OPATOSHU · Music by JOHN ADDISON · Written by BRIAN MOORE
Directed by ALFRED HITCHCOCK · A Universal Picture

Paul Newman attempts to kill Wolfgang Kieling before he can report Newman's deceptive defection to the Communist authorities.

233

Topaz
1969

Carlos Rivas, a Cuban revolutionary, points an accusing finger at the fleeing Roscoe
Lee Browne as the chase through Harlem begins.

Production: Alfred Hitchcock; *Screenplay:* Samuel Taylor, from Leon Uris's novel; *Director of Photography:* Jack Hildyard; *Color:* Technicolor; *Set decoration:* John Austin; *Sound:* Waldron O. Watson, Robert R. Bertrand; *Editor:* William Ziegler; *Assistant directors:* Douglas Green, James Westman; *Special photographic effects:* Albert Whitlock; *Music:* Maurice Jarre; *Costumes:* Edith Head (Fashioned in Paris by Pierre Balongin); *Studio:* Universal, location work in Europe; *Principal Actors:* Frederick Stafford (*André Devereaux*), Dany Robin (*Nicole Devereaux*), John Vernon (*Rico Parra*), Karin Dor (*Juanita de Cordoba*), Michel Piccoli (*Jacques Granville*), Philippe Noiret (*Henry Jarre*), Claude Jade (*Michele Picard*), Michel Subor (*Francois Picard*), Per-Axel Arosenius (*Boris Kusenov*), Roscoe Lee Browne (*Philippe Dubois*), and John Forsythe as *Michael Nordstrom; Running Time:* 108 minutes (original release at 125 min.); *16mm Rental Source:* Audio-Brandon.

If *Marnie* and *Torn Curtain* seem sloppy in their poorly realized rear projections and Universal studio sets, *Topaz* dazzles with location photography in Paris, Copenhagen, and New York, and meticulously recreated sets in Hollywood. But they are of no avail because the material enacted in their environs is as confusing as it is apathetic. The plot was as brittle as the characters were cardboard.

In need of a project, Hitchcock impulsively selected Leon Uris's *Topaz,* the best-selling spy novel about Cold War espionage. Staying close to the original, Hitchcock had to shoot excessive footage just to develop the incident-crammed story. In so doing, he created a picture that got bogged down in too many explanations. The expected Hitchcock surprises which make his films move so well are consequently missing.

The story revolves around André Devereaux (Frederick Stafford), as the film's central character, assisting the C.I.A. in finding out about Russian activities in Cuba in 1962. He also must uncover those responsible for leaks to the Soviets from

NATO. He completes both his tasks with little compassion or bother and provides little with which the audience can easily identify. To further complicate the basic story, Devereaux and his wife, Nicole (Dany Robin) are bitter towards each other because she suspects he is unfaithful to her. Her assessment is correct, and we see that he is in love with Juanita de Cordoba (Karin Dor), the widow of a former Cuban revolutionary hero. His affair with Juanita in Cuba leads to her death when Rico Parra, a new leader in the Cuban government, suspects them and finds out that she is the leader of an underground group plotting to overthrow his government.

Rico is cast as a Castro look-alike and his appearance at the Hotel Theresa in Harlem, where Castro himself stayed when he came to the United States, is one of the few true-to-life sequences in the film.

The theme of betrayal pervades. André and Nicole's marriage fails because of his affair with Juanita. The central plots of NATO leaks, of a Russian defector to the United States, and of Juanita's underground work against Rico and Cuban dictatorship, are only some of the betrayals. The problem is that there is so much of this going on that none seems more important than the other.

Hitchcock, always savvy to picturing death lyrically and realistically, designed one of his most effective death sequences in *Topaz*. Rico has learned of Juanita's betrayal. He knows that she will be tortured for it and kills her quickly as they embrace. They speak passionately but tenderly. They are embraced and Hitchcock lets the camera encircle them at shoulder height in a style characteristic of many of his love scenes. Suddenly there is a gunshot. Juanita suddenly, almost sexually, jerks back. She begins to fall. The camera is elevated now as we see her purple dress flow open like a flower bloom on the cold checkered black and white marble floor. The shot adds intensity to the scene and makes the death more painful.

On the whole, the acting in *Topaz* is poor. John Forsythe, as Michael Nordstrom, the American, gives a pedestrian performance, and Frederick Stafford as Devereaux tries to bring some emotion to a role that screenwriter Samuel Taylor has not shaped too carefully. John Vernon is a convincing, Castro-like Cuban tyrant, and Phillipe Noiret and Michel Piccoli as the two French quislings probably do the best acting job of all.

The film cost some four million dollars to produce with location shooting eating about a third of this budget. A rather elaborate reconstruction of the Hotel Theresa (which had been torn down in New York before shooting began) alone cost one hundred thousand dollars. In fact, part of the four-laned Seventh Avenue outside the hotel had to be built as well, for authenticity, and was done with the aid of newspaper and other photographic accounts of the Castro visit to the United States.

There were reports that as many as five different endings were filmed by Hitchcock, but only three can be accounted for. Given the choice, it was still difficult to find the one that is a satisfactory conclusion to the more-than-two-hour movie. The first ending, which was probably dropped because it was too melodramatic, was a duel between Andre and Granville in a cavernous stadium. A few men enter and the duel begins. Then one of the men tries to stop the duel, but the referee refuses. At the very moment the men take aim, a sharpshooter at the top of the stands shoots the spy in the back with a telescopic rifle. Someone asks the Frenchman what happened, and he replies, "Obviously the Russians have no further use for him."

The second version had Granville on his way to Moscow, cheerfully waving goodbye to André and Nicole, who were off to Washington. The third ending has Granville enter his home and close the door behind him. The frame freezes on this shot and a gunshot is heard on the soundtrack. Granville has committed suicide. It was this third, least convincing ending, that was finally used.

An additional half-minute epilog was tacked on before the end credits, as an unidentified reader rises from a bench along a large Parisian boulevard and coldly drops a newspaper which states that the crisis is at an end. It is only we lucky few in Row J, center, who are aware of what occurred behind the headlines.

Hitchcock's foray into yet another spy adventure was not well timed. By its December, 1969, release, interest in spy stories and Cold War drama had all but dissipated. We had been sated with them, and as it happens, the first of the litter had been Hitchcock's own *North by Northwest*. Even if we hadn't been jaded with one too many tales of espionage and even if *Topaz* had not arrived too late for audience interest instead of apathy, the film would probably still not succeeded because of its intrinsic inadequacies. Even the *déjà vu* Maurice Jarre musical score was misplaced. Lacking Bernard Herrmann's virtuosity, and sounding

Karin Dor with Frederick Stafford.

Karin Dor with John Vernon.

Karin Dor with John Roper, Lewis Charles, and Anna Navarro, as they plan for picnic-spy mission with cameras in food basket.

Roscoe Lee Browne, Carlos Rivas, and John Vernon.

John Forsythe escorts Sonja Kolhoff, Per-Axel Arosenius, and Tina Hedstrom, a defecting Russian scientist and his family.

more like his famous *Dr. Zhivago,* Jarre's score was sadly commercial and, like the film itself, did not evoke any emotions from the audience.

Topaz was Hitchcock's final film in Technicolor. Even though his next production, *Frenzy,* carried a "Technicolor" credit, the actual prints, in the United States at least, were several steps down —Eastmancolor—a process which by 1972 was in itself excellent, but still lacked that extra bit of gloss and density present in the original dye-transfer Technicolor.

The sixties closed for Hitchcock with two hits and three misses, in that order. Critics and the public alike began to wonder aloud, "Has Hitchcock lost his touch?" "Is it time for the old man to retire?" In 1972 they were to get their answer: no.

Frenzy

1972

Barry Foster.

Producer: Alfred Hitchcock; *Associate Producer:* William Hill; *Screenplay:* Anthony Shaffer, from the novel GOODBYE PICCADILLY., FAREWELL LEICESTER SQUARE by Arthur Labern; *Production Manager:* Brian Burgess; *Assistant Director:* Colin M. Brewer; *Director of Photography:* Gil Taylor; *Special Photographic Effects:* Arthur Whitlock; *Editing:* John Jympson; *Sound:* Peter Handford, Gordon K. McCallum, Rusty Coppleman; *Music:* Ron Goodwin; *Color:* Eastman Color, CRI by Technicolor; *Production Design:* Sydney Cain; *Art Direction:* Robert Laing; *Set Decoration:* Simon Wakefield; *Assistant to Mr. Hitchcock:* Peggy Robertson; *Location Scenes:* Filmed in London, interiors at Pinewood Studios; *Distributor:* Universal; *Principal Actors:* Jon Finch (*Richard Blaney*), Alec McCowen (*Inspector Oxford*), Barry Foster (*Bob Rusk*), Barbara Leigh-Hunt (*Brenda Blaney*), Anna Massey (*Babs Milligan*), Vivien Merchant (*Mrs. Oxford*), Billie Whitelaw (*Hetty Porter*), Bernard Cribbins (*Felix Forsythe*), Clive Swift (*Johnny Porter*), Michael Bates (*Sergeant Spearman*); *Running Time:* 116 minutes; *16mm Rental Source:* Universal 16.

If the opening of *Frenzy* seems slightly familiar, it is because it is almost identical to the first frames of Hitchcock's *Young and Innocent*. In the latter, a woman's body is washed ashore with the belt from a raincoat, obviously used to strangle her, floating nearby. *Frenzy*, Hitchcock's first film made in England in almost twenty years, opens with a Parliament official declaring that there will no longer be pollution in England's waters. Just then a woman's nude body floats down the Thames, a tie around her neck, revealing that she is the latest victim of a killer that is terrorizing London.

The initial exposition of the film invokes memories of many of the early Hitchcock films made in England, *The Lodger* in particular, with its motifs of a panic-stricken city swept with fear of a psychopath on the loose.

Perhaps one of the reasons for *Frenzy's* success was Hitchcock's return to the subject matter that made *Psycho* into one of the most profitable films of the early 1960s. *Frenzy* mirrors the chaos of today's society, but it is tempered with Hitchcock's disarming use of understated comedy. Just as *Psycho* was about a maniac, so too was *Frenzy*. This was blended with Hitchcock's favorite theme of the innocent man. The script was brilliantly penned by Anthony Shaffer, based on the novel *Goodbye Piccadilly, Farewell Leicester Square* by Arthur Labern. Shaffer was the author of the mind-teasing play *Sleuth*. He was able to assimilate Hitchcock's brand of humor with the harsh realities of the crimes committed by the psychopath.

The story adheres to the plot of the novel but strays with additional subplots obligatory to any film made by Hitchcock. Adding a comedy relief from the otherwise grim proceedings, we catch the police inspector, played by Alec McCowen, being treated to his wife's gourmet cooking. All the poor man wants is a hearty and filling meal. Instead he is the recipient of an assortment of exotic foods. It is during the undelectable repasts, that he relates to his wife the events up to date. Not only does it help the audience understand what has happened but it reduces the tension for a brief time, before it again tightens.

Richard Blaney (Jon Finch), a former RAF pilot now down on his luck, quits his job as a pub bartender when the boss accuses him of stealing drinks. Momentarily upset, he talks with his friend, Bob Rusk (Barry Foster), a fruit-and-vegetable dealer. He then drops in on his ex-wife Brenda (Barbara Leigh-Hunt), the owner of a matrimonial agency. His pentup frustration causes him to lash out at her verbally, while her secretary overhears from the outer office. The next day, Bob Rusk comes to Brenda's office and is told that her agency can not satisfy his peculiar tastes in women. She tells him to go alsewhere but instead he stays, brutally attacks and rapes her, then strangles her with his necktie.

Scotland Yard puts out an arrest warrant for Blaney based on Brenda's secretary's identification. He learns of his new problem from Babs Milligan (Anna Massey), a co-worker at the pub he has just quit. He escapes from the police with Babs and gets shelter with an old-time war buddy, Johnny Porter (Oliver Swift). Babs stays with Rusk, who rapes and kills her. He dumps her body in a potato sack but, when he realizes that his monogrammed stickpin is missing, torn off in the struggle before the rape, he rushes back to the truck. He finds the right sack and then coldly breaks her fingers to release the pin clenched in her fist. Blaney goes to Bob for help. Instead Bob frames him and after a quick trial and conviction, Blaney cries out that he will get revenge on Rusk. Inspector Oxford (Alec McCowen) hears this and checks into the possibility of Blaney's innocence. His wife (Vivien Merchant) provides him with inedible gourmet cooking along with her suspicion that Blaney is not the right man. The information begins to build against Rusk but Blaney, impatient for revenge, escapes from prison. He sneaks to Rusk's room and bludgeons what he thinks is Rusk's body but actually is the latest rape victim. Inspector Oxford arrives and tells

239

Anna Massey and Barry Foster.

Jon Finch, and Jimmy Garner, with Anna Massey in the background.

Jon Finch throws himself down a prison stairwell so that he will be put in the hospital, where he can escape.

Barry Foster and Barbara Leigh-Hunt.

Jon Finch.

Blaney to be still. Rusk comes in shortly with a trunk intended as the coffin for the body in the bed. Oxford, surprising Rusk, remarks, "Why Mr. Rusk—you're not wearing your tie." Blaney is exonerated.

Frenzy is a festival of Hitchcock touches and production values. Every shot and movement fits together with perfection.

Police rush to the body of a young girl that floats up to the scene of a political speech in the film's opening. The tie with which she has been strangled is still hanging around her neck. The speaker hopes it is "not his club tie." We cut to a shot of John Finch putting on *his* tie. We immediately, although incorrectly, assume that he is the murderer. Rusk, the real murderer, is identified symbolically with his gold and diamond initial stickpin in the form of an *R*. He often uses it to pick his teeth after eating a piece of fine English fruit. He removes it from his tie and places it in his lapel before his bout with Barbara Leigh-Hunt. The pin becomes a symbol of violence and murder.

When Babs leaves the pub in hope of helping the hiding Blaney prove his innocence, she is followed by her friend Rusk. She walks out of the pub with the sounds of the city around her. Suddenly the sound fades out and we hear Rusk behind her, asking if she needs a place to stay. A chill runs through the audience. Soon after Hitchcock again uses sound (and camera movement) to add yet another magnificent touch. Babs and Rusk arrive at his flat. The noise of London fades as the camera follows them to the top of the stairs. "You know, you're my kind of woman," says Rusk. The camera slowly tracks back down the stairs in a single movement and the noises of traffic cover any screams that might be made. We know that we will never see Babs alive again. When we do see her again, she is stuffed in a potato sack. Rusk is trying to regain his stickpin, which has somehow disappeared. He remembers that she grabbed it during her murder. Rusk finds the pin tight in her rigor-mortised grip. He must break her fingers to set it free. Later, as Mrs. Oxford gives her ideas to her husband the inspector, she gingerly breaks breadsticks. Hitchcock takes us immediately back to the breaking of the fingers with exactly the same sound.

After his trial, Blaney is pulled from the courtroom screaming, "I'll get you, Rusk!" and is placed in a small cell. Hitchcock returns to the *Paradine Case* technique as the camera looms above the cell and the door closes behind him with a resounding clang.

After a spate of films that did not have that Hitchcock polish to them, *Frenzy* was full of luster. The idea of assembling a cast of excellent but generally unknown (in the United States) actors gave the story a look of urgency and reality which would have been lost with familiar faces. The scripts of Hitchcock's previous three films were his undoing. With *Frenzy* he had first-class material. *The New York Times* noted, for example, that Hitchcock has been able to make a trite situation thoroughly absorbing with a "marvelously funny script" and "with a superb English cast" and with his gift for implicating the audience in the most outrageous acts which often as not, have us identifying with the killer."

The *Washington Post* on the other hand, perceptively pointed out that the film is a pastiche of recreated classic sequences from the director's preceding films. "There's a coarse variation of a classic sequence in *Strangers on a Train*—Walker's attempt to retrieve a cigarette lighter from a sewer drain, intercut with Granger frantically trying to complete a tennis match in order to intercept Walker. In *Frenzy* the situation involves only the killer, whom we watch trying to retrieve a stickpin from the death grip of one of his victims. Perhaps it is a matter of taste, but I don't think the sight of Barry Foster scrambling around in a potato sack with a naked corpse and then breaking her grip is quite inspired, funny or reputable as true vintage Hitchcock."

Quibbling aside, almost every film critic declared *Frenzy* to be Hitchcock the way we remembered him to be—funny and frightening. If Hitchcock was acclaimed for his sense of originality and ingenuity, the critics who expounded this did so in the most remarkably dull and unoriginally uniform style:

- "Hitchcock is back in good form"—Kathleen Carroll, New York *Daily News*
- "Hitchcock is in fine form in *Frenzy*"—Joseph Gelmis, *Newsday*
- "Hitchcock is still in fine form"—Jay Cocks, *Time*
- "A return to old forms by the master of suspense"—Roger Ebert, Chicago *Sun-Times*

And so on. But that's all the public had to hear. After three successive disappointments, his popularity, although still high, was descending. The raves for *Frenzy* brought people to the theaters and in its first run earned $6.5 million in the United States and Canada. The "return to old form" was manifested in the same techniques

Jon Finch

Barbara Leigh-Hunt.

that made *Psycho* so nerve-racking. There is only one scene of brutal violence in the film, but others are implied or are not particularly graphic. Nevertheless, the tempo of violence remains instilled in our minds throughout the film. In fact, it was the first Hitchcock drama to receive the MPAA restricted-adult rating of *R*.

If he accepted sloppy, perfunctory performances from his cast in his last few pictures, in *Frenzy* he gets riveting portrayals and gutsy acting, making every part of the story and characterizations believable.

Jon Finch, as the innocent loser caught up in a circumstantial nightmare, evokes a balanced amount of outrage. Alec McCowen as the methodical Sherlock Holmes–type inspector is properly subdued in his role. Vivien Merchant as his doting wife is perhaps understated in her comic role, but she provides Hitchcock with the required foil, and Anna Massey as the doomed Babs Milligan is likable with that blend of Thelma Ritter commonness and Patricia Neal sexuality.

Time magazine's summation of the picture was the consensus of most critics and viewers: "Hitchcock's *Frenzy* is the dazzling proof that anyone who makes a suspense film is still an apprentice to this old master."

Barry Foster with Anna Massey.